MASTERPIECES
2001-2015
世界の住宅

MASTERPIECES

《世界の住宅》別冊03
MASTERPIECES 2001-2015
発行・編集：二川由夫

2015年11月25日発行
エーディーエー・エディタ・トーキョー
東京都渋谷区千駄ヶ谷3-12-14
電話(03)3403-1581(代)
ファクス(03)3497-0649
E-mail: info@ga-ada.co.jp
http://www.ga-ada.co.jp

ロゴタイプ・デザイン：細谷巖

製本・印刷：図書印刷株式会社

取次店
トーハン・日販・大阪屋
栗田出版販売・西村書店・中央社
太洋社・鍬谷書店

禁無断転載

ISBN978-4-87140-355-9 C1352

GA HOUSES SPECIAL 03
MASTERPIECES 2001-2015
Publisher/Editor: *Yoshio Futagawa*

Published in November 2015
© A.D.A. EDITA Tokyo Co., Ltd.
3-12-14 Sendagaya, Shibuya-ku,
Tokyo, 151-0051 Japan
Tel. (03)3403-1581
Fax.(03)3497-0649
E-mail: info@ga-ada.co.jp
http://www.ga-ada.co.jp

Logotype Design: *Gan Hosoya*

Printed in Japan by
Tosho Printing Co., Ltd.

All rights reserved.

Copyright of Photographs:
© *GA photographers*
All drawings are provided by
architects except as noted.

04		*"Masterpieces 2001-2015" by Yoshio Futagawa*
		"マスターピーシズ 2001-2015" 二川由夫
08	*2001*	*Ettore Sottsass, Mourmans House, Lanaken, Belgium*
		エットーレ・ソットサス，モーマンズ邸
14	*2001*	*Glenn Murcutt, House in Southern Highlands, New South Wales, Australia*
		グレン・マーカット，サザン・ハイランドの家
20	*2001*	*Georg Driendl, "Solar Tube", Vienna, Austria*
		ゲオルグ・ドリエンドル，"ソーラー・チューブ"
26	*2001*	*Osamu Ishiyama, Setagaya-Mura, Setagaya, Tokyo, Japan*
		石山修武，世田谷村
32	*2001*	*Jun Aoki, I, Tokyo, Japan*
		青木淳，I
36	*2002*	*Masaki Endoh + Masahiro Ikeda, Natural Ellipse, Shibuya, Tokyo, Japan*
		遠藤政樹+池田昌弘，ナチュラル・エリップス
40	*2002*	*Sean Godsell, Peninsula House, Victoria, Australia*
		ショーン・ゴッドセル，半島の家
44	*2002*	*Akira Yoneda + Masahiro Ikeda, Bloc, Kobe, Hyogo, Japan*
		米田明+池田昌弘，ブロック
48	*2003*	*Ryoji Suzuki, Experience in Material No. 45 House in Jingumae, Tokyo, Japan*
		鈴木了二，[物質試行45]神宮前の家
54	*2003*	*Peter Stutchbury, Bangalay, Upper Kangaroo Valley, New South Wales, Australia*
		ピーター・スタッチベリー，バンガレイ
60	*2003*	*Kei'ichi Irie + Masahiro Ikeda, Y House, Chita, Aichi, Japan*
		入江経一+池田昌弘，Y House
64	*2003*	*Steven Ehrlich, Ehrlich House, Venice, California, U.S.A.*
		スティーヴン・アーリック，アーリック邸
70	*2003*	*Tokyo Institute of Technology Tsukamoto Lab. + Atelier Bow-Wow, Gae House, Setagaya, Tokyo, Japan*
		東京工業大学塚本研究室+アトリエ・ワン，ガエ・ハウス
74	*2003*	*Kazuyo Sejima, House in Plum Grove, Tokyo, Japan*
		妹島和世，梅林の家
78	*2004*	*Katsufumi Kubota, I-House, Hatsukaichi, Hiroshima, Japan*
		窪田勝文，I-House
82	*2004*	*Will Bruder, Sky Arc Residence, Marin County, California, U.S.A.*
		ウィル・ブルダー，スカイ・アーク・レジデンス
88	*2004*	*Steven Holl, Writing with Light House, Eastern Long Island, New York, U.S.A.*
		スティーヴン・ホール，光に描かれた家
92	*2004*	*Alberto Kalach, Bross House, Santa Fe, Mexico City, Mexico*
		アルベルト・カラチ，ブロス邸
98	*2004*	*Hiroyuki Arima, Second Plate, Fukuoka, Japan*
		有馬裕之，Second Plate
102	*2005*	*Steven Holl, Planar House, Phoenix, Arizona, U.S.A.*
		スティーヴン・ホール，プラナー・ハウス
108	*2005*	*Álvaro Siza, House Armanda Passos, Porto, Portugal*
		アルヴァロ・シザ，アルマンダ・パッソス邸
112	*2005*	*Blank Studio, Xeros Residence, Phoenix, Arizona, U.S.A.*
		ブランク・スタジオ，ゼロス・レジデンス
118	*2005*	*Ryue Nishizawa, Moriyama House, Tokyo, Japan*
		西沢立衛，森山邸
124	*2005*	*Sou Fujimoto, T House, Gunma, Japan*
		藤本壮介，T House
128	*2005*	*Hiroshi Sambuichi, Stone House, Shimane, Japan*
		三分一博志，ストーン・ハウス
134	*2005*	*Kengo Kuma, Lotus House, Japan*
		隈研吾，ロータス・ハウス
140	*2006*	*Gurjit Singh Matharoo, Patel Residence, Ahmedabad, India*
		グルジット・シン・マタロー，ペイテル邸

2001-2015

144	2006	*selgascano, House in the Florida, La Florida, Madrid, Spain* セルガスカーノ，フロリダの家
150	2006	*Will Bruder, Feigin Residence, Reno, Nevada, U.S.A.* ウィル・ブルダー，フェイジン邸
156	2006	*Ryue Nishizawa, House A, Tokyo, Japan* 西沢立衛，House A
162	2007	*Randy Brown, Laboratory, Omaha, Nebraska, U.S.A.* ランディ・ブラウン，ラボラトリー
168	2007	*Peter Stutchbury, Avalon House, Avalon, New South Wales, Australia* ピーター・スタッチベリー，アヴァロンの家
172	2007	*Terunobu Fujimori + Keiichi Kawakami, Yakisugi House, Nagano, Japan* 藤森照信＋川上恵一，焼杉ハウス
178	2008	*Antón García-Abril, Hemeroscopium House, Las Rozas, Madrid, Spain* アントン・ガルシア＝アブリル，ヘメロスコピウム・ハウス
182	2008	*Enric Miralles Benedetta Tagliabue, House in Barcelona, Barcelona, Spain* エンリック・ミラージェス・ベネデッタ・タグリアブエ，バルセロナの家
188	2008	*Studio Mumbai, Belavali House, Belavali, Maharashtra, India* スタジオ・ムンバイ，ベラヴァリの家
194	2008	*Tadao Ando, House in Sri Lanka, Mirissa, Sri Lanka* 安藤忠雄，スリランカの住宅
202	2008	*Sou Fujimoto, House N, Oita, Japan* 藤本壮介，House N
206	2009	*Keisuke Maeda, Atelier-Bisque Doll, Minoh, Osaka, Japan* 前田圭介，アトリエ・ビスクドール
210	2009	*Makoto Takei + Chie Nabeshima/TNA, Square House, Karuizawa, Nagano, Japan* 武井誠＋鍋島千恵／TNA，方の家
214	2010	*Aires Mateus, House in Leiria, Leiria, Portugal* アイレス・マテウス，レイリアの住宅
220	2010	*Andra Matin, AM Residence, Jakarta, Indonesia* アンドラ・マティン，AM邸
226	2010	*Kengo Kuma, Glass/Wood House, U.S.A.* 隈研吾，Glass/Wood House
232	2010	*Tadao Ando, House in Utsubo Park, Osaka, Japan* 安藤忠雄，靭公園の住宅
238	2010	*Kengo Kuma, Bamboo/Fiber, Japan* 隈研吾，Bamboo/Fiber
244	2011	*Ryue Nishizawa, Garden & House, Japan* 西沢立衛，Garden & House
248	2011	*Tadao Ando, House in Monterrey, Monterrey, Mexico* 安藤忠雄，モンテレイの住宅
256	2011	*Sou Fujimoto, House NA, Tokyo, Japan* 藤本壮介，House NA
260	2012	*Smiljan Radic, Red Stone House, Santiago, Chile* スミルハン・ラディック，レッド・ストーン・ハウス
266	2012	*Smiljan Radic, House for the Poem of the Right Angle, Vilches, Chile* スミルハン・ラディック，「直角の詩」のための住宅
274	2012	*Bercy Chen, Edgeland Residence, Austin, Texas, U.S.A.* ベイシー／チェン，エッジランド・ハウス
278	2013	*SPBR Arquitetos, Swimming Pool in São Paulo, São Paulo, Brazil* spbrアルキテートス，サンパウロのスイミング・プール
284	2013	*doubleNegatives Architecture, House in Nagohara, Minamisaku, Nagano, Japan* ダブルネガティヴス・アーキテクチャー，なご原の家
288	2014	*Ryue Nishizawa, Terasaki House, Kanagawa, Japan* 西沢立衛，寺崎邸
292	2015	*Wespi de Meuron Romeo Architects, New Concrete House in Caviano, Ticino, Switzerland* ウェスピ・ド・ムーロン・ロメオ・アーキテクツ，カヴィアーノの新しいコンクリートの家

Key to Abbreviations

ALC	alcove
ARCD	arcade/covered passageway
ART	art room
ATL	atelier
ATR	atrium
ATT	attic
AV	audio-visual room
BAL	balcony
BAR	bar
BK	breakfast room
BR	bedroom
BRG	bridge/catwalk
BTH	bathroom
BVD	belvedere/lookout
CAR	carport/car shelter
CH	children's room
CEL	cellar
CL	closet/walk-in closet
CLK	cloak
CT	court
D	dining room
DEN	den
DK	deck
DN	stairs-down
DRK	darkroom
DRS	dressing room/wardrobe
DRW	drawing room
E	entry
ECT	entrance court
EH	entrance hall
EV	elevator
EXC	exercise room
F	family room
FPL	fireplace
FYR	foyer
GAL	gallery
GDN	garden
GRG	garage
GRN	greenhouse
GST	guest room/guest bedroom
GZBO	gazebo
H	hall
HK	house keeper
ING	inglenook
K	kitchen
L	living room
LBR	library
LBY	lobby
LDRY	laundry
LFT	loft
LGA	loggia
LGE	lounge
LWL	light well
MBR	master bedroom
MECH	mechanical
MLTP	multipurpose room
MSIC	music room
MUD	mud room
OF	office
P	porch/portico
PAN	pantry/larder
PLY	playroom
POOL	swimming pool/pool/pond
PT	patio
RE	rear entry
RT	roof terrace
SHW	shower
SIT	sitting room
SHOP	shop
SKY	skylight
SL	slope/ramp
SLP	sleeping loft
SNA	sauna
STD	studio
STDY	study
ST	staircase/stair hall
STR	storage/storeroom
SUN	sunroom/sun parlor/solarium
SVE	service entry
SVYD	service yard
TAT	tatami room/tea ceremony room
TER	terrace
UP	stairs-up
UTL	utility room
VD	void/open
VRA	veranda
VSTB	vestibule
WC	water closet
WRK	workshop/work room

Masterpieces 2001-2015 *Yoshio Futagawa*

From as early as the beginning of the 20th century, the great wave of modern architecture has had a major lasting impact, despite a temporary stall due to WWII, on architecture throughout the world, and especially on residential architecture that is directly connected to lifestyles of everyday people. This surge has directed our living spaces to move into a different phase, while it continued to mature with the changes of society, delivering the "contemporary house" to every corner of the world by the end of the century. Never before the 20th century has there been a time when such amount of space was devoted to works of residential architecture in the history of architecture around the globe, representing the extent of popularization and individualization that architecture has undergone. While standardization, industrialization and manualization in response to vast/diverse masses were in keeping with the principles of modern architecture, they simultaneously brought about many examples of "facilitation" and "losing of substance" that only rely on imageries of silhouettes. Expendable "silhouettes" transformed themselves as "styles" such as Mod, PoMo and Decon, but in a larger context, they have been, since the modern times, a "bird in a cage" of modernism that remained unchanged. No matter how the style changed, the fundamental frame and its requirements never did: the house was always there to wrap around people's everyday living i.e. lifestyle, reflecting what goes on inside to show it to the outside.

At the turn of the century, popularization of internet that united the world has, along with the precedent personalization of visual media and emergence of virtual space such as video games that rapidly permeated the public, caused immediate changes in the real lives of people. As lifestyles shifted their timeline from real to virtual, people started to spend more time of their daily life immersed in screens, leading to the rapid declination of the significance of real spaces. The richness of real spaces was complex and diverse as a result of physical quantity and resolution, while on the other hand virtual spaces, still in the process of further development, directly stimulated the sensitivity of those who experience them in a "drug-like" manner by sharpening up the effects that their limited specs are able to produce. With the emergence of this drug-like space, concern over the real space, interest in residential architecture and the meaning of it came to be radically transformed in terms of both individuals and society.

As we entered the 21st century, the first and most probably the greatest event was the 9/11 attacks that hit New York, marking a start of the new century predictive of future hardships. Real life was uncertain and undependable, and re-

20世紀初頭に始まった近代建築の大波は，途中WWIIによる停滞に遭うものの確実に世界の建築，そして日常のライフスタイルに対して住宅建築に直接的かつ多大な影響をもたらし続けた。この大波は我々の住空間をそれまでと違うフェーズに向かわせ，それ自体は社会の変化に伴い成熟し続け，世紀末には世界の隅々まで「現代住宅」を行き渡らせた。20世紀ほど住宅建築作品が世界の建築史に多くのページを割く時代は無かったのであり，それは建築が如何に大衆化，個人化したかということを意味していた。多大／多様なマッスに対応する規格化，工業化，マニュアル化は，そもそもの近代建築の理念に沿ったものであったが，同時に多くの「簡便化」，輪郭のイメージだけで成立するような「形骸化」を生み出していった。そして消費される「輪郭」は，その姿を「スタイル」として，「モダン」，「ポストモダン」，「デコン」と様々に変化させてみたものの，大きな枠組みにおいては，近代以降，変わらない近代主義の中の「籠の鳥」であった。いかにスタイルを変えても，根源的なフレームとその要請は変わらず，住宅は常にそこに繰り広げられる日常＝人々の暮らし＝ライフスタイルを包み込み，その様子を外に向けて映し出す鏡であった。

世紀末，世界中を一つにしたインターネット／WEB世界の普及は，それ以前に始まる映像メディアのパーソナル化，テレビゲームなどのヴァーチャル空間の出現と，その大衆への急激な浸透とともに，人々のリアルな暮らしに急激な変化をもたらした。ライフスタイルはリアルからヴァーチャルへ時間軸をシフトさせ，人々は日常の多くの時間をスクリーンの中で過ごすようになり，リアル空間の意味は急激に衰退していった。リアル空間のもつ豊かさ，それは物理的な量や解像度がもたらす複雑で多様なものであったが，それに対し，ヴァーチャル空間は依然として途上にあるものの，限られているそのスペックがつくり出せる効果を先鋭化することで，「麻薬的」に体験者の感性をストレートに刺激するものである。この麻薬的な空間の出現によって，リアル空間への関心，住宅建築への興味やその意味を急激に個人的，社会的に変質させていくことになった。

21世紀に入り，最初にして多分最大の事件になることであろうニューヨークを襲った9.11は，新世紀の苦難さを予感させるスタートとなった。先の見えない，頼りにならないリアルな暮らしはヴァーチャルな快楽への逃避を要求し，日々の暮らしは断片化し，

quired taking refuge in virtual pleasures. Internet filled in the gaps between fragmented pieces of daily life. By the time smartphones came to fit everyone's hands, people spent most of their time in virtual spaces, leisure and business alike. Stock trading took on more and more the character of video games as transactions took place on personal computer screens. Real spaces became mere properties for trade, houses mere objects of investment. It eventually gave itself away with the failure of Lehman Brothers in 2008, revealing a picture of continued collapse. At the end of the day, residential architecture's visions and goals nurtured by the 20th century resulted in total destruction.

From then on, residential architecture, in spite of its face/codes that remained the same, has been bound to express itself as a presence with a completely different meaning, and been forced to an apparent shift. Ready-built houses that are mass-produced in countries such as America under the initiative of housing developers were clad in styles with high popular appeal, whose utmost importance was in the generality of their specs, resaleability, and how easily they can be turned into financial commodities—any architectural cultural character was deemed an utterly unnecessary excess. On the other hand, residential architecture for specific locality/culture that has been attracting interest in terms of particularity came to be globally welcomed by patrons (i.e. amateurs/otakus) with specific architectural cultural preference, though being in the minority quantity-wise. The process, like an internet-mediated exchange on the web, crosses the distance between localities and cultural differences, creating sympathy along the way to keep people committed. This is what is happening at the forefront of today's residential architecture so it continues into the future. What is required in the living space is not an everlasting daily life but things catering to parts of the fragmented daily life: imperfectness of principles and functions in the virtual space will be complemented by time, as imagery and particularity are given higher priority in the so-called "adjective" space that is in demand. The current world-wide popularity of the system of renting spare rooms such as Airbnb is quite interesting as a phenomenon which clearly indicates the change in the idea of living space on the part of both the letters and renters. The similarity between a home and a hotel is gradually increasing. Owners are willing to let their individual spaces that used to accommodate privacy, while renters experience a fragment of other people's daily life as a primary space for their stay. The essence of daily life is no longer in the real space.

Japanese residential architecture, with its small scale

その間をインターネットが埋めていく。そして、スマートフォンが人々の手に収まる頃にはヴァーチャル空間での暮らしが主となり、余暇も仕事もその中で行われるようになる。ゲーム化が加速した証券取引は、パーソナルコンピュータの画面で行われ、リアル空間はそのための取引の物件＝住宅は投資対象でしかなくなり、ついに2008年に起こるリーマンショックでその馬脚を現し、破綻し続ける構図を露呈した。ここに20世紀が育んできた住宅建築の目指したヴィジョンは完全に崩壊してしまった。

以降、住宅建築は、それ以前と同じ様相／コードをまとっていても全く意味の違う存在を表明しなくてはならず、明らかなシフトを余儀なくされてくる。アメリカを筆頭に量産されるデヴェロッパー主導の建売住宅は、大衆性の高いスタイルをまとい、その仕様が如何に一般性を持って金融商品化可能か、リセール可能かということが最重要であり、余分な建築文化的な特質をまったく求めないものとなった。それと対極に、量的にはまったくもってマイノリティーであるが、限られた建築文化的な嗜好を持ったパトロン（＝オタク）に対して、今までその特殊性において注目を集めていた特定の地域、文化のための住宅建築が、世界同時的に迎えられることになる。インターネットを介したWEB上のやり取りのごとく、文化的な差異や地域間の距離を越えて、他人事ではないようにシンパシーをもたらしながら。これが現在の住宅建築が未来に存続していく最前線である。住空間に対する要請は、永続する日常ではなく、断片化した日常の一部のためのものであり、理念や機能が不完全であってもヴァーチャル空間での時間はそれを補完し、イメージや特殊性が優先される、所謂「形容詞」的な空間が求められている。現在、世界的に流行している「Airbnb」などの空き部屋貸しのシステムは、貸し手、借り手双方の住空間に対する考え方の変質を如実に表していてとても興味深い現象である。住宅とホテルは相似化してきている。貸し手はプライバシーを収めていた個人空間を容易に他人に貸し、借り手は一次的滞在空間として他人の日常の断片を経験する。日常の本質はもはやリアル空間にはない。

戦後、日本の住宅建築はそのスケールの小ささやそこに詰め込まれる密度のある突出したアイディアによって世界的に注目されてきたが、それは「ウサギ小屋」と揶揄され、アメリカやヨーロッパの文化圏にとっては決して自分たちの住宅ではない「見世物」

Masterpieces 2001-2015

and dense, unusual ideas tucked inside, had gathered worldwide attention after WWII. Ridiculed as the "rabbit hutch" it was seen by the American and European cultures as a "freak show" that was totally different from their own homes: there was indeed an aspect of self-deprecation and fake stoicism. However, following the drastic global change in what is required in the living space, it is almost natural that the international world is willing to incorporate certain properties of Japanese residential architecture, which is a phenomenon reminiscent of its accommodating perspectives of the world of manga and anime. The tiny space of the Hojo (small abbot's chamber)-like rabbit hutch came to gain support, as a new concept of "nothingness," from residents of the new virtual space from around the world who are not interested in the amount of space. Like a play equipment or a furniture, it is closer to a space for transit where people spend just a portion of daily life. Its out-of-the-ordinary spatial characteristics, consisting of suggestions for a radical spatial composition and living space as an additional device that only involves image manipulation, is fueling the accelerated process in a positive manner. The output is diverse, delivered to every corner of the world. Japan remains a housing kingdom, but it is entering a new phase.

In South America, Australia and Asia, residential architecture has localized and modernized over a period of time as it emerged from within each nation's rich contexts such as unique environment and culture, maturity of society and economic development—a move that looks as if it switched places with the residential architecture lead by America, Europe and Japan up to the end of the 20th century that transformed with the arrival of the 21st century. Some examples of architectural characteristics found in many of them are: real, conventional richness that comes from the way a certain distance is kept from the environment or a boundary is set between indoor and outdoor spaces; expansive sense of scale that had been lost in America and Europe; and generous, utopian/out-of-the-ordinary space that seems to be the opposite of the actual fractionating/diminishing situation. Imagery of these characteristics is, with the addition of interpretation similar to that of out-of-the-ordinary spaces found in such places as resort hotels, transmitted around the world in a superficial manner. Residential architecture today is evaluated for its out-of-the-ordinary amusement factor.

Without doubt, America has been a housing kingdom during the 20th century. After WWII, Case Study Houses had a major effect on residential architecture all around the world. The subsequent Post-Modernist movement produced a myriad of residential masterpieces designed by individual

であった。それらはある種の卑屈なやせ我慢といった性格を側面に持っていた。しかし世界同時的な住空間に対する要請の激変によって，もはや日本の住宅建築の特性を世界が迎え入れていることは，漫画やアニメの世界観への迎合に似た現象であるように思われる。ウサギ小屋だった，方丈のような狭小空間は，新しい「無」の理念として，世界中の空間量を必要としない新しいヴァーチャル空間の住人たちからの支持を得る。それらは遊具的，家具的であったり，ある種の日常の一部を過ごす通過空間のようなものである。そして，ラディカルな空間構成の提案や，イメージ操作だけの付加的な装置としての住空間など，その非日常的な空間特質はさらにポジティブに進化を加速させて，多様な形でアウトプットされ，世界に発信される。日本は依然として住宅王国であるが，その状況は新しいフェーズに入っている。

南アメリカ諸国やオーストラリア，アジア諸国においては，時間をかけてその地域にローカライズされ，現代化されてきた住宅建築が，独特な環境や文化，社会の熟成，経済の発展といった豊かなコンテクストの下，台頭してきた。これは，アメリカ，ヨーロッパ，そして日本が20世紀まで先導してきた住宅建築が，21世紀に入って変質するのと入れ替わるかのような動きと言える。それらの多くが備える建築的特質は，内外空間の境界，環境との距離感の取り方によってもたらされる旧来的，リアルな豊かさであったり，アメリカやヨーロッパが失ってしまったおおらかなスケール感であったり，断片／縮小化する状況に対極するかのようなおおらかでユートピア的／非日常の空間である。これらの特質はリゾートホテルなどがもつ非日常としての空間と同様な解釈が付加されて，そのイメージは表層的に世界に発信される。今日の住宅建築は非日常的なアミューズメント性を評価されている。

20世紀，アメリカは疑いのない住宅王国であった。戦後，一連のケーススタディハウスは世界中の住宅建築に大きな影響を与え，その後のポストモダンムーブメントにおいても個人作家による大量，多様な名作住宅をアウトプットしてきたが，世紀末以降急激にその姿は縮小した。しかしながら，この国の別の特質である例外的な富裕層による大型住宅がつくられる特殊な国であることが今日でも変わらないのは興味深い。これらの大型住宅はクライアントと取り巻くビジネスソサエティをつなぐパーティーハウス的な性格を持っていたり，プライベートギャラリーのような文化的

architects. Then the turn of the century saw a rapid scale-down. Nonetheless, it is interesting to note the fact that it still is a unique country where large-scaled residences are built by the exceptionally wealthy, the presence of the latter being another peculiarity of this country. These large-scaled residences sometimes serve as party houses where clients connect with their business societies, or as private galleries as a demonstration of their cultural demeanor: such singularity is alive and well, with no parallel in the world. Another current matter of interest is that in recent years, large-scaled residences comparable to those in America by the super wealthy from resource-rich countries and emerging nations are growing from ostentatious to sophisticated. There are also signs of accelerated homogenization of cultural values.

European nations still remain, by and large, conservative in regard to their residential architecture. Rigidity of the existing system in the urban area; restriction by traditional cultural/social rules in provinces; basic conventional vision toward living spaces, all make up for the continuation of a situation in which it is difficult to create a detached residential architecture. But gradually, a younger generation of architects with new sensitivities is starting to emerge alongside elders with a long career on their back. Taking advantage of the global information overload, they bring significance to new materials, forms and space, and create new landscapes in challenging contexts.

Following the accelerated homogenization of global information traffic, there may soon be a time when residential architecture as information will race around the world—but the real space itself will still be unable to move. Architecture is basically a body of information that can only be acquired through real experience. It appears that lack of understanding of the inherent quality of space as well as the absence of sensitivity for space caused by a misapprehension that parts of information from a handful of images are all that it takes to recognize a space, is becoming seriously worse. Will making a false assessment as a result of casually ignoring information of real spaces out of contentment through illusions in virtual spaces cause a problem in the future? Or will the resolution of the virtual space be enhanced to the same level as the real space? Will residential architecture ever reinstate its perpetual completeness, from its status as the adjective, fragmented space for temporary stay that the present situation is headed for?

Foreseeing the future and whereabouts of residential architecture will not be easy.

English translation by Lisa Tani

振る舞いの表明であったりするが，世界に例のない状況は未だに生きている。資源国や新興国のスーパー富裕層によるアメリカに準じるような大型住宅が近年，成金的なものから良質化してきていることも興味深い昨今の現象である。文化的価値観の均質化も加速している。

ヨーロッパ諸国は依然として住宅建築に概して保守的な地域である。都市圏の既存システムの剛性，地方における伝統的な文化的／社会的ルールによる縛り，そもそもの住空間に対する伝統的なヴィジョンなど，戸建の住宅建築が生まれにくい状況に変わりはない。しかしながら，キャリアの長い作家たちとともに新しい感性を持った若いジェネレーションが少しずつ出現している。世界的情報過多の状況を味方に，新しいマテリアルや造形，空間の意味性を創出し，その手強いコンテクストに新しい風景をつくり出している。

世界中の情報トラフィックの均質化が加速して，今後いよいよ情報としての住宅建築が世界同時的に駆け巡る状況になっても，依然としてリアルな空間自体は移動できない。建築は本来，実体験でしか得ることのできない情報である。わずかなイメージによる一部の情報だけであたかもその空間が認知されるような状況がもたらす，空間が本来持ち得る質への不理解と空間に対する感受性の欠如は，いよいよ深刻になってくるように思われる。ヴァーチャル空間における幻覚的な充足レベルでリアル空間の情報を軽く受け流し，間違った評価を下すことが将来問題化するだろうか，それともヴァーチャル空間の解像度がリアルと同等に高まっていくのだろうか。現状が向かう形容詞的，断片的な一時滞留のための空間から，いずれ再び住宅建築は永続的な完結性を復権するのか。

住宅建築はどこに向かうのか，未来を予想することは容易ではない。

Ettore Sottsass 2001

Mourmans House, Lanaken, Belgium

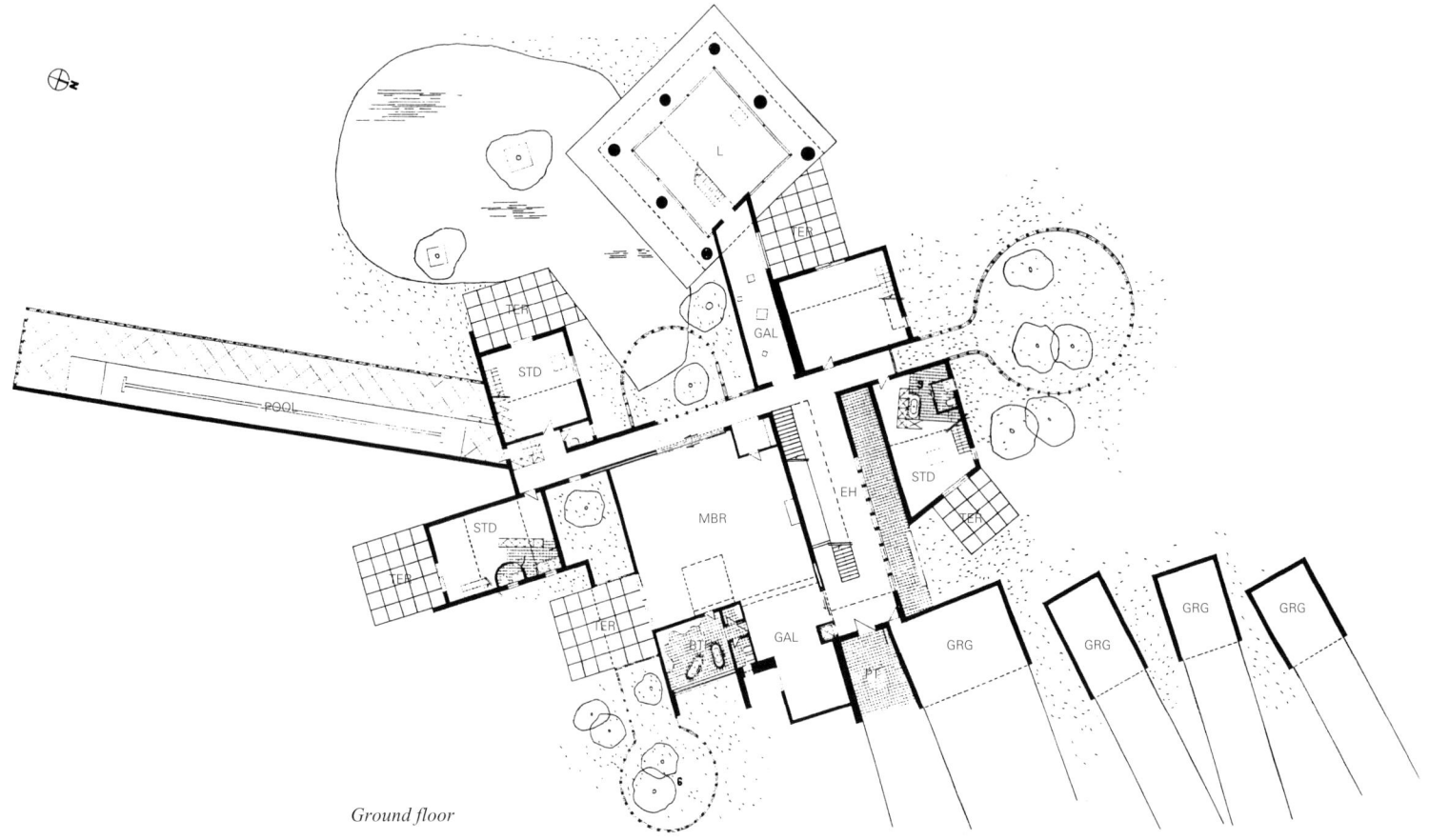

Ground floor

The project consists of a private single family home of 1,100 square meters with an integrated aviary of 300 square meters for exotic birds.

Ernest Mourmans' request for a situation in which the birds and the people were continuously interacting (visually) throughout the different areas of the house was resolved by architecturally incorporating the volumes and corridors for the birds (a custom-designed greenhouse construction system), into a series of volumes and corridors for people. The people spaces use simple construction methods (concrete and steel) and local materials such as glazed brick, colored concrete block and metal roofing, as well as ceramic tile cladding and slate.

Together the two environments form a bi-level, three-dimensional dialogue between the birds, the gardens and courtyards, the people and the architecture. The custom-designed interiors include the more architectural built-in specialities, such as the lemon-wood staircase in the living room, or the large master bathroom with dual bathtubs and mirrored walls, to the actual furniture including all sofas, tables, beds, libraries, cabinets and so on.

The interior finishes are extremely detailed with unusual materials: blue Brazilian marble for the large gallery/entry hall, exotic natural woods for the wardrobe walls, custom made ceramic tiles for the bathrooms and kitchen, rare marble for the fireplaces, bleached wood or fiber-laminate for doors.

Throughout the house there is a collection of art installations, including a ceramic tile wall printed entirely with a Helmut Newton photograph from the "Big Nudes" series, a Dan Flavin "light" in the stairwell and plans for a Sol Lewitt wall installation in the sculpture gallery, and a Francesco Clementi fresco in the living room.

外来種の鳥を飼う300平米の鳥小屋を組み入れた1,100平米の住宅である。

鳥と人が，どこにいても常に視覚的に交流できる家というアーネスト・モーマンズの要望には，鳥のための空間と廊下（特注の温室工法システム）を人のための空間と廊下の連鎖のなかに統合することで応えた。人のための空間には単純な工法（コンクリートと鉄）とセラミック・タイル被覆やスレートに加え，施釉煉瓦，着色コンクリート・ブロック，金属屋根のような地元の材料を使用した。

2種類の環境が一つになって，鳥たち，庭や中庭，人間たち，そして建築の間に2層に広がる，3次元の対話が生まれる。

特別にデザインしたインテリアには，居間にあるレモン・ウッドの階段，浴槽が二つあり，壁全面が鏡になっている主寝室の広い浴室のように，建築と一体化した造作部分から，家中のソファ，テーブル，ベッド，書棚，戸棚などの個々の家具に至るまでが

Southwest view from garden

含まれる。
　内部仕上げは，珍しい材料を用いた非常に精緻なものである。広いギャラリー／エントリー・ホールにはブラジル産の青大理石，ワードローブの壁にはエキゾチックな自然木，浴室と厨房には特注のセラミック・タイル，暖炉には稀少大理石，扉には漂白した木またはファイバー・ラミネート等々。
　家全体に，インスタレーション・アートが配されている。ヘルムート・ニュートンの"ビッグ・ヌード"シリーズから選んだ写真を全面にプリントしたセラミック・タイルの壁，階段室にあるダン・フラヴァンの"ライト"，そして計画されている，彫刻ギャラリーのソル・ルイットによる壁のインスタレーション，居間のフランチェスコ・クレメンティのフレスコ画等々。

Living room

Studio

Glazed space for birds

Entrance hall

Staircase to dining room

Dining room on first floor

Dining room: view from kitchen

Fireplace and sofa at dining room

Cupboard for kitchen

Fireplace at living room

Living room

Living room: view toward garden

Gallery next to bedroom

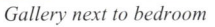

Master bedroom

Glenn Murcutt 2001

House in Southern Highlands, New South Wales, Australia

This house stands amid the countryside in Southern Highlands, south of Sidney, richly endowed with the beauties of nature.

The first sight caught from the approach is the artificial pond that focalizes the site. It functions not only as a reservoir impounding rain water, but also to attract wild animals and provide chances to observe them from inside the house.

The building features a linear organization: the hall placed along the southern side in the longitudinal direction connects all of the spaces in this house. The main space is placed north of this hall, and the roof covering the entire building and the overhung that consists the hall's wall are both designed to serve as sunshade during summer and to introduce the southern hemisphere sunshine deeper into the house during winter. Galvanized corrugated sheets on the wall along the longitudinal side is similar in figure to the roof, protecting the privacy as well as shielding the chilly wind from the south.

Five bedrooms and two living rooms make up this residence's main living space, with flexibility of purposes accommodating family members and friends.

The main structure is steel-framed. Its roof is given a peculiar shape reminiscent of traditional methods of farming architecture, a gentle silhouette in harmony with the surrounding natural environment. This roof and the wall of the southern hall are covered with galvanized corrugated sheets. External walls are finished with gray slate or cement painted gray. Wood is finished with oil stain. Pillars of exposed concrete and galvanized corrugated sheets are unsurfaced. The structural steel frames are painted metallic gray. Inner walls and ceilings are painted white. Floors are covered with stone.

View from northeast

Overall view from north

Entrance on east

View toward main entrance from hall

Detail: drain

Detail: roof

Living room

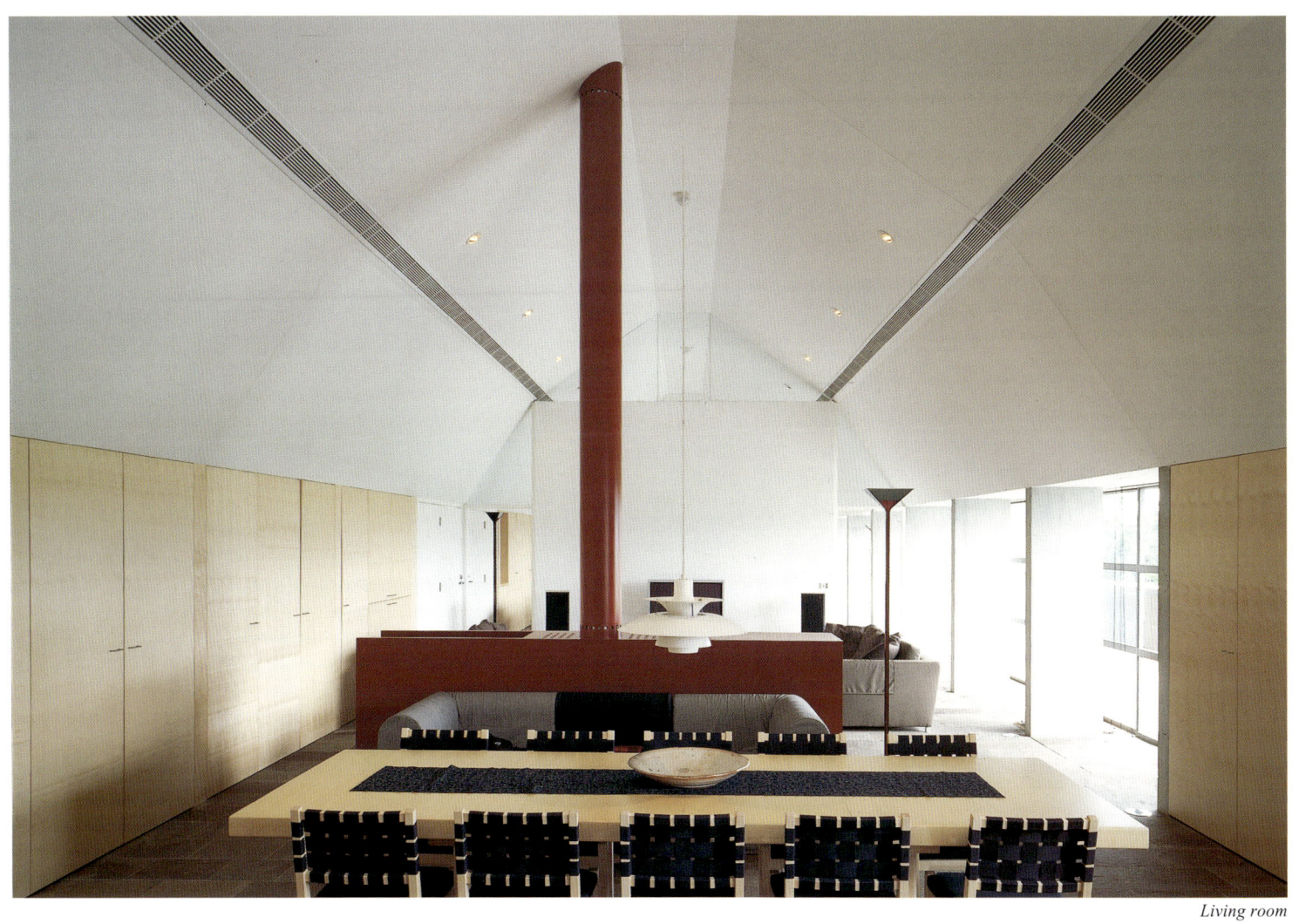

View toward dining room and kitchen

Guest bedroom

View toward living room from kitchen

　この住宅はシドニーの南，美しく豊かな自然の残るサザン・ハイランドの田園地帯に位置する。
　アプローチで最初に見ることとなる人口池は，敷地に焦点をつくりだす。この池は雨水を貯める貯水池として機能するとともに，野生動物を呼び込み，住宅内からそれらを観察する機会を提供する。
　建物は東西方向にリニアな構成で，その長手方向南側に沿って置かれるホールはこの住宅のすべての空間を結んでいる。主要空間はそのホールの北側に配置され，建物全体を覆う屋根の形状とホールの壁面であるオーバーハングは，夏期には日除けとして作用し，冬期には，南半球の陽光を室内深くまでもたらすように設計されている。建物長手方向に沿うように配置される亜鉛引き波板の壁は屋根の相似形であり，この住宅の内部のプライバシーを守ると共に，南からの冬の冷たい風を防ぐ役目をする。
　この住宅の主要な空間である五つの寝室と二つの居間は家族やその友人達のためのフレキシブルな用途に対応出来るようになっている。
　主構造は鉄骨による。特徴的な形態の屋根は，伝統的な農業建築の様式を喚起させるようなもので，周囲の自然環境と共存する優しいシルエットが与えられている。その屋根と南側ホールの壁面は亜鉛引き波板葺きである。外壁は灰色のスレートが暖かな灰色に塗られたセメント仕上げ，木材はオイルステイン仕上げによる。また，打放しコンクリートの柱と亜鉛引き波板は無塗装である。そして，構造材である鉄骨はメタリックグレーに塗装される。内部の壁，天井は白く塗られ，床は石貼りである。

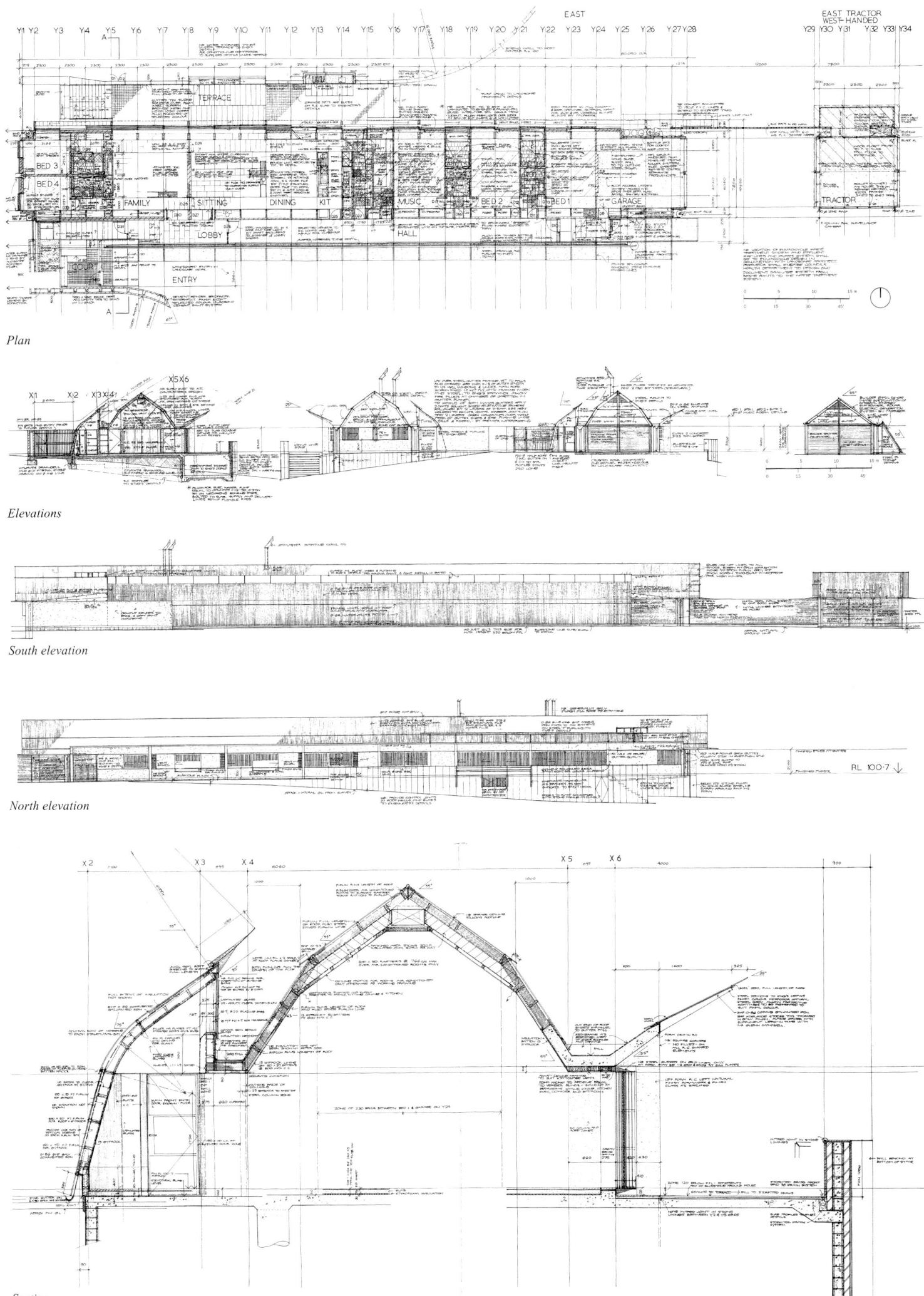

Plan

Elevations

South elevation

North elevation

Section

Overall view from street on north

View from garden on south

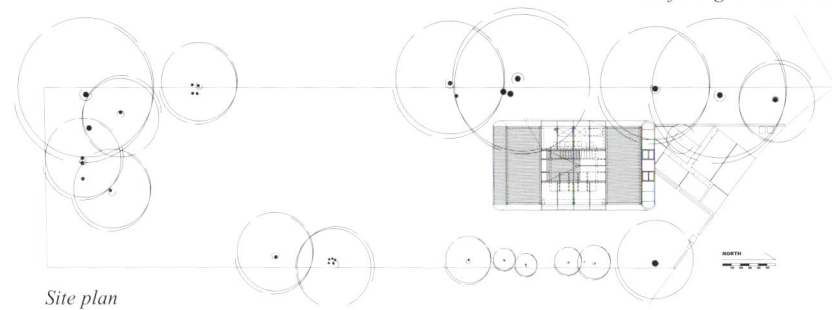

Site plan

Starting position
The property, where *Solar Tube* was built, is situated in Döbling, a north-western outskirt of Vienna. Döbling is a quiet, rather wealthy residential area with mostly single-family-homes. The property itself is rather narrow but long with a high tree stock. The size of the property totals 1,300 square meters.

Before the actual design process could be started, the opportunities had to be checked. The opportunities are always defined by the characteristics of the location, the plot and the landscape. The sun's position is needed to be taken into account as well as the number of hours of sunlight and a range of other weather aspects before starting the actual design process.
Why "solar tube"?

A "solar tube" in general is a small light-and-heat captor which is usually installed on the roofs of houses. In this case, the entire house serves as a collector, opening to light-and-heat on all sides. The wooded site has enabled the architect to use generously glazed elevations, which are sloping or curved in various parts. Since the roof and floors are also partly transparent, the core of the house works like an integrated atrium. As for the glass "tube" that forms the uppermost level, it helps cut heating costs in winter. Apart from its energy-saving virtues, glass also offers intimacy with the surrounding nature. Therefore one gets the feeling of living in a tree-house. It's a symbiosis between nature and architecture.
Built in only 5 months
Solar Tube was built in only 5 months, from April till August 2001. This fast construction was possible due to the usage of mostly prefabricated or in-stock units and base materials. Custom designed and manufactured elements do not necessarily produce better results. At the same time, choosing an alternative solution saves a lot of money, energy and time.
Low energy concept
Overheating in summer is avoided by the trees as well as by a special ventilation system that works like a chimney. In winter the heating costs can be cut to a minimum because of the compact coat of the building that is designed in a way of absorption and reflection that allow a high amount of sun energy to be used. On the other hand of course the defoliated trees in winter allow the sunlight to shine through the glazed facade and roof and therefore also help cutting the heating costs.
Design and functionality
Seeing *Solar Tube* from the street is an experience on its own. Passer by's are attracted by the remarkable shape of the house as well as by the glass facade, although the facade facing the street is more closed (compared to the sides facing the garden) to give the inhabitants more intimacy.

The integrated atrium that builds the core of the house is open to all sides. Even from the ground level one can see through to the sliding roof. This is possible due to the partly transparent floors on one hand and on the other hand due to the fact that the bedrooms in the uppermost level are reached over a gallery. The interior is also characterized by the spirit of "open living". Most of the furniture was also designed by Georg Driendl and therefore fits in perfect harmony to the design of the building itself. The library for instance is very remarkable, as the movable book-shelves are installed on a rail in the upper level and extract over 2 levels.

East elevation

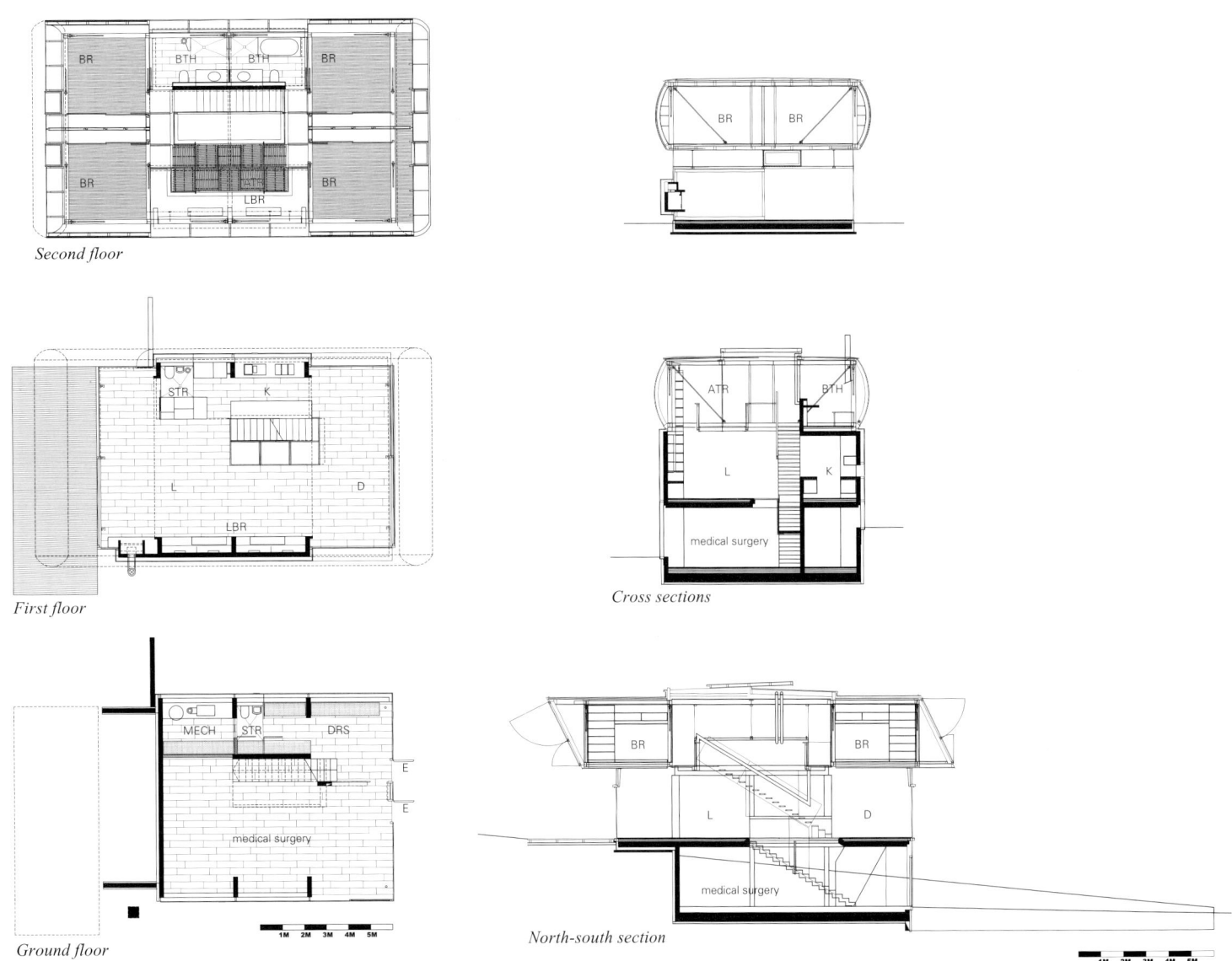

Second floor

First floor

Ground floor

Cross sections

North-south section

〈出発点〉
敷地は、ウィーンの北西郊外、デブリンクにある。デブリンクは大半が一戸建て住宅が並ぶ、比較的豊かで、静かな住宅地である。敷地そのものは、かなり幅が狭いが、奥行きが深く、背の高い木立に恵まれている。敷地の広さは全体で1,300平方米である。

デザインを始める前に、太陽熱を利用できるかチェックする必要があった。そういった状況は常に、ロケーションの特徴、計画構想、ランドスケープによって判断される。実際の作業に入る前に、日照時間、その他の気象状況と同様に、太陽の位置についても計算に入れる必要がある。

〈なぜソーラー・チューブか？〉
"ソーラー・チューブ"は通例、屋根の上に設置された、光と熱の小さな捕獲装置である。今回のプロジェクトでは、家全体が、全面を光と熱に開いたコレクターとして働く。木立の多い敷地は、立面の様々な部分に、斜めになったものやカーブしたガラス面を豊かにとることを可能とした。屋根と床もまた一部が透明なので、住宅のコアは、全体を統合するアトリウムのように働く。最上階を構成するガラスの"チューブ"は、冬場の暖房費を節約するのに役立つ。その省エネルギーという長所の他に、ガラスは、周囲の自然を身近なものにしてくれる。このためツリー・ハウスに住んでいるような感覚を得られる。自然と建築の共生である。

〈わずか5ヶ月で完成〉
「ソーラー・チューブ」は、2001年の4月から8月にかけてのわずか5ヶ月で完成した。この迅速な工事は、プレハブや規格ユニットと基盤材料を大幅に使用することで可能となった。注文設計や手工芸でつくられたエレメントは必ずしもより良い結果を生むわけではない。同時に、二者択一的な方法は経費、エネルギー、時間を大幅に節約してくれる。

〈省エネルギー・コンセプト〉
夏の過熱状態は、煙突のような作用をする特別な通気システムと同時に木立によって防ぐ。冬には、暖房費を最小限に節減できる。熱を吸収し反射するようにデザインされた建物のコンパクトな外皮によって、太陽熱エネルギーを大量に利用できるからである。一方、もちろんのこと、冬の落葉によりガラス張りのファサードや屋根を透過して太陽が差し込むことも、暖房費の節減を助けている。

〈デザインと機能性〉
道路から「ソーラー・チューブ」を見るのは、ちょっと変わった体験である。通りがかりの人は、ガラスのファサードと同時にこの家の珍しい形態に惹きつけられる。とはいえ、道路側のガラス面は（庭に面した側よりも）、住む人により心地よさを与えるために比較的閉ざされている。

コアを形成し、家全体を統合するアトリウムは周囲すべてが開かれている。1階からでさえ、スライディング・ルーフまで見通せる。これは、一つには、床面が部分的に透明であること、一つには、最上階の寝室が両端に位置し、ギャラリーでつながっていることによる。内部空間はまた、「オープン・リビング」という考えによって特徴づけられている。

大半の家具もドリエンデルのデザインであり、建物のデザインと完璧に調和している。例えば、ライブラリーは特に目を引く。可動の書棚は上階に設置されたレール上に装填されていて、二つの階から本の出し入れができるのである。

First floor: living room

Living room: double height bookshelves

24

Second floor: view toward bedrooms on south

Kitchen

Bathroom

Osamu Ishiyama   2001

Setagaya-Mura, Setagaya, Tokyo, Japan

Distant view from south

View from southwest: sliding walls

Garage

Partial south elevation

My philosophies of life, my views on the world, and my architectural perspectives are all clear and present within this house—my own home. It is located in Setagaya Ward, some 15-minute train ride from Tokyo's subcenter, Shinjuku. Setagaya Ward is an area where land plotting as a product of the former feudalistic agricultural society was left intact upon its growth into a city. My house stands in the midst of such landscape typical of Setagaya where no traces of modern urban planning can be found. To the north is a grove of a Shinto shrine, and to the south is the 'green-zone preserve', premodern crop fields that the local administration has secured according to its nature-conservation plan.

The site is presently carrying a wooden, single-storied house that my wife's mother has built. She was much concerned about its physiognomy, and had consulted the carpenters. This 50-year-old house is an average, traditional Japanese house. We have been living there in good comfort, but the day came when all of a sudden a sliding shutter fell off. Then glass doors came off. The veranda crumbled. In a word, it's had its day. Anyway, it was the eldest in the vicinity: all of the neighboring houses have been either rebuilt or repaired for the last 10 or 20 years. Incoherence and chaos always go together with residential quarters in Japan. And my house was inevitably part of it. Despite its humble fifty years of life and its orthodox yet average features, the house was cherished by our family. Never pretentious, this house built by nameless carpenters has never ceased to please me. Its life has simply come to expire, and its prolongation would be just too much costly.

So I took my decision to rebuild it. However, all family members wished to live in the old house for as long as possible, and would not want to move temporarily elsewhere during construction. With this, I managed to go on with the construction works by bringing the old house up in midair over the site. Hence comes this structure where a pair of floors is suspended from a set of four masts, as a mini-model of artificial ground.

I am currently engaged in a concept of open-system technology. Architectural technology has always been considered not as pertaining to individuals, but to architects and construction companies in a social manner, that is, accumulated inside the construction industry. But my opinion is that in an information society, technologies of architecture, especially of houses, ought to be nurtured among the individuals, the dwellers' side. In brief, I believe that housing and living environment must be developed among the individuals.

This house is the first prototype of my open technology theory. There have been several studies of the kind in the past, but with this one, I have succeeded for the first time in materializing my theory in a clearly comprehensible way. Every detail of the living environment built on the artificial ground of this tension structure was put together by my staff members and myself.

Osamu Ishiyama

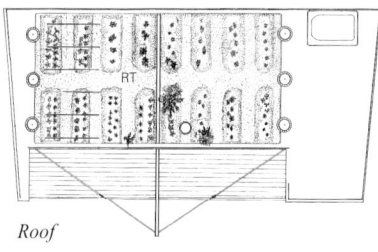
Roof

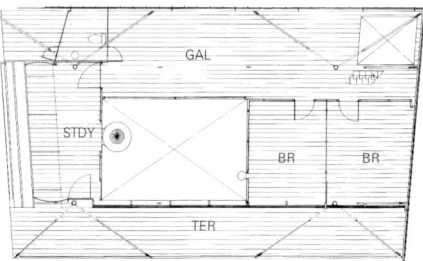
Third floor

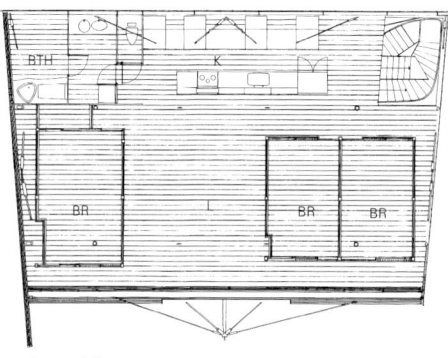
Second floor

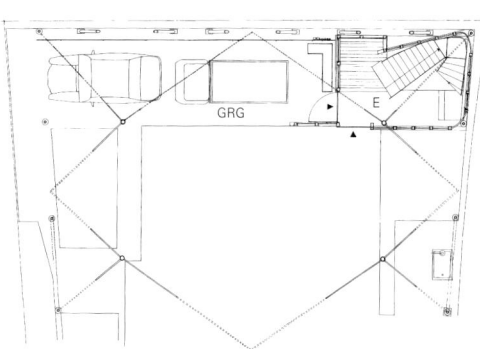
First floor S=1:300

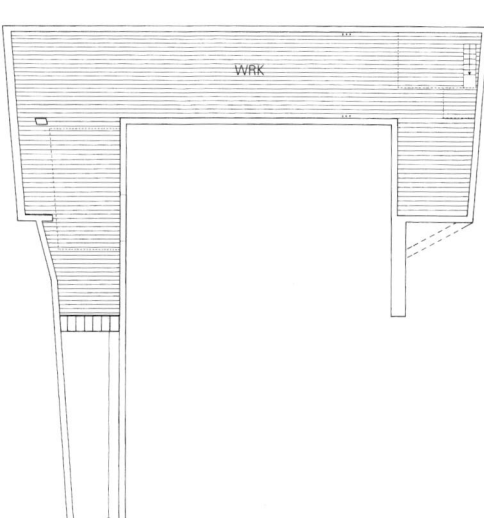
Basement

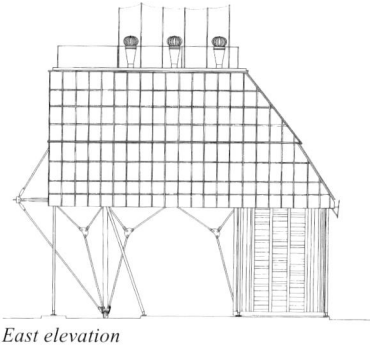
East elevation

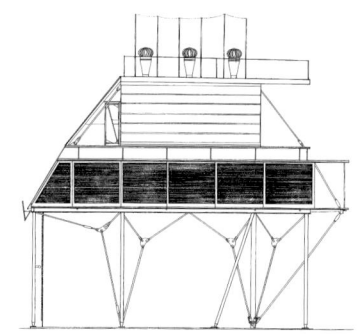
West elevation

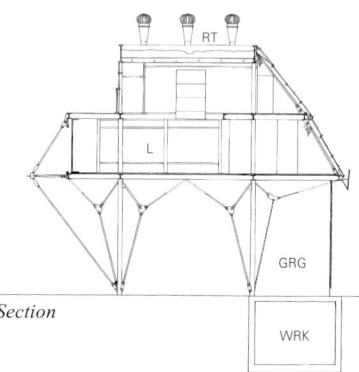
Section

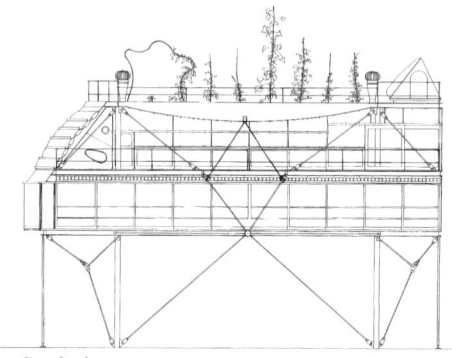
South elevation

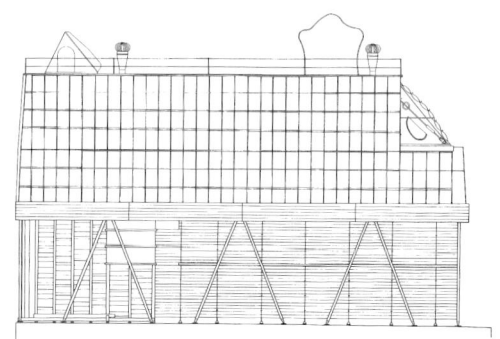
North elevation S=1:300

View of living room from third floor

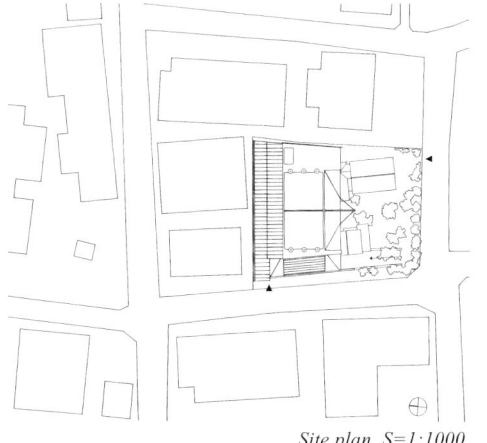

Site plan S=1:1000

　私の自宅である。それゆえに私の人生観，世界観，建築観が鮮明に表れている。自宅は東京の副都心新宿から電車で15分程の世田谷区にある。世田谷区は近代的な都市と呼ぶには余りにも無計画な，前近代の農耕社会の土地割がそのまま都市の姿になってしまったところで，私の家はそんな世田谷の典型的な風景の中に建っている。北には神社の森があるし，南は保護緑地という畑で，都市内の緑を守るために行政が計画的に残した前近代の畑である。

　現在敷地には木造平屋の住宅が建っている。家内の母が大工さんと家相を相談しながら建てた家である。築50年になるこの家は極々普通の日本の伝統的家屋だった。その家に私も何不自由なく暮らしていたのだが，ある日突然雨戸が落ちた。ガラス戸も自然に落ちた。縁側もボロボロになった。つまり家の寿命が来たらしかった。それでも私の古い家は周辺では一番古い家だった。周りの家は全てここ10年20年で新築改築されていた。とりとめのない住宅地の無秩序は日本に典型的な風景でもあるが，私の家もその只中に建てなければならなかった。高々築50年の古い家であったが，私の家族は皆その古い伝統的な普通の家を愛していた。私も名も無い大工が建てた何気ない家を好ましく思っていた。ただ，古い家の寿命が来たのだ。それを延命するには余りにもコストが掛かり過ぎた。

　それで新築することにした。しかし家族は皆，古い家に可能な限り住み続けたいという。新築工事中に仮住まいに引越すのも嫌だという。それで古い平屋の上空に古い家を残したまんま新築することにした。4本のマストから人工土地のミニモデルとしての床を2枚吊り下げる構造は，そうした理由から決定された。

　次に私は開放系技術という技術体系を構想しつつある。建築技術は従来個人に属するものではなくて，社会的に建築家や建設会社，ようするに建設産業の側に蓄積されていると考えられてきた。それに対して，私は情報化社会における建築，特に住宅は，生活者としての個人の側に技術が育られてるべきだと考えている。端的に言えば住宅，あるいは住環境は個人の側から構築されるべきだと考えている。

　この住宅は，私の開放系技術論の試作品一号である。これまでも様々な習作はあったが，初めて解りやすい形で理論を形にできた。テンション構造の人工土地につくり込まれた住環境は全て，私と私のスタッフが組み立てたのである。

（石山修武）

View of kitchen from living room

Gallery on third floor

Kitchen

Living room

Entrance: staircase

Living room

Jun Aoki
2001
I, Tokyo, Japan

View from street on northeast

First floor: bedroom above

First floor: view toward street

Study on second floor △▽

A sculpture-like, concrete outer shell placed within the space between two houses. A 50 mm-thick coat of Styrofoam. Covering up the whole thing are planks of imported wood; steel and aluminium-framed windows; and stainless-steel mesh.

Two independent volumes stuck inside the shell. The upper level's floor, which encloses the mezzanine, which in turn confines the only hermetic space of the house. The ground level's floor, which encloses the basement space. The space between the outer shell and the two volumes, that are sometimes open vertically, or filled up with steel-framed windows. Inner and outer spaces generated inside the outer shell.

Handrails of the simplest form, of thick steel pipes, whose impressive thickness reminds us that they are pieces of rectangular steel tubes rather than handrails. The stainless-steel water sink placed on the floor as if it had appeared out of the blue, and an over-sized desk of recycled timber, whose horizontal plane exerts the same level of strength as the floor or the ceiling. A series of stand-alone units of steel furniture that have nothing to do with the outer shell. Wall in an inverted L-shape, suspended from a set of two pipes parallel to one another, to provide storage space or to serve as a partition.

The elements that constitute the building were not assembled to form any hierarchical structure destined for the materialization of some kind, nor to merge to become one integral space. Instead, each of them exists as a single unit of substance. And the aggregation of such units has accidentally produced a space. Such attitude gives transparency to something that lies behind the substances and spaces that the act of creation has brought about and forced to take onto itself. Its purity is a source of wildness and liberty.

家と家の隙間に存在する彫刻のような形をしたコンクリートの外殻。その外側に取り付けられた50ミリ厚のスタイロフォーム、それらをカバーするように被せられた南洋産の木板、スティールとアルミのサッシュ、ステンレスのメッシュ。

外殻の内側に挟まっている二つの独立したヴォリューム。2階となる床面と、その内側である中2階となる唯一の内気の閉ざされた空間。1階となる床面と、その内側である地下階となる空間。ある部分は吹抜となり、ある部分はスティールのサッシュが嵌められている、外郭と二つのヴォリュームの間に生まれる隙間。外郭の内側に生まれる内部空間と外部空間。

太さによって手摺であること以前に角パイプであることを認識させる、太いスティールの単純な手摺。床面に唐突に置かれたステンレスのシンクと、床や天井と同じ強さの面として存在している、古材を並べたオーバーサイズの机。外郭とは無関係に取り付けられた、独立した単体の反復によるクロカワ付きスティールの家具。収納や間仕切りとなる2本の平行するパイプから吊り下げられた逆さL字形の壁。

建物を構成する要素が、ある何かの実現のためにヒエラルキーをもって構築され、融合し一つの空間として存在するのではなく、それぞれがある単体の物質として、存在しているというようなあり方、そしてそのことによってたまたまできた空間。それは、つくるという行為によって生じ、担わされてしまう物質や空間の背後にある何かを透明に近づけ、純粋であることの、荒々しさと自由さを生んでいる。

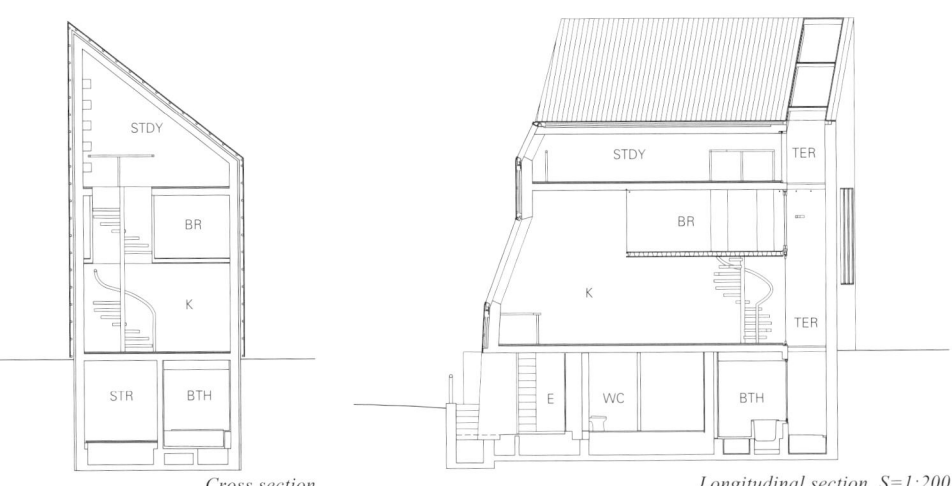

Study

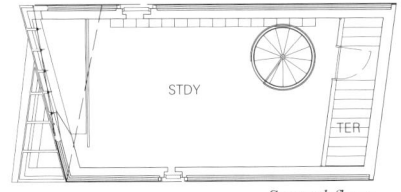

Second floor

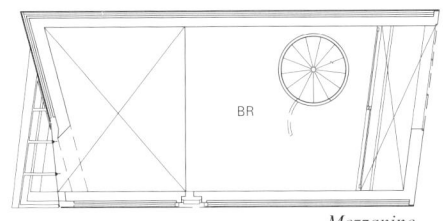

Mezzanine

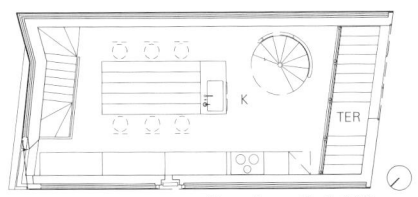

First floor   S=1:200

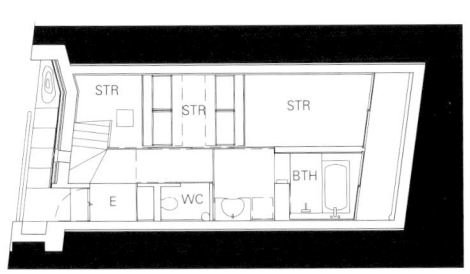

Basement   *Cross section*   *Longitudinal section   S=1:200*

Masaki Endoh + Masahiro Ikeda 2002

Natural Ellipse, Shibuya, Tokyo, Japan

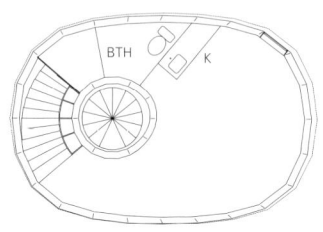
Second floor

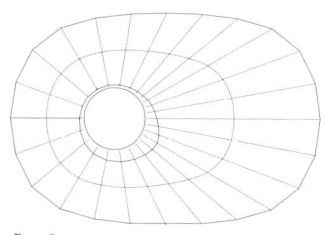
Roof

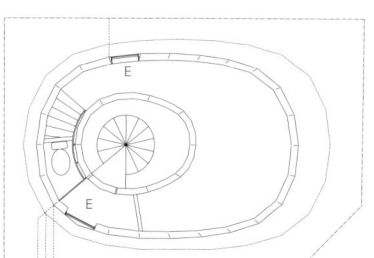
First floor S=1:200

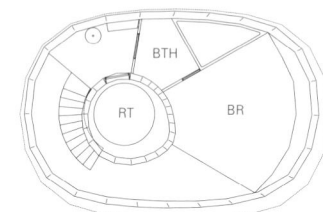
Fourth floor

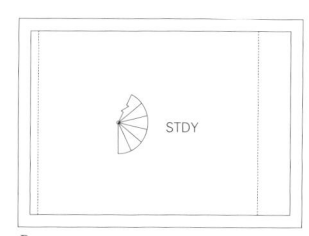
Basement

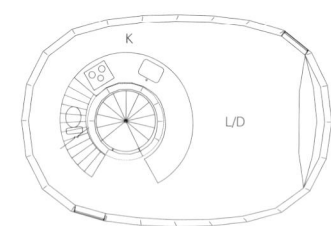
Third floor

Site
The site is located on the edge of Shibuya, Tokyo's shopping and entertainment district. There amid a riot of color of glaring neon lights, a duplex house was planned. The type of design that would close itself to such exterior to ensure a decent environment inside, would not satisfy the owner who has purchased this particular plot of land without reluctance. A design in competence with the surroundings is most likely to be swallowed up sooner or later. In both cases, perception of environment is partial and one-sided: here, flexibility to manipulate the environment is a must. We have finally come up with a concept of an architecture that would enable such action.

Elliptical Ring / Body of Rotation
The geometry adopted was the ellipse. By varying the ratio between its major and minor axes, the ellipse makes it possible to adjust its form according to the external requirements, or modify the allocation of floor spaces.

Also, its double focus deprives this figure of centrality, making it possible to erase the hierarchy of details such as the pillar or the beam, and to create a continuity from the outside toward the inside. The overall shape takes the form of a body of rotation made of 24 units of elliptical rings placed along a horizontal elliptical orbit. It represents at the same time, the structure itself: a sequence of what has been formed inside each ring.

Plan
The plan consists of a cylindrical central block composed of these rings and zones for natural lighting and longitudinal flow lines that continue from the exterior, radiating outward.

Exterior = FRP
FRP is employed for external finish, as a material capable of joining the rings and expressing such continuity. It has the merit of being waterproof, and can be molded and applied at will, to realize a seamless exterior.

Architecture with freedom
This architecture is endowed with a flexibility of form, with various design terms such as material or structure defined by elliptical rings, as transition parameters. A rather biased freedom based on a certain hypothesis, that has nonetheless accomplished an architecture to take root in the environment through nifty and precise footwork.

Masaki Endo + Masahiro Ikeda

〈敷地〉
敷地は東京の繁華街渋谷の外れに位置し，百花繚乱としたネオンが連なるところである。ここに2世帯の住宅を計画した。こうした条件下の，外部に閉口し，良好な環境条件を内部につくり込むようなデザインでは，この土地を進んで購入した建築主を満足させることはできず，逆に周囲と競い合うデザインでも，いずれ呑込まれてしまう結果が予想される。どちらも環境を一面的にしか捉えてなく，自在に環境を操ることが必要とされている。そうした行為を可能にする建築を考えた。

〈楕円リング・回転体〉
その手段として，楕円という幾何学を採用した。楕円という形は，長短辺の比率を変えることができ，それによる床面積の割振り，外部条件からの形の調整を可能にする。また，焦点が二つの中心性のない形でもあることで，柱と梁といった部位のヒエラルキーを消し，外から内への連続性をつくることも可能にする。全体の形は，その楕円形のリング24個を水平の楕円軌道に沿って並べた回転体として成立している。これは同時にストラクチャーでもある。個々ののリング内で成立していたものが連続したものである。

〈プラン〉
プランは，このリングが集まってできる中央の筒状部分を，外から連続する採光部兼縦動線に充てた放射状にのびた形をしている。

〈外装=FRP〉
外装には，リングの繋ぎとその連続性を表現を可能にするものとして，FRP材を採用する。この素材の長所となる防水材であること，自在に成型施工できることに加え，シームレスな外装を可能にしている。

〈自在性をもつ建築〉
こうした建築は，楕円リングによって定義される構造，材料等の様々なデザイン条件をパラメータとして，形を変化させる自在性をもっている。ある仮説に基づく偏った自在性であるのだが，それによって環境へ，微細にフットワークよく定着していく建築になっている。

（遠藤政樹+池田昌弘）

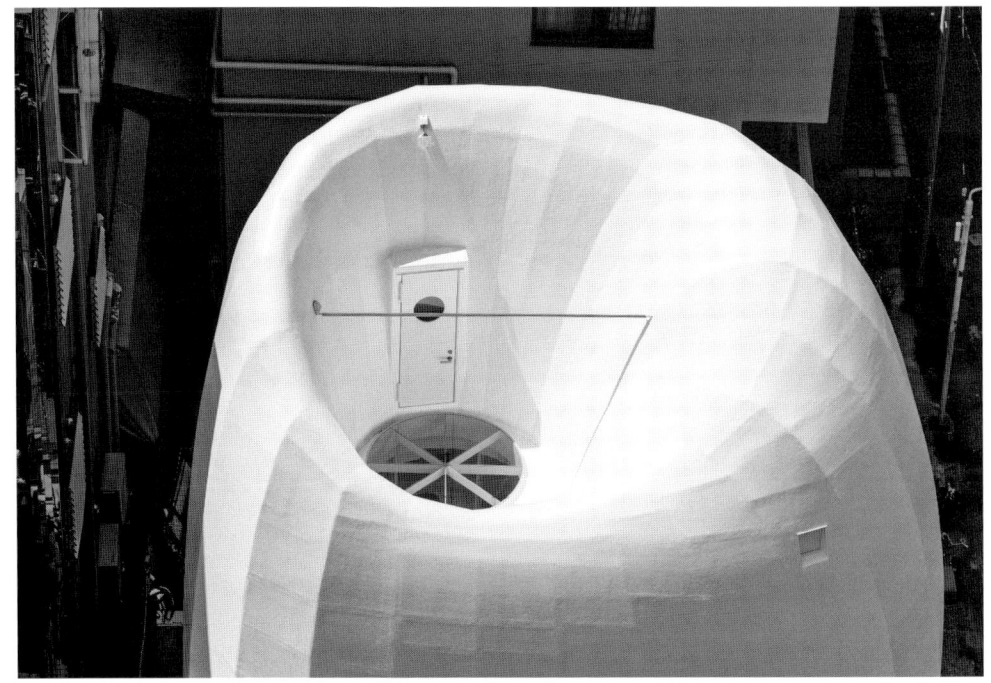

Roof terrace

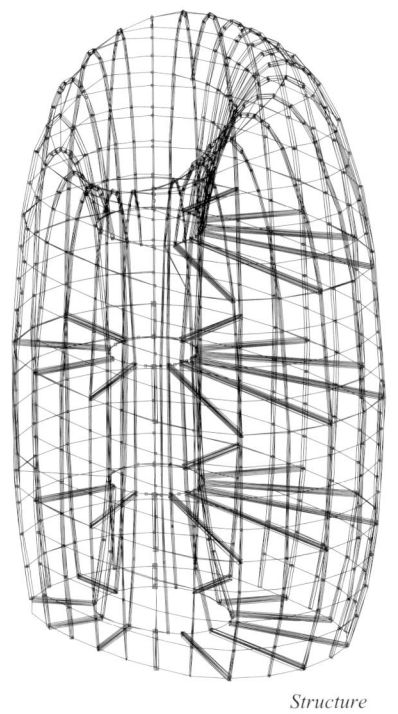

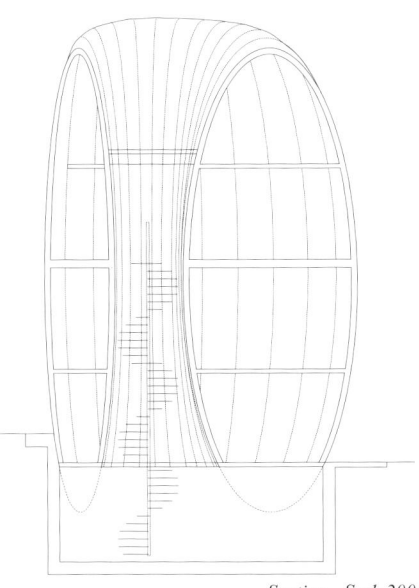

Structure

Section   S=1:200

Overall view

Bedroom

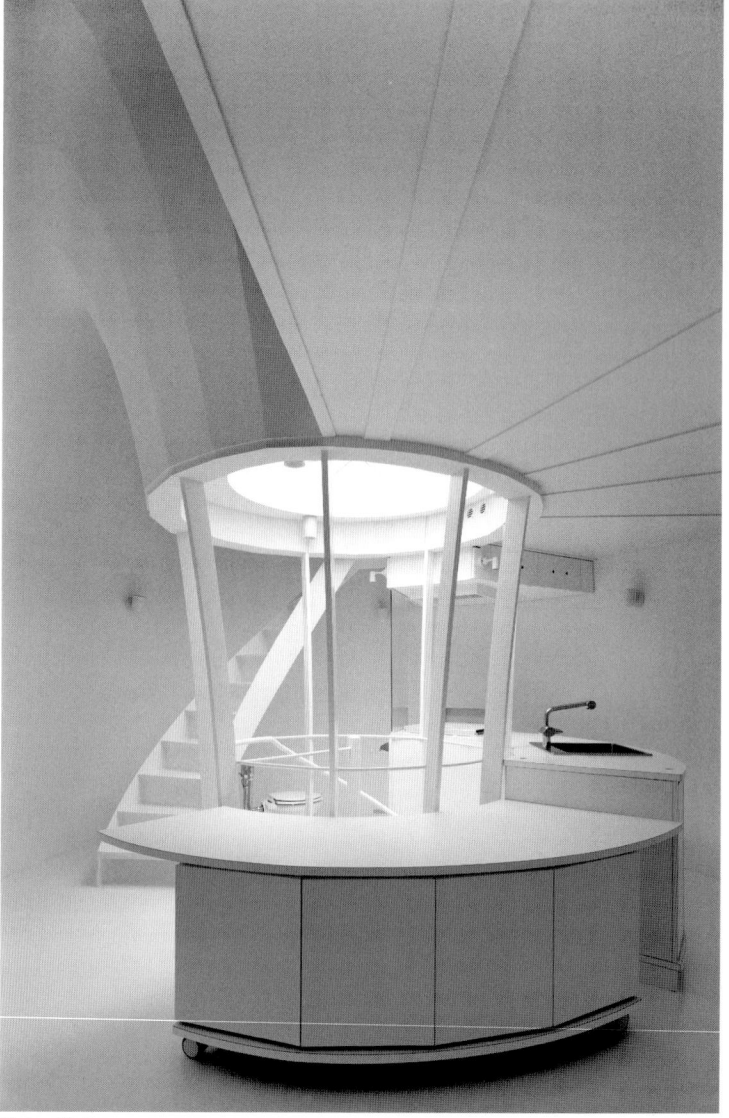

Basement

Living/dining room

Downward view through skylight

Staircase

Sean Godsell

2002

Peninsula House, Victoria, Australia

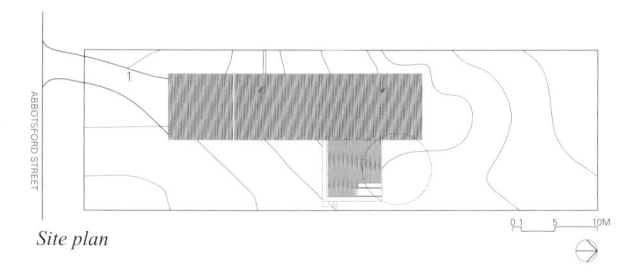

Site plan

Roof

Upper level

Lower level

East elevation

West elevation

Sections

A 30 x 7.2 meter-oxidized steel portal structure has been embedded into the side of a sand dune. This structure forms the 'exoskeleton' of the house upon which the weather controlling outer skin—operable timber shutters, glass roof and walls, membrane roof—are mounted. The simple programme of the house—a living/eating room, library and sleeping room forms the 'endoskeleton' of the building. The sleeping room is an inner room accessed by a private stair. These notions of inner room (moya) and enclosed verandah (hisashi) were explored in an earlier work (the Carter/Tucker House, GA HOUSES 69) where the idea of fluid (aisle) space formed the basis of the design for that building. The verandah has become further abstracted in this work to become the protective outer layer of the building. There is no distinction in that sense between the function of the roof and the function of the walls. The house itself is the nurturing inner room, protected from the elements by a coarse outer hide. The interplay of the occupant between these two elements activates the simple form of the building (by the opening and closing of the facade) and transforms it into an organic domain. This effect is further accentuated by the emptying and filling of the building with light, filtered through the timber screens, which maps the course of the day and the time of the year in the shape and extent of the shadows cast by the screens.

This is a further investigation into the similarities between the enclosed verandah of the traditional Japanese house and the 'sun room' of the Australian house. My interest lies in the iconic nature of these elements to both cultures—Asian and European—and the common architectural ground which they afford to the region.
Sean Godsell

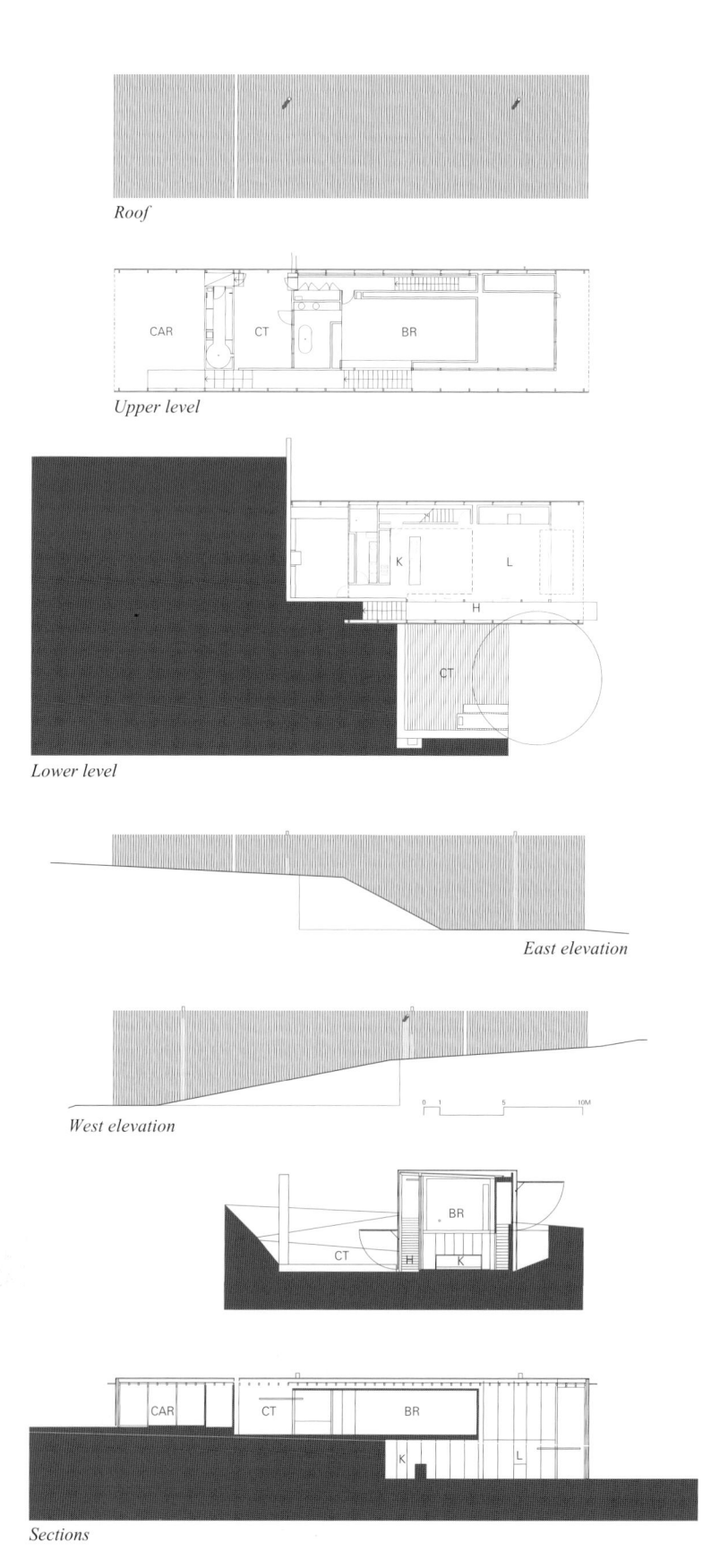

View from northeast

View from east

Living room: looking east

Living room: looking north

Bathroom

Living room (right) and hall (left)

Living room and terrace on east

Hall: dining room/kitchen on right

　砂丘の斜面に，酸化被膜処理したスティールでつくられた，30×7.2メートルの門型を埋め込む。この構造物は住宅の"外骨格"をかたちづくり，その上を，調節可能な木製シャッター，ガラスの屋根と壁，薄い膜製の屋根など，天候に対応して調節される外皮で覆う。リビング／食事の場，書斎，眠りの場から成る単純な部屋割りが"内骨格"を構成する。眠りの場はプライベートな階段から入る，奥の間である。奥の間（母屋）とそれを取り囲むベランダ（庇）という考えについては，少し前の作品（『カーター／タッカー邸』，『GA HOUSES 69』）で試していた。そこでは流動的な空間（側廊）というアイディアが建築デザインの基礎になっていた。今回の建物では，ベランダは内部を保護する外側の層にするために，より抽象化されている。その意味では，屋根の機能と壁の機能の間に違いはない。家そのものは，粗い外皮で自然から守られた，人を育む内奥の部屋である。これら二つの要素と住む人との間の相互作用が建物の単純な形を（ファサードを開閉することで）活性化させ，それを有機的な領土へと変貌させる。その効果は，木製スクリーンから浸透し，投射される影の形や長さによって1日の，1年の時の推移を地図のように描いていく光で，建物を空にし，また満たすことで強調される。

　このプロジェクトは，日本の伝統的な住宅の，部屋を取り囲む縁側とオーストラリアの住宅が持つ"サンルーム"との間の類似性をさらに深く研究したものある。私の関心は，アジアと西欧という両方の文化にとってのこれらのエレメントの持つアイコン的な性格と，この地域にそれらが与えてくれる共通の建築基盤にある。

（ショーン・ゴッドセル）

Akira Yoneda + Masahiro Ikeda   2002

Bloc, Kobe, Hyogo, Japan

Evening view

Entrance hall

Staircase on second floor: looking south

Overall view from southeast

View toward tatami room (left) and patio (right) from living/dining room

View toward dining room from patio

East elevation

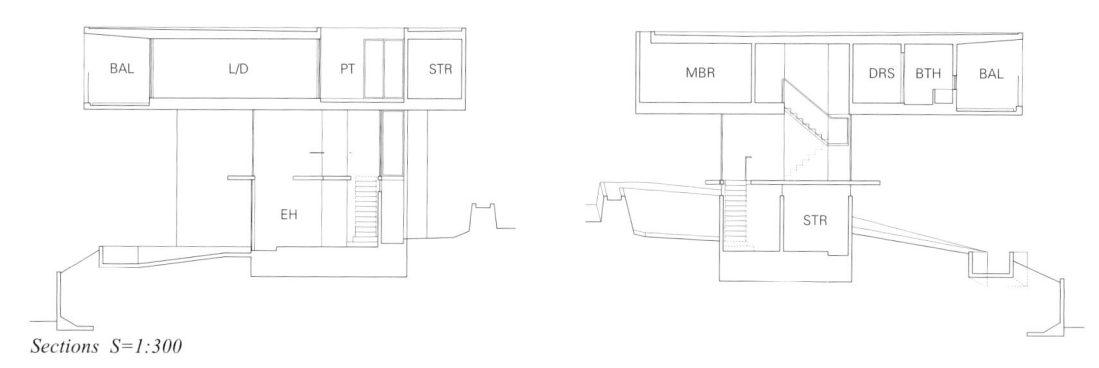

Sections S=1:300

This house was planned and constructed for an elderly lady who has lost her European-style house when the recent Great Hanshin Earthquake has destroyed her dear old home, and had no other choice than to live in a temporary residence for a long time. With its panoramic view over the Inland Sea (Setonai-kai), the site is situated in a tiered, fine residential zone developed in proximity of a terminal station of a cable car offering access to the top of the Rokko Mountains. The area gives an impression that the topological undulation from the Rokko Mountains is progressively transformed into an artificial one as it approaches the urban area.

In retrospect, Kobe consists of a narrow strip of urban land that was developed in the east-west direction between the Inland Sea shoreline and Rokko Mountains. The adjacent sea and mountains have been connected by sloping streets running north and south throughout the city. Whereas such horizontality and verticality attribute to Kobe's landscape a unique characteristic as a dialectic of the city and the nature, this building is organized in a manner that the topological undulation and the artificial rectangular volume are mediated by the geometry of orthogonal walls.

In other words, the first and second levels composed of white planes function as indexes suggesting the urban landscape's latent structure: the second-floor slab floating over the entrance hall corresponds to the horizontal shoreline along which stretches a highway; the elevator's side walls correspond to the slope connecting the sea and the mountains and to the cable car.

The overhung green rectangular volume on the top floor accommodates the old lady's self-contained residential space. Openings in limited forms of balcony and patio have been prepared to provide the same privacy and views over Seto Inland Sea and Rokko Mountains as the former house. Underneath this volume are: a room to lodge her children—who are now on their own and involved in international activities—on their visit home; the library to keep the archive of family remembrances; the entrance hall decorated with Western furniture and the fresco from the old house that have escaped damage, all housed in such manner that they seem to open outward.

The cantilever on the third floor measuring 10 meters in maximum is made structurally possible through the reinforcement supplied by the inner partition walls of the water utilities. The second-floor slab is hung down from the staircase leading to the third floor by four thin glass plates.

The outer structure features a stone fence that had originally existed on the premises, onto which lava rocks, scrap wood and a palm tree sent over from the old lady's hometown were arranged. They represent a narrative expression of destruction and regenesis derived from the earthquake.

Here is an attempt to create a hybrid field in which conflicting senses such as nature and man-made, sea and mountain, past and future, memory and expectation, fixation and separation, destruction and regenesis, opening and closure are formed to coexist, through a command of vocabulary pertaining to modern architecture that has once claimed to uphold universality or balance.

Akira Yoneda+Masahiro Ikeda

Dining room: view of Kobe Harbor

Site plan S=1:600

Third floor

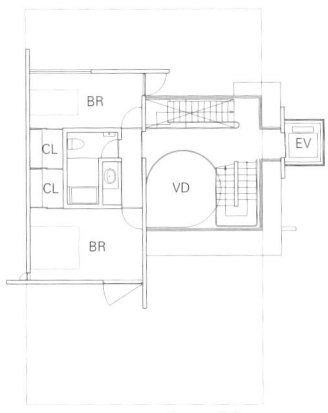

Second floor

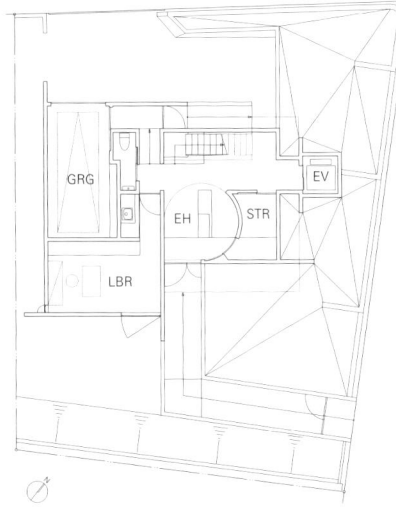

First floor S=1:300

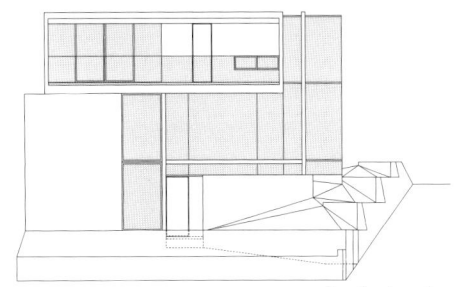

South elevation

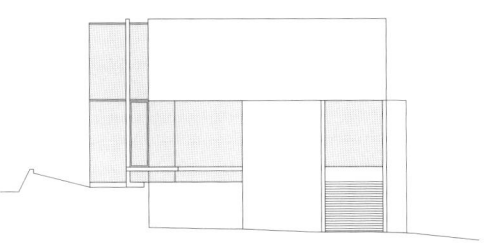

North elevation

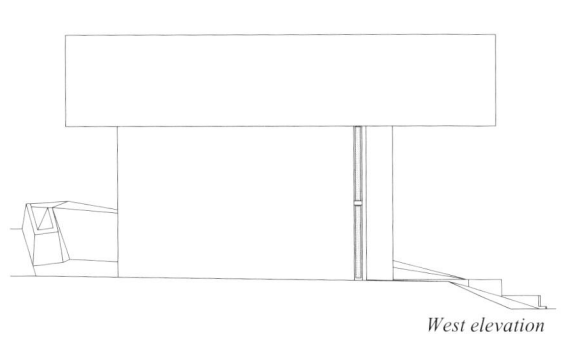

West elevation

East elevation S=1:300

阪神大震災で神戸の住み慣れた自宅洋館を失い，その後長らく仮住まいを余儀なくされてきた年配の婦人のために，この住宅は計画，建設された。六甲山頂にアクセスするケーブルカーの始発駅近い敷地は，瀬戸内海をパノラマ状に見渡せる，ひな壇状に造成された良好な住宅地にあって，六甲山からの地形の起伏が徐々に市街地に向けて，人工的なものへと変化しつつある印象をもっている。

そもそも神戸は，瀬戸内海の海岸線と六甲の山並に挟まれた幅の狭い市街地が東西方向に展開し，近接した海と山が市街地を縦断する南北方向の坂道によって結びつけられている。こうした東西方向の水平性と南北方向の垂直性が，神戸の景観に都市と自然の弁証性として固有の性格をもたらしているのに対し，この建物は地形のアンデュレーションと人工的な直方体のヴォリュームが，直交する壁の構成によって媒介されるような組み立てがなされている。

すなわち，1，2階の白い平面による構成は，都市景観の潜在的な構造を示唆するインデックスとして機能し，例えばエントランス・ホール上部の宙に浮いた，2階スラブは，海岸線もしくはそれに沿って水平に伸びる高速道路に対応し，エレベーターの側壁は，海と山を結ぶ坂道，さらにはケーブルカーと対応している。

最上階3階のオーバーハングした緑色の直方体が，完結した婦人の居住スペースであり，プライバシーを確保しながら見晴しのよかった旧宅同様，瀬戸内海と六甲の山並への眺望を得るために，バルコニーとパティオに限定された開口が設けられている。一方そのヴォリュームの下には，既に独立しインターナショナルに活躍している子供たちが滞留する居室，家族の記憶のアーカイブとなるライブラリー，さらには損失を免れた旧宅の壁画や南蛮家具を設置するエントランス・ホールが，むしろ外界へ向かって開いた形でおさめられている。

3階の最大10メートルに及ぶキャンティレバーは，構造的に内部水まわりの間仕切壁と上下のスラブを一体のストラクチャーとすることで可能とされ，2階スラブは，3階からの階段隔壁と4本の細いガラスの方立によって吊り下げられている。

外構は，元々の敷地の石垣を残した上に，溶岩石や廃材，そして婦人の郷里より取り寄せた1本のフェニックスを配して，震災による破壊と再生をナラティブに表現している。

こうして，かつてユニバーサリティーや均衡を標榜した近代建築のボキャブラリーを駆使して，自然と人工性，海と山，過去と未来，記憶と希望，定着と離脱，崩壊と再興，開放と閉鎖などの相反するものの感覚が，同時に生成され，共存するハイブリッドな場を形成することが目論まれている。

（米田明＋池田昌弘）

Ryoji Suzuki

2003

Experience in Material No. 45
House in Jingumae, Tokyo, Japan

Overall view from northwest

For this type of low-rise housing, environment at ground level is similar to that of a basement in terms of both natural lighting and ventilation. It is thus reasonable to assume that the actual ground level that may be called above ground can be found at around 5 meters above ground where the increase in the ratio of open space becomes apparent.

A view of the site's vicinity from this virtual ground level reveals that the crowd of houses and condominiums can be pictured as a topographic mass, a plateau 5 meters high. Planting there a house would mean boring a cavity into the massive plateau, cutting slits, and setting up a dry area. Partial boundaries such as external wall, roof and facade become vague. They are no longer independent constituents of a house mold, but things with a role of illustrating the undulating motion of the plateau that emerges somewhere around 5 meters above ground.

The figure of the spiral volume that is the most distinctive feature in this house; the L-shaped grand staircase on rooftop; and the court cut open in ground level on the south, are all consequences of speculations upon the plateau into which this residence has come to be inserted anew.

The structure consists of a 'stepped monocoque' in reinforced concrete. Thin walls that make up the rigid frame are supported in midair by steel 'cross-shaped columns' so they also function as wall girders, accounting for the double-faced 'convexity' of profile which gives this house's interior/exterior a distinction.

Partition walls, sliding door, paper panel doors, storage fittings are among those that segmentalize the spaces. Their height is limited to 2.4 meters, leaving out the upper space as transoms. In this manner, the 'concave' undulation on the reverse side of the 'convexity' is internalized in a direct continuum.

Ryoji Suzuki

Third floor

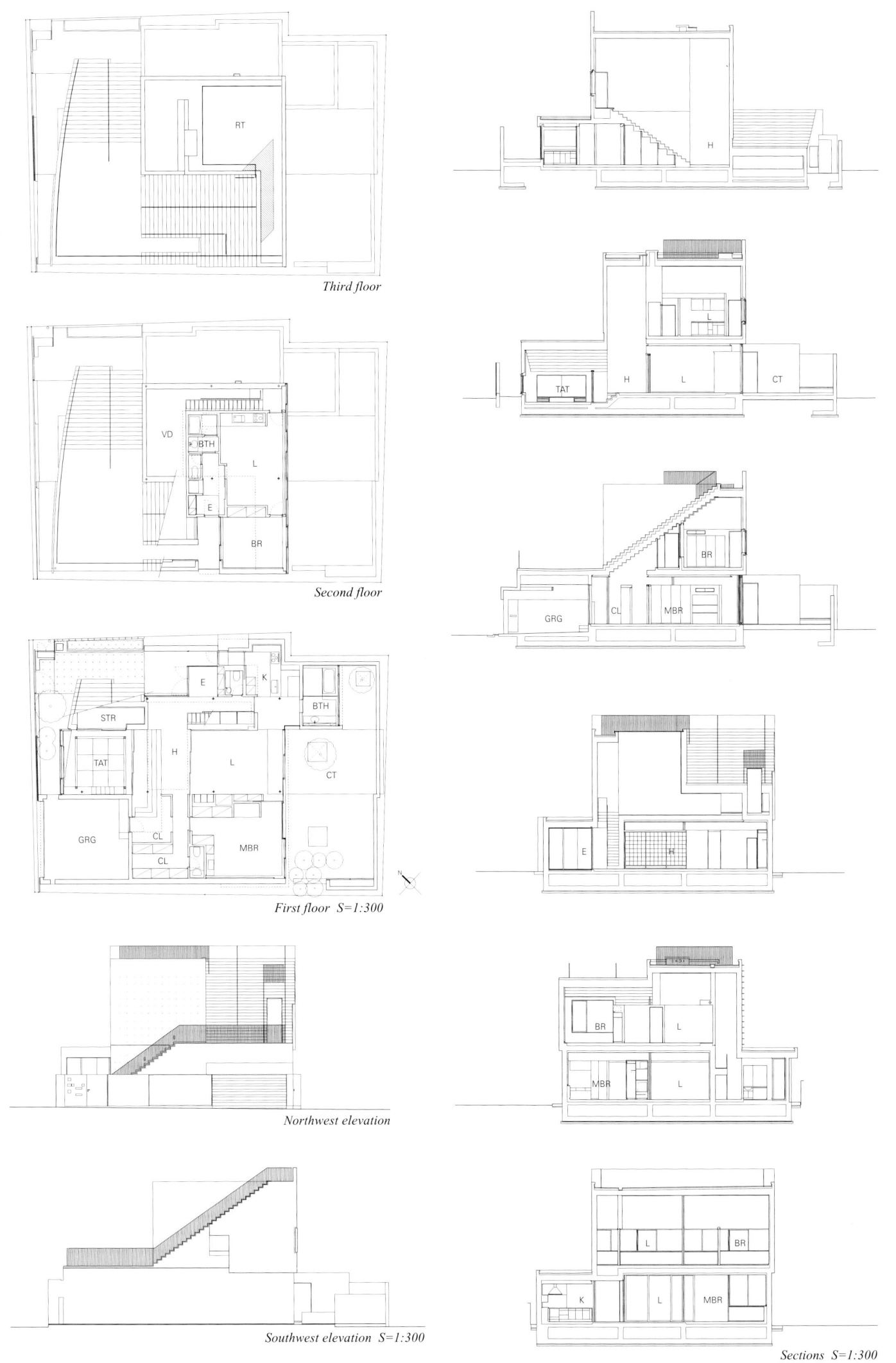

Second floor

First floor S=1:300

Northwest elevation

Southwest elevation S=1:300

Sections S=1:300

49

Hall: living room (left) and tatami room (right)

View toward tatami room from living room

View toward living room from tatami room

Detail of pillar, ceiling and staircase

Kitchen and bathroom

View toward hall from entrance

　原宿の表参道から少し奥に入ったこの一画だけ,なぜか古い記憶をとどめているかのようだ。とはいえ,かつてはゆったりとした住宅地であったに違いないこのあたりも,周辺が商業化し高層化するに伴い,マンションなどの建て込む高密度な住宅地区へと急速に変貌しつつある。したがって敷地周辺のグランドレベルでの空地率は極めて少なく,この住宅のような一戸建ての低層住宅にとってのグランドレベルの環境は,採光的にも通風的にも地下のそれに近いものとなり,地上と呼びうる実質的なグランドレベルは,空地率が明らかに増加する地上5メートルあたりに想定するほうがむしろ適切だ。

　この仮想されたグランドレベルから敷地の周辺一体を見直すと,密集する住居やマンションはひと塊りの,高さが5メートル程度の台地のような地形として把握できる。そこに住宅を置くことは,このようにマッス化した台地に空洞を穿ち,スリットを切り,ドライエリアを開くことになる。そこでは,外壁や屋根やファサードといった部位の境界は曖昧となり,それらはもはや独立した一個の家型を構成するものとしてではなく,地上5メートルあたりに出現している台地の起伏運動を明らかにするものとしての役割を持つ。

　この住宅の特徴といえる螺旋状に旋回するヴォリュームの形状もL型に曲がった屋上の大階段も,その踊り場にあたる空地も,また南側のグランドレベルに切り開かれたコートも,この住宅が新たに差し込まれることになった台地に対する考察の結果である。

　構造は鉄筋コンクリートによる「階段状モノコック」である。薄肉ラーメンを形成する壁は,スティールによる「十型柱」で宙に支えられることによって壁梁の役割をも果たすこととなり,この住宅の内外部を特徴づける「凸型」の断面が生まれた。

　スペースを分節化するものは間仕切り壁,引き戸,障子,収納家具,などであるが,それらの高さを概ね2.4メートルに止め,上部をすべて欄間状に空けることによって,「凸型」の裏側,すなわち反転した「凸型」の起伏は,そのまま直接的に内部化されている。

（鈴木了二）

Peter Stutchbury

2003

Bangalay, Upper Kangaroo Valley, New South Wales, Australia

Overall view across dam from north

1. COURTYARD
2. VEGETABLE GARDEN
3. DAM
4. TIMBER JETTY
5. WATER TANK (existing)
6. WATER JET

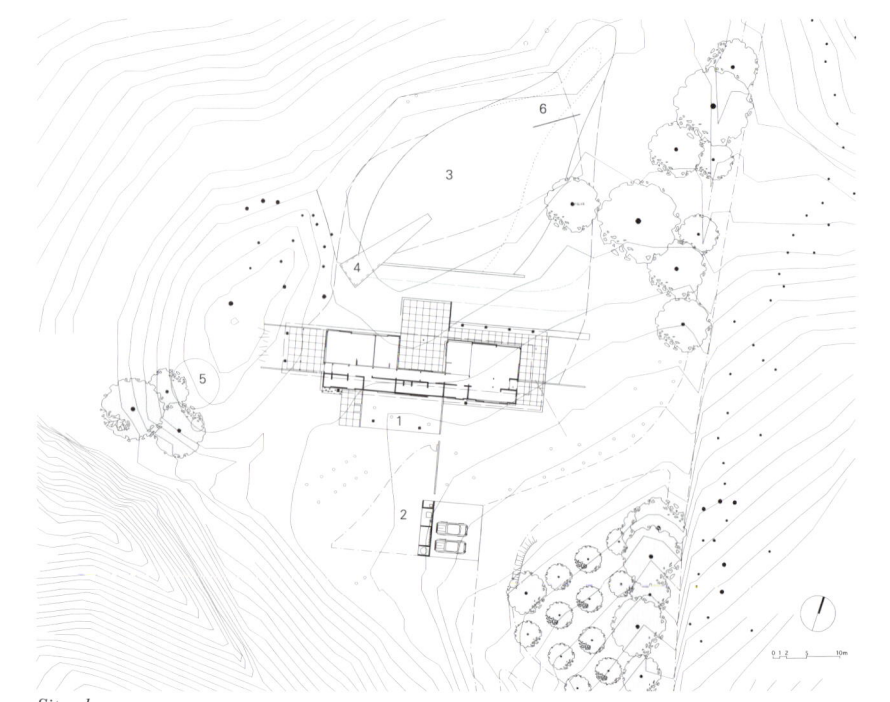

Site plan

Bangalay is located on a property that was once part of the Buderoo National Park on the South Coast of New South Wales. It is a temperamental area, where the environment changes from fog, to sunshine to heavy winds regularly. The site itself is positioned on a large flattened clearing on a hill overlooking the valley.

The brief from the clients was simple: a place for entertaining, eating, sleeping and a study from which to run their olive plantation business. It was important to them that the house respected the land as they did, for they had spent many years "camping" there and knew the place well.

The house is an elegant shed. The building's uncomplicated circulation runs off a long central corridor. The openable glazed living areas and bedrooms are positioned to the north, to make the most of passive solar gain. The heart of the house is a large sheltered courtyard, which serves as mediator between the public and private spaces of living and sleeping. To the south of the corridor, robust concrete blockwork bays, used for their thermal mass, accommodate service areas such as washing and storage. A simple skillion roof rises toward the east, providing a greater sense of space to the living areas, and allows the morning light to stream in. The bedrooms are positioned on the western side, and the roof gently lowers to provide a sense of containment and security. The roof then kicks up as a gesture to the view beyond. The roof floats above Comfort Plus (used for it's thermal properties) glazed highlights. Small opening within the highlights ensure that cross ventilation is always possible during the hot summer months.

One of *Bangalay*'s greatest attributes is its connection with the land. Large timber framed sliding glass doors surround the house, allowing the building to open and close and frame the landscape it so comfortably sits within. A large cantilevered verandah roof hangs above these openings providing uninterrupted shelter to the area below. The house's ability to open to the environment permits its inhabitants to live at the edge of nature.

The building's palette is a simple, controlled, sophisticated one of timber, plywood, steel, and concrete. Timber and plywood are used extensively to soften the austerity of the other materials. The main structure of the house is a series of recycled hardwood portal frames, which gently step down to the west. A double head beam, with hooppine plywood or glass panel infills, allow the doors to be externally mounted and slide in front of walls clear out of the way. Hooppine plywood is used significantly for the ceiling, cupboard joinery and gusset infills.

The sophistication of the timber structure of this building is veiled by the simplicity of the end result. The double beam structure allows enough inherent strength to cantilever verandah trusses, and provides a working cavity for all horizontal services. The development of the double post and beam structure is paramount in this building. Stutchbury and Pape have pioneered many aspects of this approach to timber post and beam assembly, and *Bangalay* illustrates the accuracy and maturity of such a structural proposition. The integrated cleating systems, locking plates, glazing infills and structural stiffening plates are all elements of this timber technology.

Whilst the building is a memorable combination of recycled timber and decorative plywood, the infusion of concrete and steel balances what would otherwise be too much of a timber palette.

The property is totally self-sufficient. All water is stored in a large dam at the top of the property and is fed by gravity to a manifold contained in the garage. The manifold controls all water, power, telephone and heating requirements of the building. Solar panels located further up the site provide power for lighting and all electrical appliances. Fluorescent lighting fixtures were used wherever possible to ensure minimal power usage.

The heating of the house is mainly through hydronic heating pipes laid within the concrete floor slab (used logically for the thermal mass properties). Water from the dam is heated by a heat exchanger (powered by solar electricity) in the garage, then pumped into the floor slab warming the house. A wood burning wet back stove is located within the garage that allows for a backup heating source should the stored power cells be low.

A dam sited to the north of the building enhances the peacefulness of the place. The dam serves not only as water feature and swimming pool, but in times of high fire risk becomes a vital fire fighting resource. The house is surrounded by carefully positioned sprinklers, which in times of fire danger, are fed by the dam to spray the house with water. The water feature also serves as a natural cooling means for the house. Breezes which blow over the dam into the house are naturally cooled by the water, and can therefore reduce the temperature inside.

Entrance

Plan S=1:300

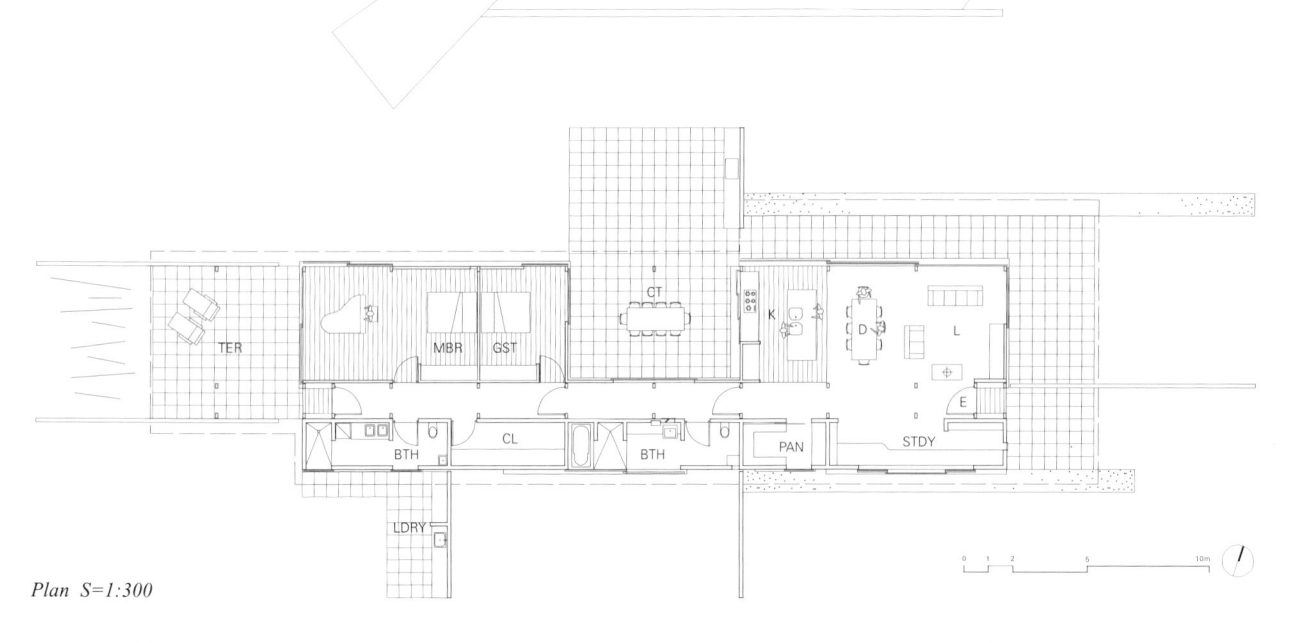

「バンガレイ」は，かつてニュー・サウス・ウェールズの南海岸に面したブデルー国立公園の一部であった土地に建っている。この地域の気候は移ろいやすく，霧が出たかと思うと晴れ渡り，強い風が吹き始め，状況は何度も変わる。敷地は，谷間を見晴らす丘の上の平坦で広い空き地にある。

クライアントからの要望は簡素である。オリーブ園を運営しながら，人をもてなし，食事し，眠り，勉強するための場所。一家はここで"キャンプ"生活を長い間営み，この場所を知り尽くしていたので，これまでそうしてきたように，この土地に敬意を払った家であることが大切であった。

この家は優雅な小屋である。明快な動線は，長い中央廊下から流れ出る。開放できるガラス張りのリビング・エリアと寝室は，パッシブソーラーによる熱取得を最大限にするために北側に配置されている。家の中心は，屋根に覆われた広いコートヤードで，居間と眠りの場所という公私の空間のあいだの仲介役を担っている。廊下の南には，コンクリートブロック積みの堅い壁で包まれた区画があり，サーマル・マスとして利用され，洗濯室や収納などのサービス・エリアを納める。東に向かって立ち上がる単純な片流れ屋根によって，リビング・エリアは広々と感じられ，朝日が差し込んでくる。寝室は西側にあり，屋根は寝室を包み込み，安心感を与えるように西に向かって緩やかに低くなる。次には前方に広がる風景に応えて上昇する。屋根はガラス張りのハイライトを構成するカムフォート・プラス(その蓄熱特性のために使われている)の上に浮かんでいる。ハイライトの中の小さな開口により，暑い夏のあいだ自然換気が常におこなえる。

「バンガレイ」の最大の特徴は土地との繋がりである。木材で枠取られたガラスの大きな引き戸は，建物を開きまた閉ざし，風景を枠取って家の中を居心地よくする。片持ちで張り出した広いベランダの屋根がこれらの開口の上にかぶさり，その下に連続するシェルターを提供する。環境に開くことができるこの家は，人を自然のきわに住まわせてくれる。

建物に使われている材料は，木材，合板，スティール，コンクリートと，単純で，抑制され，洗練されたものである。木材と合板はその他の材料の厳しさを和らげるために広く使われている。家の主構造は，再生利用された硬木の門型フレームの連なりで，それらは西に向かって緩やかに低くなって行く。ナンヨウスギの合板やガラス・パネルを充填したダブル・ヘッド・ビームによって，ドアは外側に取り付けられ，壁の前に引き入れられるため邪魔にならない。ナンヨウスギの合板は天井，指物細工の食器棚，ガセットプレートなど，かなり広範に使われている。

この建物の木構造が持つ複雑さは，仕上がりの単純性によって覆い隠されている。二重梁構造は，ベランダのトラスを片持ちで支えるに十分なだけの強度を持ち，水平方向にサービス用の空隙を提供する。ダブル・ポストとダブル・ビームの構成はこの建物の中で最も重要な部分である。私たちは，木造の柱梁構造について，多くの面で先駆的な仕事をしてきたが，「バンガレイ」は，提案してきたものの中でも精度と完成度が高い。一体化されたずれ止めの支持システム，ロッキング・プレート，ガラスの充填材，構造強化プレートなど，全てこの木造技術に含まれる。建物では再生利用の木材と装飾的な合板を印象的に組み合わせているが，コンクリートとスティールを導入することで，木の存在感を過剰なものにすることなく均衡をとっている。

この土地と建物は完全に自給自足している。敷地の一番高い場所につくられた大きなダムに貯えられた水は，ガレージ内にあるマニホルド(多岐管)から供給される。マニホルドは建物が必要とする水，電力，電話，暖房のすべてを制御する。敷地のさらに高い位置に置かれたソーラーパネルが，照明とすべての電気器具に電力を提供する。最小限の電力で済む場所にはすべて蛍光灯が採用された。

暖房は主にコンクリート床(サーマル・マスの効力を論理的に利用)に通された温水管で行われる。ダムから引かれた水はガレージの熱交換器(太陽熱により動力を得る)で暖められ，床スラブに送り込まれ家を暖める。背面にパイプがあり温水も供給できる薪ストーブがガレージ内にあり，補助熱源となって蓄電池の使用量を減らすだろう。

建物の北にあるダムは，この場所の静けさを強める。ダムは水風景をつくり，水泳プールとしても使われるが，消火の際の重要な水源となる。家の周りにはスプリンクラーが設置され，火災の危険が迫ればダムから給水をして家に放水する。ダムはまたこの家を自然に涼める役割も果たす。ダムの水面を渡って家のなかに流れ込む微風は水で冷されているので，室温を下げてくれる。

East elevation S=1:300

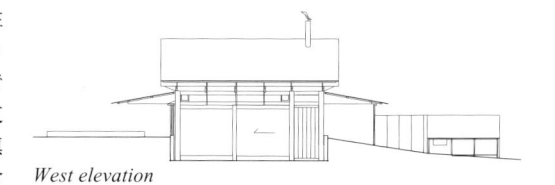

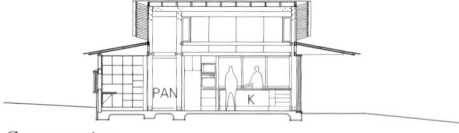

West elevation

Cross section

View from entrance

Court

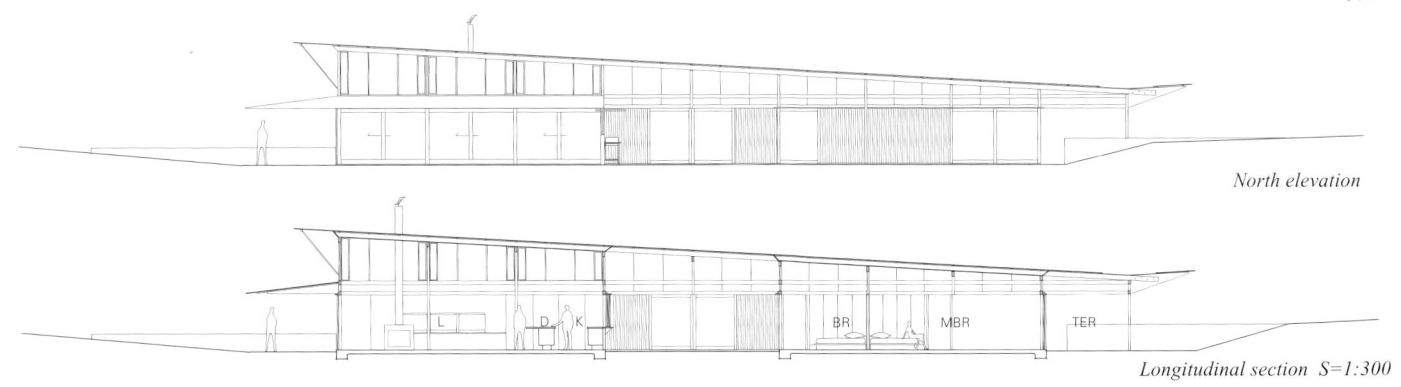

North elevation

Longitudinal section S=1:300

Fireplace

Court: looking west

Living/dining room: looking west

Living room: looking east

Court

Master bedroom *Bathroom*

Kei'ichi Irie + Masahiro Ikeda 2003

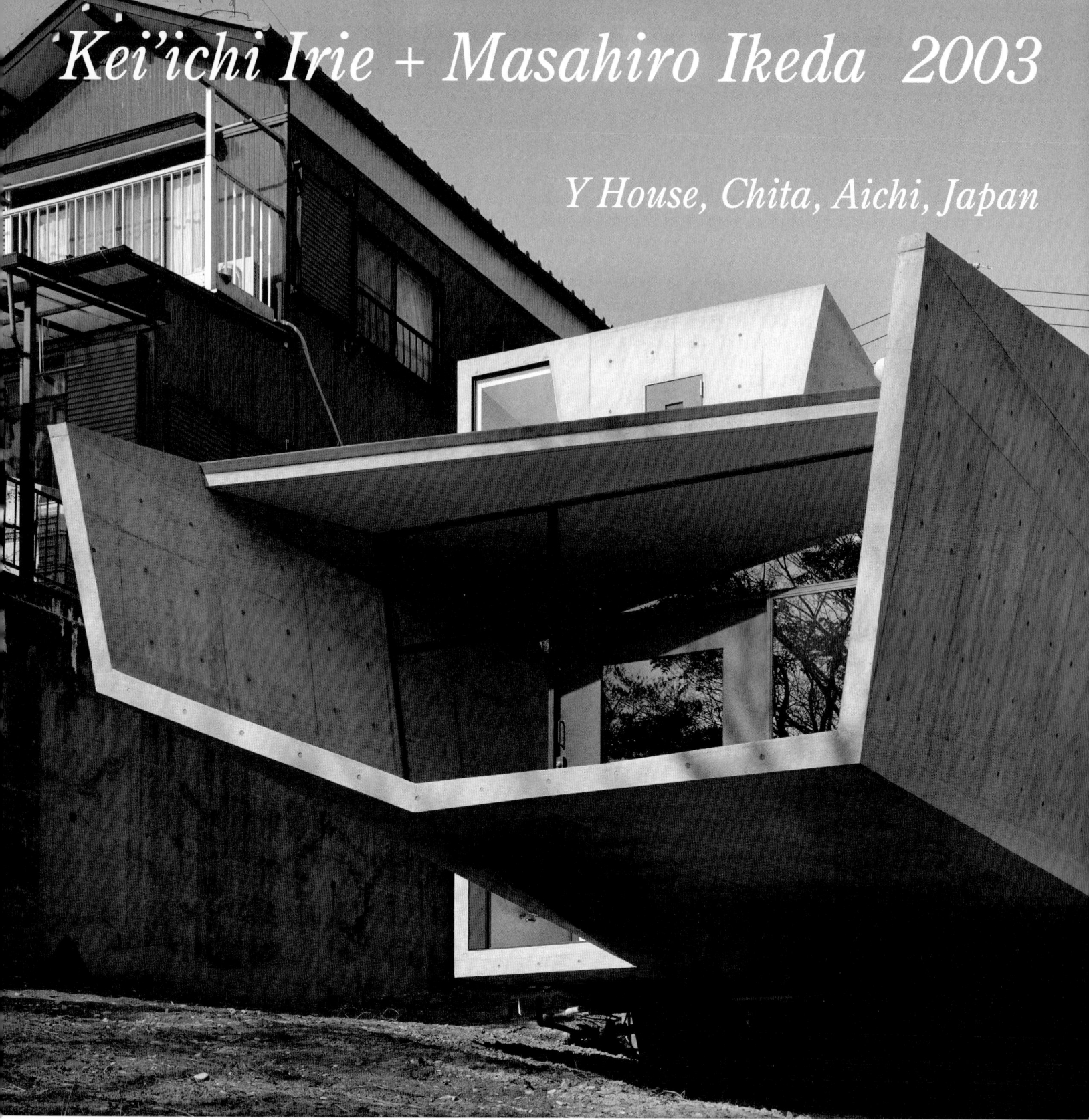

Y House, Chita, Aichi, Japan

Overall view from southeast

Sad Suburbs
Suburban sceneries are sad. Modernization, industrialization, and IT innovation have ripped down the cities' inner landscapes, destroying to shreds what had been left of nature in the suburbs. Cities in the pre-modern times used to devise ways of reconciling and co-existing with nature that they had destroyed in the course of their own construction. But the suburbs have abandoned it, swayed by stereotyped urban models. To this day, excessive faith in industrial development and forces of technology is conducting hideous violence across the country. Such historical bruises would continue to prevail among suburbs throughout Japan as long as there are those who believe that urban recovery may be improved by means of industry, science and technology. Dignity and serenity of landscape are now on the way of extinction.

Y House is found among a row of houses up on a hillside. A landscape with retaining walls in conflicting wilderness as a result of leveling off the steep inclination for housing land development—its imperviousness is just menacing. It is in no way possible to impose a full-scale change on such devastation. But we may build a house that is neither destructive nor violent.
Like a Musical Instrument
We decided to avoid tinkering with the inclination as much as possible and create a space isolated from the surrounding painful landscape. Once inside the building, the floor slopes down along the topography leading to a large cantilever floor, directly open to the forest. The only major opening in this house, it frames the forest scenery through the big sliding doors with black rims. The opening facing the street serves only to introduce light through the translucent glass, except for one black-rimmed window which frames a small view of the town.

Walls on both sides of the cantilevered space are slightly slanted outward to avoid assimilating themselves into the surrounding retaining walls. These slanted surfaces intersect, preliminary to being named floors or walls, and res-

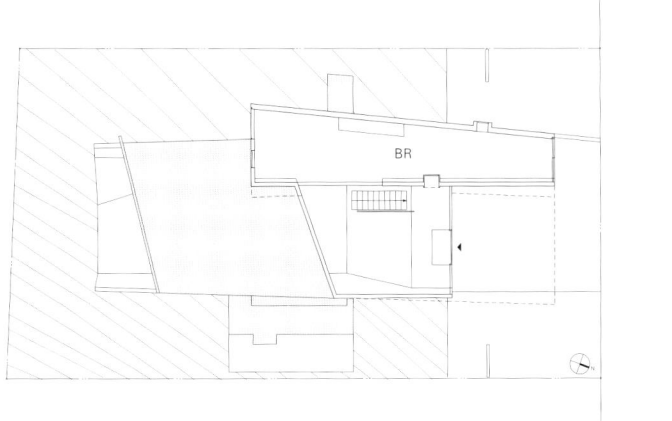

onate with each other to create a soundless acoustic space. The plates of the body (as in a violin) producing such echoes is the thin surface of concrete, only 15 cm thick. The realization of uniformity of thickness (15 cm) among all surfaces allowed the architecture to take on such musical property. Motions such as the slow sway of forest trees, birds' flight, or traces of rain feed the space with a variety of speeds. They reverberate between slanted surfaces and reach the ear.
Kei'ichi Irie

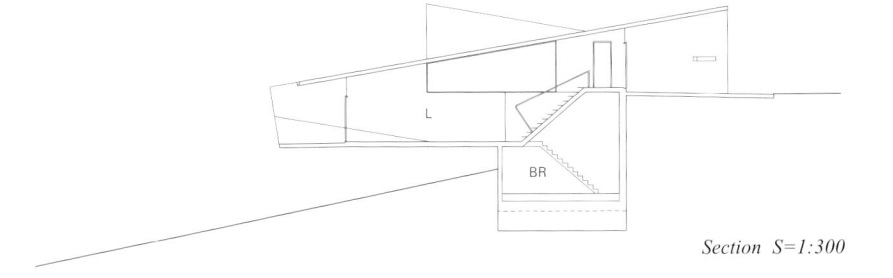

First floor S=1:300

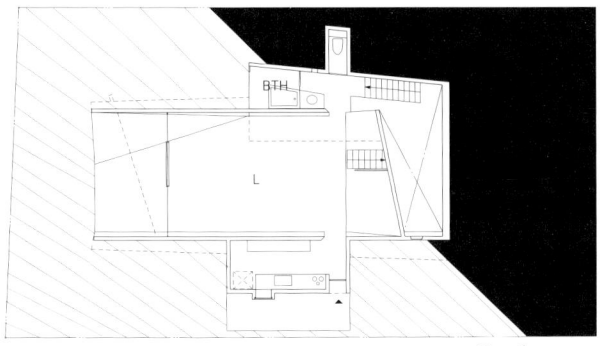

First basement

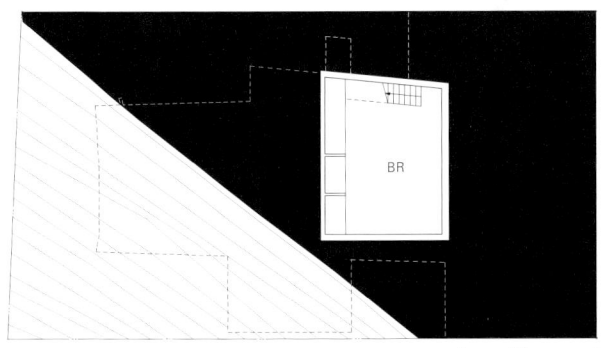

Second basement

Section S=1:300

Evening view of main entrance

Living room on left, bathroom on right

View toward bedroom on first floor from living room

〈悲しき郊外〉
地方都市の風景は悲しい。近代化，産業化，IT化が都市内部の風景を引き裂き，その郊外に残った自然をずたずたに破壊している。近代以前の都市はその建設のために破壊した自然と，折り合いをつけながら共存するための工夫をしてきたが，都市のステレオタイプ化したモデルに振り回される地方都市はそれを捨て去った。産業の発展とテクノロジーの力への過信は，いまでも日本中に醜い暴行を加え続けている。こうした歴史的な傷は，都市の再生を産業の発展や科学技術の力で改善できると考える人々がいるかぎり拡大し，あらゆる郊外にも及ぶ。風景から，威厳と静謐が消えつつある。

「Y House」の敷地は山の上に家が立ち並ぶ一角にある。山を切り崩し，急な斜面に平らな地面をつくるために擁壁がせめぎあう風景はその鈍感さ故に危険だ。こうした惨状を全面的に変えることなどできない。だがその中に破壊的でも暴力的でもない住宅を建てることはできる。

〈楽器のように〉
斜面をできるだけ加工せず，また周囲の痛々しい風景からは隔絶した空間をつくることにした。建物に入ると地面の傾斜にそって床が斜面状に下り，大きなキャンティレバーで張り出したフロアへと続く。その空間はまっすぐに森へと開かれている。この住宅で唯一大きく開かれているのが森へ向かう開口部であり，そこには大きな黒い額縁をもった引き戸があって，森の風景を切り取っている。道路側の開口部は乳白色のガラスから光だけを取り入れるが，一つだけ黒い額縁の窓が，小さな町の風景を切り取っている。

キャンティレバーで張り出した空間の両側の壁は，微妙に外へ傾斜させているので周囲の擁壁に同化することがない。このような傾斜面は，床や壁と名付けられる前の状態で交錯し，反響し合いながら，音にはならない音響的空間をつくる。その響きを生み出す響胴（バイオリンのそれのように）にあたるのが，コンクリート面の15センチという薄さだ。すべての面を等しく厚さ15センチにすることが可能になったことが，建築にこうした音楽的特性を与えた。森の木々のゆっくりとした揺らぎや鳥の飛行，雨の軌跡などの動きが，空間に様々な速度を入力してくれる。それらは傾斜した面の間を反射しながら，耳へと届く。

（入江経一）

View from main entrance

Living room: view toward main entrance

Steven Ehrlich

2003

Ehrlich House, Venice, California, U.S.A.

The Ehrlich House was designed as a flexible compound for large family gatherings and overnight guests. Key requirements were to maximize volume, light and privacy on a narrow urban lot, employ sustainable initiatives and design with a particular sensitivity to scale and context. Built of raw, honest materials appropriate to the bohemian grittiness of Venice, the house dissolves the barriers between indoors and out creating multi-use spaces that fully exploit the benign climate.

The site is a 43 x 132 foot lot on the corner of a street of traditional beach bungalows, lined with palms. At two stories plus a mezzanine level, the house as well as its separate garage/guest house is taller than most of its neighbors. The mass has been peeled back and mitigated on the upper levels by two large sheltering pine trees and a palm, one of which graces each of three distinct courtyards. Walls and landscaping screen the two street facades.

Flexibility and transformation have been fully realized. The wood-and-steel frame structure is outlined by a steel exoskeleton, from which automatic light scrims roll down to shield the front facade from the western sun. The fifteen-ft. high living-dining area opens up on three sides: to the lap pool on the west with sliding glass doors; to the north courtyard and guest house with pocketing glass doors; and to the garden to the south through pivoting metal doors. When opened entirely to the elements, the structure is an airy pavilion with temperate ocean breezes that make air-conditioning unnecessary. Environmental sensitivity was a major concern; the concrete slab absorbs the sun's warmth in the winter and has a radiant heat source for cold nights, and photovoltaic sunshades at the roofline store and augment energy.

Shifts from confined to lofty spaces animate the design. Space is compressed at the low front entrance of the house, and then explodes into the main volume. Stairs lead up to a pair of mezzanine-level sleeping/lounging lofts with decks; a glass bridge spans the living room and leads to another flight of stairs up to the master bedroom and study. The top floor is flooded with light from a shed roof that opens a long clerestory to the western sky.

Rough and smooth surfaces are contrasted throughout the house. The western front facade, a clearly defined mass, is clad inside and out in rusted steel. Ample roof overhangs and fascias are of metal and parklex. The interior back wall of shot-blasted structural concrete masonry is a backdrop for artwork.

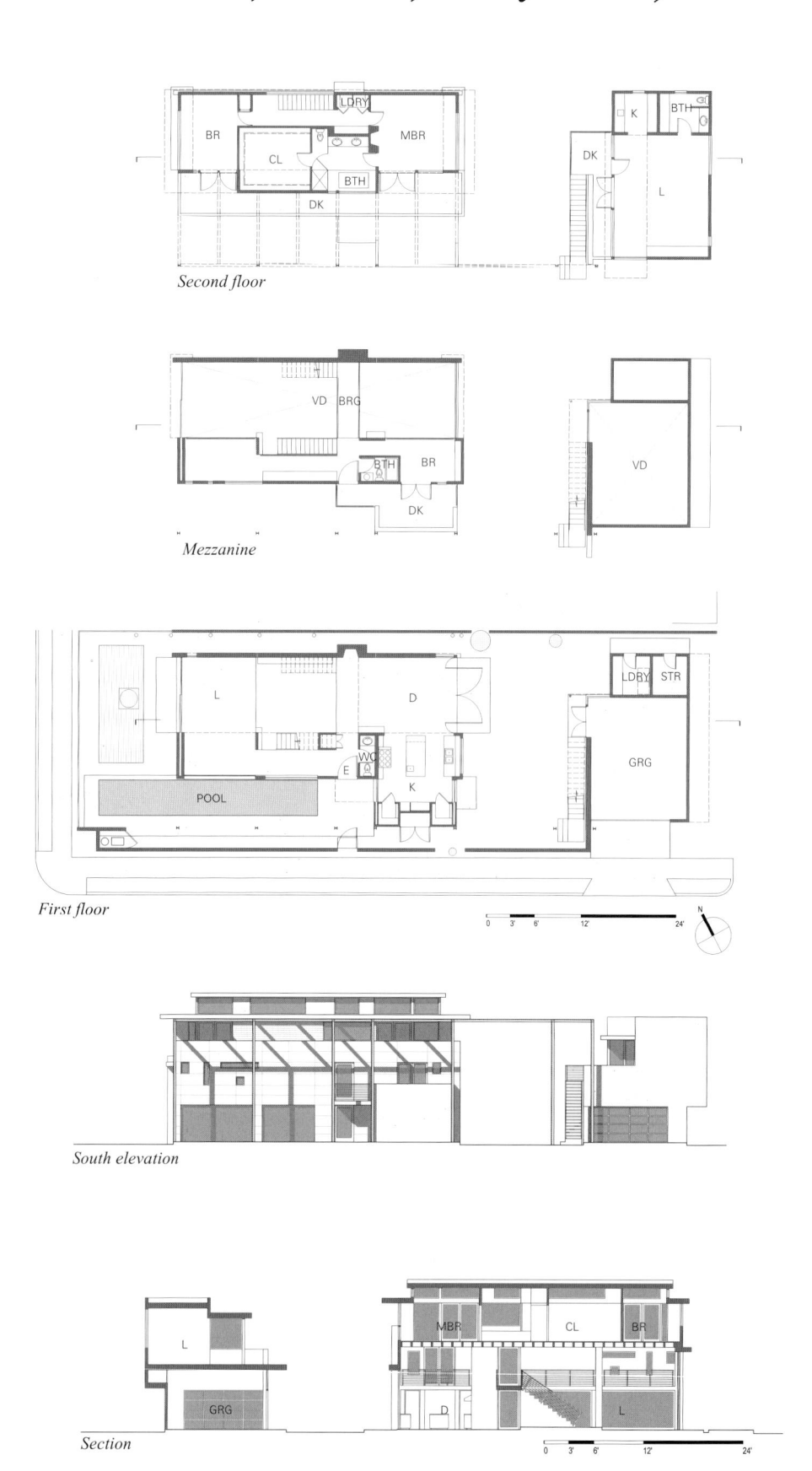

Second floor

Mezzanine

First floor

South elevation

Section

Street view from southwest

Main house: view from east

65

Pool: looking east

Pool (left) and living room (right)

「アーリック邸」は，大家族での集いや，泊まっていく客のためのフレキシブルな複合体としてデザインされている。持続可能性を先取りし，スケールと周辺環境に特別な注意を払ったデザインによって，狭い都会の敷地に，ヴォリューム，光，プライバシーを最大限に取り入れることが課題だった。ヴェニスの町のボヘミアン的気風に相応しい，素地を生かした，正直な材料でつくられた家は，温和な気候を十分に利用して内部と外部の障壁を溶解させ，多目的空間をつくりだす。

ヤシの木が並び，伝統的な海辺のバンガローが続く道路の角地にある43×132フィートの敷地。2階建てに中2階が付加されている建物は，別棟のガレージ／ゲスト・ハウスともども，近所の大半の建物より背が高い。かさ高な躯体は背後を剥ぎ取り，大きく覆うマツやヤシの木によって上階の高さを緩和させている。マツやヤシの木は，三つのコートヤードのそれぞれを美しく飾る。壁と景観構成によって道路側の二面が覆い隠されている。

柔軟に変貌可能な住宅で，木造鉄骨枠組構造をスティールの外骨格が縁取っている。この外骨格から，軽い布地のロール・カーテンが自動制御で降りてきて，正面ファサードにあたる西日を遮る。高さ15フィートのリビング・ダイニング・エリアは三方が開いている。西側はガラスの引戸からラップブールへ，北側は戸袋に納まるガラス戸からコートヤードとゲスト・ハウスへ，南側はメタルの回転扉から庭へ出られる。自然に対しすべてを開くと，建物は風通しのよいパヴィリオンになり，穏やかな海風が入り，空調は不要となる。環境に対する配慮が重要なテーマであった。コンクリート・スラブは，冬には太陽熱を吸収し，寒い夜にはその熱を放射する。ルーフラインに沿った日除には光起電装置が付き，エネルギーを蓄え，増大させる。

閉ざされた空間から天井の高い空間への転換はデザインに生きいきした動きを与える。背の低い正面玄関で圧縮されていた空間は，次に主空間のなかへ爆発するように広がる。階段が，デッキの付いたスリーピング／ラウンジング・ロフトのある対になった中2階へ通じる。ガラスのブリッジがリビングルームの上を架け渡し，別な階段がさらに上の主寝室と書斎へ上って行く。最上階は，西の空に面して細長い高窓が開いた片流れ屋根からの光に浸される。

荒削りな面と滑らかな面の対比が家全体に見られる。西側正面は，明快に輪郭をとった構成で，内外とも腐蝕させて錆を付けたスティールで被覆されている。豊かな屋根のオーバーハングと鼻隠はメタルとパークレックス。内部のショット・ブラストしたコンクリート・メーソンリーの構造壁は美術品や工芸品の背景となる。

Entrance

Living/dining room: looking west

Mezzanine: view from glazed bridge to south

Living room: staircase and bridge

Dining room

Bathroom

Master bedroom

Tokyo Institute of Technology
Tsukamoto Lab.+Atelier Bow-Wow

2003

Gae House, Setagaya, Tokyo, Japan

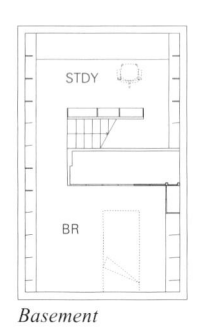

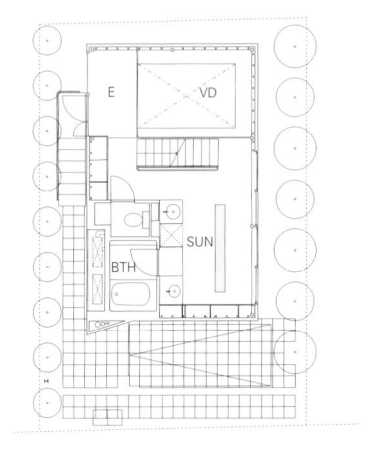

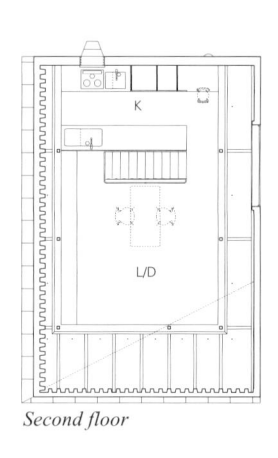

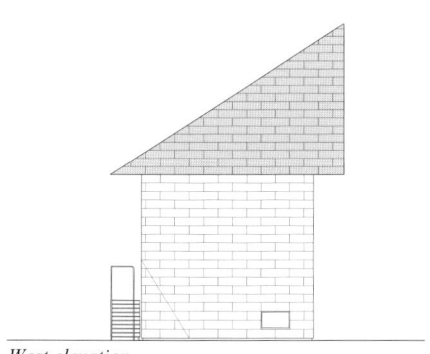

Basement

First floor S=1:200

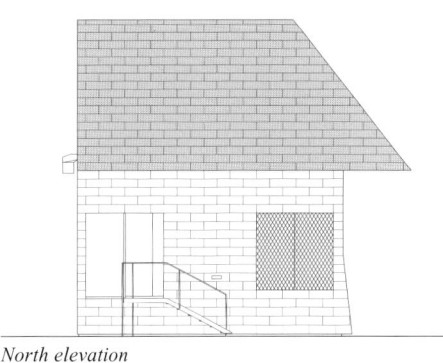

Second floor

West elevation

North elevation

Section

Located along the old railroad line of Mekamasen, the vicinity of *Gae House* is a residential zone with a little less than 80 years of history. There exist remnants of garden fences hedging around a whole block, recording the management of road boundaries and greenery of the past. However, many housing sites are being divided and sold in lots mainly due to inheritance tax dodge, leaving each frontage of such lot to measure 6 to 8 meters wide, just enough to replace the live fence with a parking space. Unfortunately, this house is no exception. But in a pursuit for a building that would embrace such intent of the surrounding environment, we have realized that by putting up the largest possible roof defined by the setback and northside slant line regulations and bringing the wall back according to the 1-meter alleviation from the edge of the eaves, the building coverage ratio would be approximately 50%. This misalignment between the roof and the wall not only provides a roof to the parking space but introduce the hedge sequence to the boundaries with the neighbors, embodying the environment's intention expressed in the presence of live fences.

Around this volume are the bedroom and the study, the husband's work place in the semibasement, and the living room and the kitchen placed inside the roof, in such manner that public spaces such as the entrance and water utilities are concentrated in the middle layer. Floor height is determined within the conflict between the outer shape and each floor's purpose. The second floor comes 900 mm below the eaves, and the section between the eave's edge and the breast wall is entirely covered with glass to create a literally 'horizontal' ribbon window. Light from outside is reflected by the white external wall and emerges from this horizontal window, scattered by the irregular surface of the deck plate to wrap the interior with shadowless soft light. This soft light blends with blurred images of adjacent green, orange sunset or figures passing through the front road, forming amplifying/summarizing relationships with the surroundings, rather than corresponding individually to each environmental element.

Such sense of envelopment was named 'granular space' in which each enveloping element stands for a grain of the texture. We have attempted to make the most of this property so that on every floor the human body would be softly enwrapped by a sequence of something small with a clear intention of its own. All secondary parts of the structure on the floors and walls are made of wood, with sequences of thin rafters and furring strips covering up the ceiling and outer perimeter. The same feature is used in the structure of bookshelves that cover the entire basement wall. The first floor is painted white for a diffused effect of light.

Elements are arranged inside the premises and the building, putting their respective distinctions and intentions forward in such way that they compete with one another, so that each element discovers not only its original intention but also its own role with respect to the entire building. I believe that placing oneself in such reciprocity between the parts would eventually lead to an organic architectural experience.
Yoshiharu Tsukamoto

Evening view: interior lights coming from opening of eaves

Living/dining room on second floor

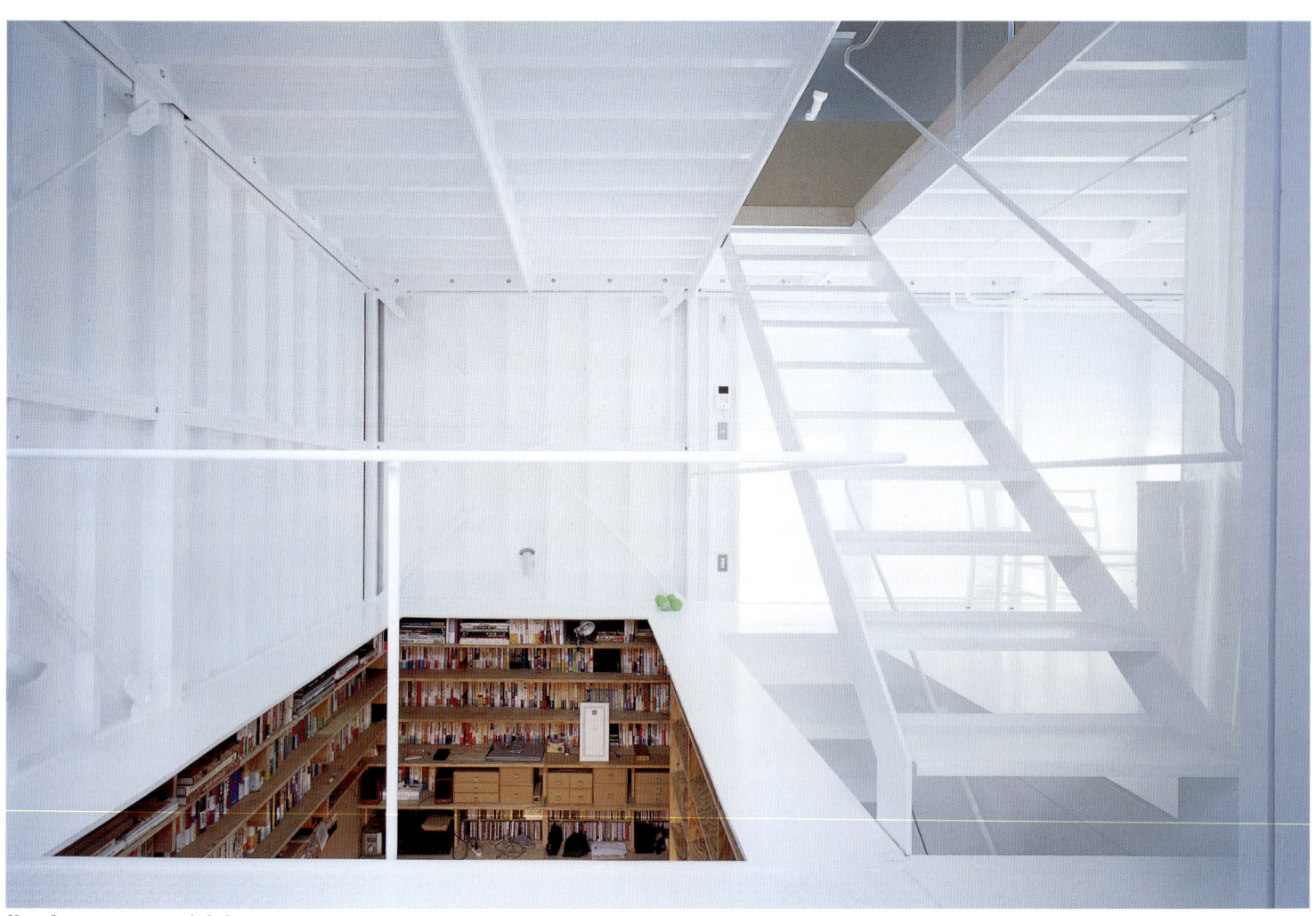

View from entrance: study below

Study: entrance above

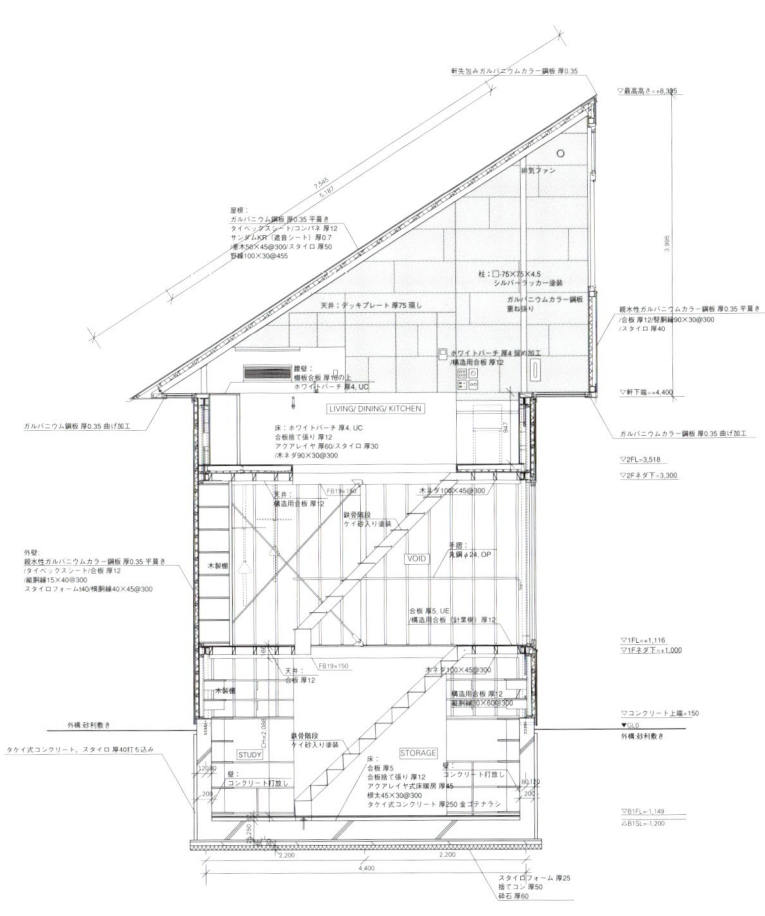

Sectional detail S=1:100

Bedroom

　「ガエ・ハウス」の敷地は1923年開通の旧目蒲線沿線にある。周囲には生け垣を連ねて一街区を丸ごと囲ったところもまだ残っていて，80年弱の歴史ある住宅地で繰り返されてきた道路境界と緑の取り扱いを見ることができる。ところが，主に相続税対策で切り売りされた敷地は，道路に対する間口が6～8メートルになってしまうので生垣は駐車場に置き換えられてしまう。残念ながらこの住居もその例にもれない。それでも，そういう周辺環境の意図を汲んだ建蔽率50パーセントの建ち方を模索したところ，敷地全体を覆うつもりで道路斜線と北側斜線で規定された屋根をかけ，軒先1メートルの緩和に従って隣地から引きをとるつもりで壁面をセットバックさせると，建蔽率が大体50パーセントになることを見い出した。この屋根と壁のズレは，駐車場の屋根になるだけでなく，生け垣の連続を隣地境界沿いに引き込む余地を生むと考えた。

　このヴォリュームに対して，寝室と夫の仕事場である書斎を半地下に，居間と台所を屋根の下に置くことにして，中間層に玄関や水回りなどの非居室を集中させた。外形と各階の意図の競合によって階高を決めると，2階の床は軒先より900ミリ下がった位置に来るので，通常なら軒裏になる軒先と腰壁の隙間をすべてガラスで覆い，字義通りの「水平」連窓とした。外からの光は外壁の白に反射してこの水平連窓から室内に沸き上がり，デッキプレートあらわしの凹凸に反射して室内を影のない包囲光で包む。この包囲光には隣地の緑や，夕日のオレンジがかった光，前面道路を歩く人影などがぼやっと写りこんで，周辺にある環境要素と1対1に対応するのではなく，それを拡大縮小するような対応となっている。

　こうした包囲感を，包囲する要素一つひとつが肌理となるという意味で，「粒だった空間」と呼んで積極的に捉え，それぞれの階で身体が何か小さな，独自の意図を持ったものの反復に柔らかく取り囲まれることを目指した。そのために，床壁ともに構造の2次部材からは全て木造とし，小さな断面の垂木や胴縁が天井や外周を反復して覆い尽くすように仕向けた。地下ではこれを棚の構造に利用して本が壁面を覆い尽くすように仕向け，1階では白ペンキが全てを塗りつぶすように仕向けて光が乱反射するようにした。

　ここでは異なる要素をそれぞれの意図が際立つように，敷地や建物の中に適宜レイアウトしていくことにより，それらを競合させて，各要素が本来の意図だけでなく，建物全体の中での独自の役割を見い出せるようにした。そういう部分同士の相互依存性に身を置くことが有機的な建築の経験をもたらすと考えたからである。

（塚本由晴）

Kazuyo Sejima

2003

House in Plum Grove, Tokyo, Japan

Overall view from northwest

Third floor

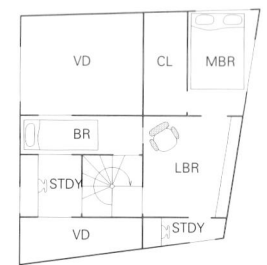

Second floor

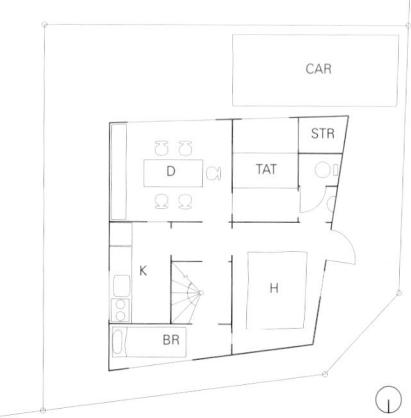

First floor S=1:200

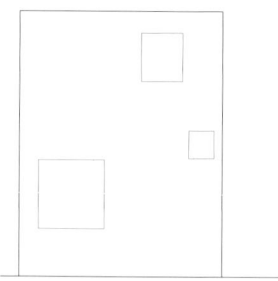

North elevation S=1:200

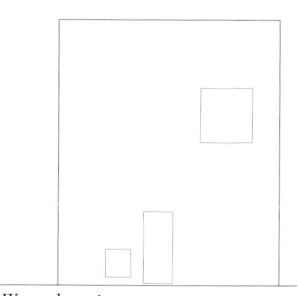

West elevation

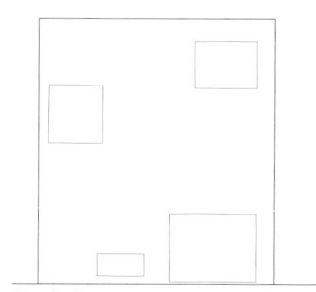

South elevation

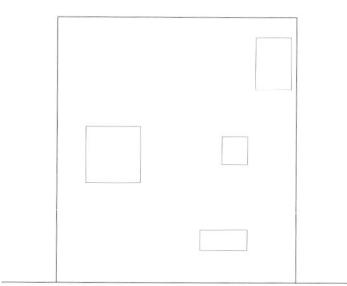

East elevation

Located in a quiet residential block of Tokyo metropolitan area, the site is the home to its 5 residents: the couple, two children and their grandmother. The site was originally full of plum trees that would blossom in early spring, garnishing this compound with its charms of a small garden. In order to retain as much as possible of this scenery, the building was isolated in the center of the site, leaving a blank space with an ambiguity with regard to the site, where the plum trees were planted back.

We have prepared a maximum number of rooms inside the house: several or them to be used as the sitting room; children's room separated into the bed room and the desk room; the book room, the detached room, the terrace room .... The number of rooms exceeding the number of inhabitants, rooms in various forms with fillings such as books, clothes, beds and built-in fittings offer new kinds of options, that is, switching rooms casually according to moods and usages.

Each room is partitioned with iron plates 16 mm thick, the main structural element, and comes with openings of various forms. These openings are not covered with doors or glass. Seen through the sheer openings, views of the adjacent rooms, the sky and the plum trees in the garden lose perspective and look like flat pictures hung on walls. Furthermore, through them, cats and children come in and go out; family members and visitors exchange words; the scent of incense and music connect the rooms as they spread out. Although the entire house is softly partitioned with thin walls, it is vaguely continuous, with a sense of openness filling the house.

South corner: 16 mm-thick wall made of steel plate, terrace on third floor

Terrace on third floor

敷地は東京近郊の静かな住宅地にある。住まい手はご夫婦と二人の子供とお母さまの五人。もともと敷地にはたくさんの梅の木が生えており、初春になると満開の梅の花が楽しめ、住宅地のなかの小庭といった雰囲気だった。できるだけこの風景が残るように、建物をぽつんと敷地のまんなかに配置して、敷地に対して曖昧な余白を残し、梅の木を植え戻した。

室内には、できるだけたくさんの部屋を用意した。茶の間のような部屋をいくつか用意したり、子供部屋をベッドの部屋と机の部屋に分けたり、本の部屋、はなれの部屋、テラスの部屋というように。住まい手の数よりたくさんの部屋があることで、本や服やベッドなどの小物や家具をしつらえたいろいろなかたちの部屋は、そのときの気分や用途によって居る部屋を気軽に変えて過ごすという、今までとは違った選択性がある。

それぞれの部屋は、主構造である厚さ16ミリの鉄板で仕切られ、いろいろなかたちの開口があいている。それらの開口には扉やガラスはない。厚みのない開口を通して、隣の部屋の風景や庭の空や梅の木は遠近感を失い壁に掛かった平坦な絵画のようにみえる。また、猫や子どもたちが出入したり、家族や来客者が言葉を交わしたり、お香の香りや音楽が部屋から部屋へと繋がって広がっていく。家全体は薄い壁で柔らかに仕切られつつも、曖昧に繋がっていて、家全体に不思議な開放感が漂っている。

Dining room

Downward view toward dining room from bedroom on second floor

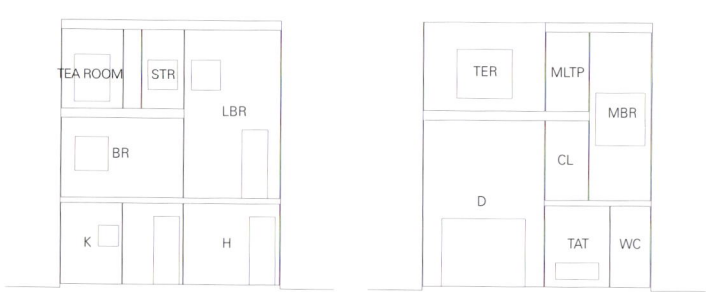

Sections S=1:200

Downward view toward library from staircase

Library: master bedroom behind wall

Downward view of bedroom on first floor

View toward study from bedroom on second floor

Dining room: tatami room on right

View toward study

View toward study from library through staircase: other one on left

Bathroom on third floor

77

Katsufumi Kubota 2004

I-House, Hatsukaichi, Hiroshima, Japan

Overall view from south

This residence stands on the opposite shore of Itsukushima Shrine in the western part of Hiroshima Prefecture. The site, located outside a curving road, is blessed with a panoramic ocean view, one which is rare for a housing site in Japan. The tide makes two cycles in a day. When the tide is in, the level difference between the sea surface and the land is about 4 meters, accounting for the magical feeling that the site is floating on the sea. When the tide has gone out, the water level drops about 2 meters, showing a totally different scenery.

The owner is a couple who has spent a long time to acquire this plot of land, out of their strong aspiration toward the ocean. The main focus in this project was thus to understand this passion and amplify it as much as possible. To start with, we have simply faced up to (something like) an intent that the location has itself. The gentle sparkle of the blue sea—an imagery of a sheet of paper rocking in the waves came to me. We decided to build a house by simply bending a sheet of slab. Converge to a method merely consisting of opening toward the sea and closing to the front road, and structure. Then a slight change in shape is added along to the site's arched form.

Details around the glass is reduced to the minimum. Much attention is paid not to break the continuity and flow of the 'space' created by the bending of slab, in order to create a comfortable space. It is our wish that the owner couple would enjoy a life full of senses of liberty and release.

Katsufumi Kubota

View from street on northwest

Southwest elevation: entrance on left

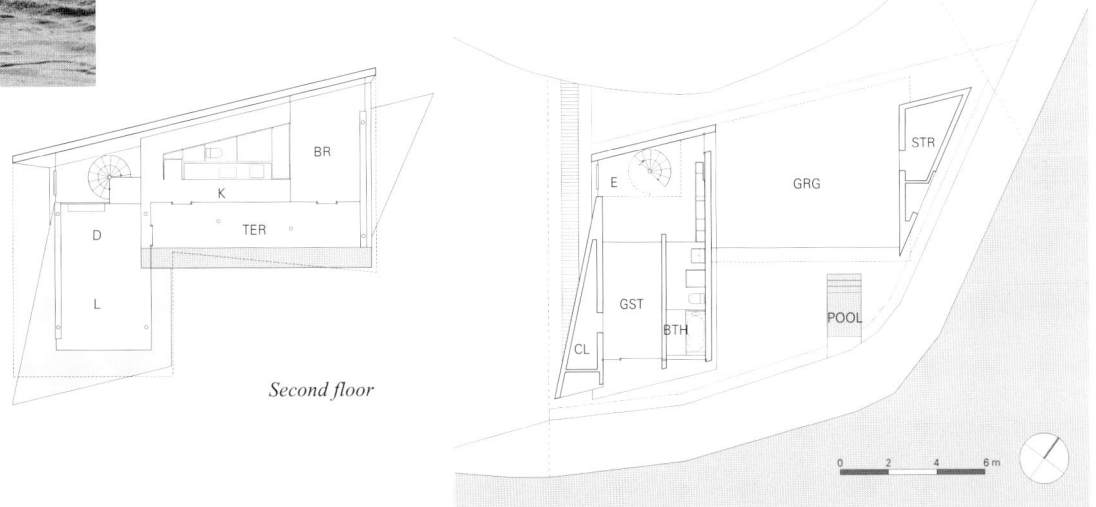

Second floor

First floor   S=1:300

View toward Seto Inland Sea on east

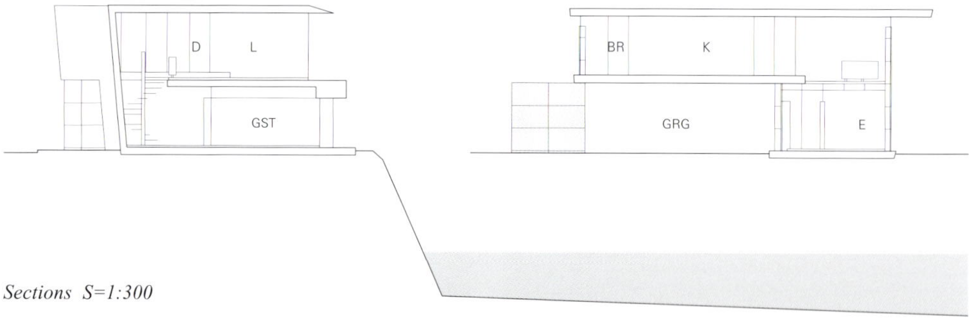

Sections S=1:300

この住宅は広島県の西部，厳島神社の対岸につくられた。彎曲した道路の外側に位置していて，道路側以外はすべて海が望める，日本国内の宅地としてはまれな敷地である。1日に2度のサイクルで潮の干満があって，満潮時には水面とこの土地とのレベル差は4メートル程となり，まるで海の上に浮かんでいるような不思議な感覚に包まれる。干潮時には海面が2メートル近く下がり，またがらりと違った景色を楽しむことができる。

オーナーは夫婦二人で，長い時間をかけてこの敷地を手に入れた経緯をみても，彼らの海への想いの強さが伝わってくる。それをどこまで汲み取って増幅させ得るかが，このプロジェクトにとっての最大の課題であった。まずは場がおのずから持っている意図（のようなもの）に素直に向かい合うことから計画は始まった。蒼くきらめくたおやかな海，その海にゆらゆらと浮かぶ1枚の紙がイメージに浮かんだ。そこで，1枚のスラブを簡潔に折り曲げて，建物をつくることを考えた。海に向かって開き，道路に対して閉じるという，たったこれだけの作法に収斂させ，構築する。そこに弓なりの敷地形状に合わせて若干の変形を加えている。

ガラスまわりのディテールは極力余計な部材を排除してあり，スラブを折曲げることで生み出される「空間」の連続性や流動感をこわさないように注意しながらも，居心地のよい空間となるように工夫してある。オーナーご夫妻には自由で解放感に満ちた生活を楽しんで欲しいと思っている。

（窪田勝文）

Bathroom

Kitchen

Dining/living room

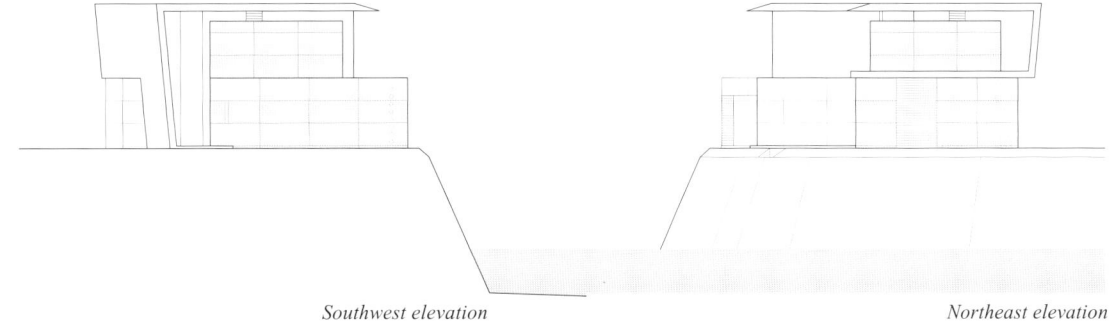

Southwest elevation　　　　　　　　　　　　*Northeast elevation*

Night view toward living room from terrace　　　　*Staircase at entrance hall*

81

Will Bruder

2004

Sky Arc Residence, Marin County, California, U.S.A.

Distant view from east

Approach

View from south: garden and terrace

Located in Kentfield, Marin County, California, the site is a forested hillside with dramatic views eastward to the bay and south toward Mount Tamalpais. Two parcels are combined, but divided by a driveway leading to a neighboring house. The steep eastern parcel is the chosen site of the new residence for this family, embracing natural contours and maximizing light, view, and connections of interior spaces and outdoor terrain. The western parcel affords a children's play yard and garden, with a recording studio outbuilding. An open-air stair descends from yard level, linking garden and residence through a gallery/tunnel under the driveway.

The crescent plan of the house derives its form from topography and landscape, embedded in the hillside and similar to the gentle curvature of the Northern California hills. Structures are placed for maximum preservation of native vegetation, including specimen Coast Live Oak and Madrone trees. The simple volumes, clad in pre-weathered pewter-grey zink, are intended to recede into the texture of the landscape. Vertical 'standing seam' fins in the cladding create a randomly-spaced shadow pattern like shadows of Pines and Redwoods on the site. Small panels of venetian plaster punctuate rooms with colors of land, sun, and sky, recalling Eames or Nelson design, or the paintings of Richard Diebenkorn. Glass is 'solex green', for visual harmony with landscape; operable windows are mahogany for their warmth, and linkage to architectural traditions of the place, including Maybeck, Moore, Esherick, Eichler, and Kahn. In lieu of overhangs, shade is provided by translucent fiberglass awnings—gossamer thin blue filters for the Bay Area sun—luminous for overcast January days.

The house choreographs light and shadow, exterior and interior, private and public. The entry opens a frame to the bay view, with naturally convecting air and arboreal aroma. Children's bedrooms are to the south, with views to the bay and Mount Tam; to the north is a modest guest suite with bay views past a redwood stand downslope. Always the movement of air—past window seats, through doors, across rooms—will carry a sensual freshness through the house. A radiused switchback stair takes one down to the main level, location of major living spaces. To the north a passage connects to the master suite and to a natural bench of land in the forest. To the south, the great room unveils an expansive panorama sweeping from bay to mountain views. This level is climatically stabilized by thermal mass, falling below grade at the rear. A curved gallery flows into a graphic design studio with a zero-edge aperture and wraparound art environment. From the great room corner the gallery tunnel leads toward the geometric center of the plan, connecting to the outdoor garden stair.

The music studio across the garden is inset several feet in the earth, placing window sills at grade. Long views are south and west, with near views of play space and a large oak. The studio and control room are shaped by acoustic considerations, their volumes sized and tuned for quality of sound. In concept lightweight foldings are origami fans within stone boxes, giving form to the experiences of making and hearing music.

This is an architecture formed of its site, an abstraction blended with the tone and topography of its natural context, deferring to the sublime wooded garden site. It will foster a lifestyle colored by the inherent beauty and wonder of the place. Constantly shifting with patterns of light, weather and season, it will be a place of continual engagement of creativity and the senses.

Entrance: orange canopy

マリン郡ケントフィールドにある敷地は，森林に包まれた丘陵の斜面で，東に向かっては湾が，南に向かってはタマルパイス山系が見晴らせる。二つの敷地を合体させているが，隣家に至る車道により物理的には分割されている。急斜面となった東側の土地が，自然の等高線に抱かれ，光，眺め，内部空間と地形との結びつきを最大限に活用した，この一家のの新しい住宅のために選ばれた。西側の土地は，録音スタジオのある子供の遊び場と家族の庭となった。野外階段が庭のレベルから降り，ドライブウェイの下を抜けて住宅へつながっている。

　住宅の半月形プランは地形と風景に由来するもので，丘の斜面にはめ込まれ，北カリフォルニアの丘の緩やかな湾曲によく似ている。建物は，ハマガシ，マドロナなどの典型種を含め，原産の植生を最大限保護するように配置された。あらかじめ風雨にさらした灰青色の亜鉛で被覆したシンプルな建物は風景のなかに沈み込むように考えてのことである。壁に付けられた垂直の"立ちはぜ継ぎ"のフィンは，敷地にあるマツやセコイアが落とす影に似た不規則に並ぶ影模様をつくりだす。ベネチアン・プラスターで仕上げたいくつかの小さなパネルが，大地，太陽，空の色を部屋に差し挟み，イームズやネルソンのデザイン，あるいはリチャード・ディーベンコーンの絵を想い出させる。ガラスは省エネルギーと周囲との視覚的調和を考え，薄い"ソレックス・グリーン"とし，開閉窓は暖かみのあるマホガニーを用いた。これはメイベック，ムーア，エシュリック，アイヒラー，カーンなど，この地の建築的伝統を意識した。半透明のファイバーグラスの薄青い色調の日除けが日影を落とす。それはベイエリアの陽射しに対応した極めて繊細で薄いフィルターであり，どんよりとした空の1月でも明るくしてくれる。

　光と影，屋外と屋内，プライベートとパブリックの対比がこの家を演出する。エントリーは湾の眺めを枠取り，空気と樹木の香りが自然に流れ込んでくる。湾とタム山が見える南には子供たちの寝室があり，北には簡素な客用寝室があって，1本のセコイアが立つ斜面の先に湾が見える。窓際の席をよぎり，扉を抜け，部屋を横切って常にそよ風が吹き渡り新鮮な空気を運び込むだろう。丸みのついたジグザグに進む階段を降りるとリビング・スペースである主階へ出る。北へ向かって，短い通路が主寝室と森の地形がつくるテラスに続く。南に向かっては，大広間があり，湾から山脈まで一気に見渡せる壮大なパノラマを見せてくれる。この階は，背面が地盤面より下に沈んでいるので，蓄熱によって室温が安定している。湾曲するギャラリーが，薄く滑らかな縁を持つ開口が付きアート環境にぐるりと囲まれたグラフィック・デザイン・スタジオへ流れ込む。大広間の角からギャラリー・トンネルが平面全体の幾何学的中心へ向かい，庭園の野外階段とつながっている。

　庭を横切る音楽スタジオは地中に数フィート沈められ，窓枠が地表面にきている。南と西に視界が開け，近くには遊び場とカシの大木が見える。スタジオと調整室は音響や音質から形態と大きさが決められ，調律されている。軽量の屏風のような壁は，音楽をつくり聴くという体験に形を与える，石の箱の中に入った折り紙の扇子という考えから生まれた。

　この家は，その場所からかたちづくられた建築であり，自然が持つ色調や地形と融合させ，木立に覆われた素晴らしい庭園を尊重し，抽象化したものである。それは敷地固有の美しさと，絶え間ない発見によって彩られた生活のかたちを育み，光のパターン，天気，季節と共に常に変わりながら，創造性と五感が魅了され続ける場所になるだろう。

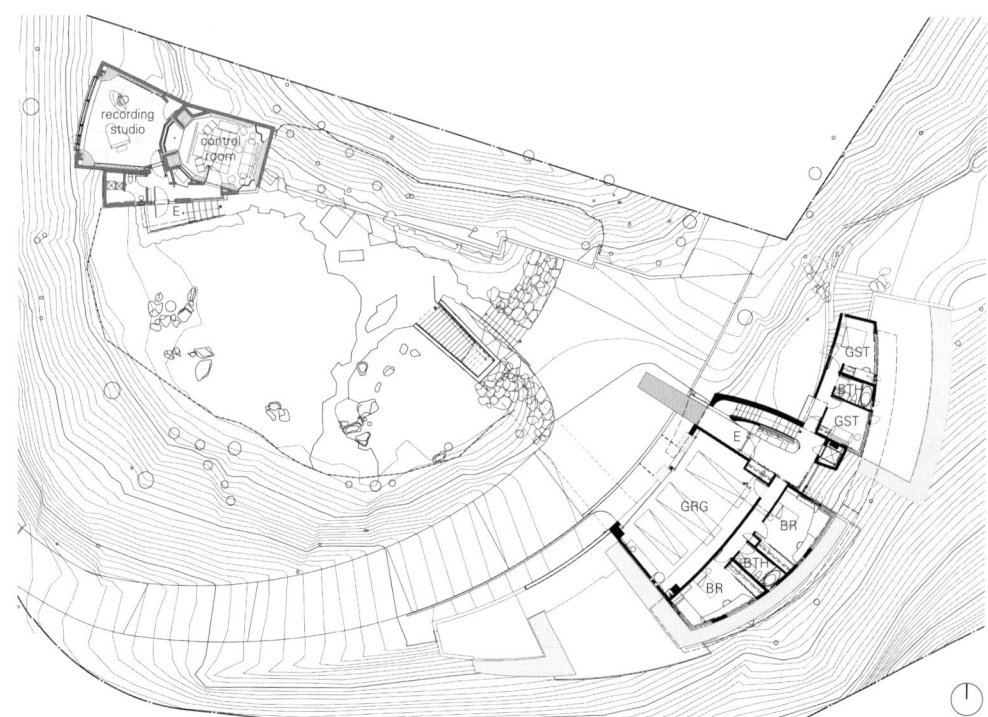

Upper level

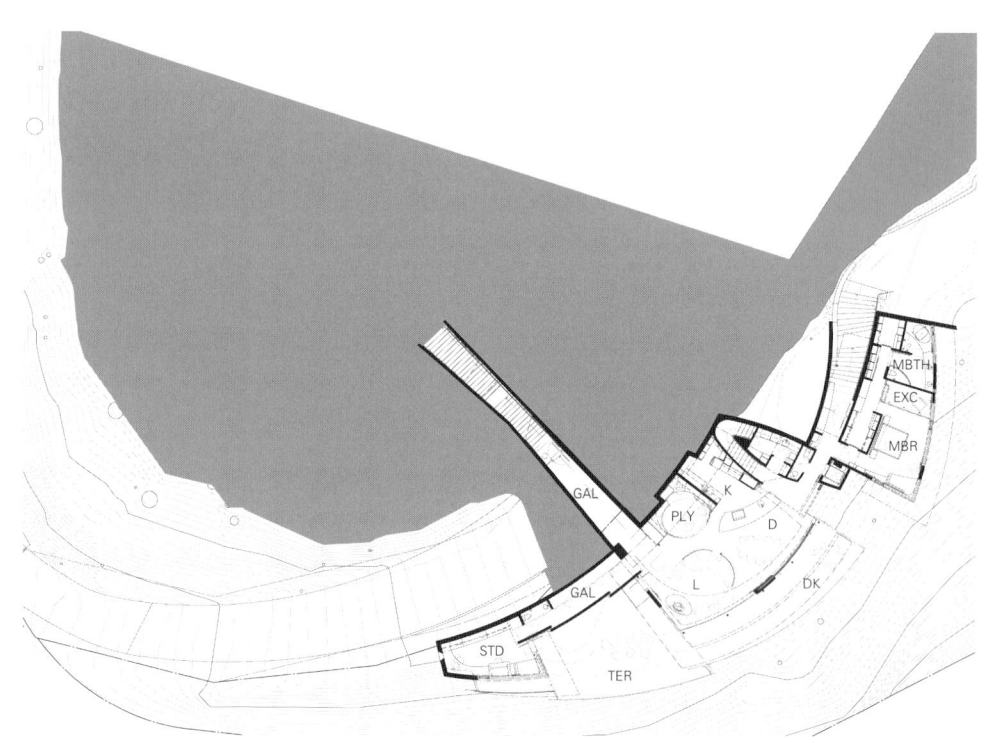

Lower level

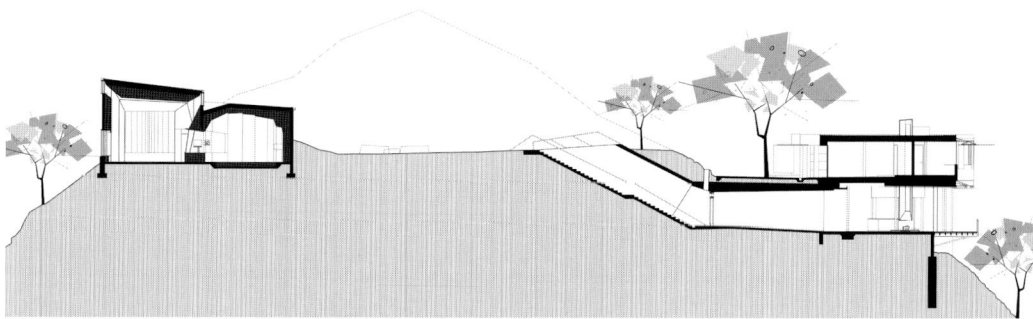

Site section: outbuilding (left) and main house (right)

View from northeast

Living room

Living room: looking east

Terrace

Corridor connects living room and office

Bathroom

Master bedroom

Steven Holl

2004

Writing with Light House, Eastern Long Island, New York, U.S.A.

View from southeast

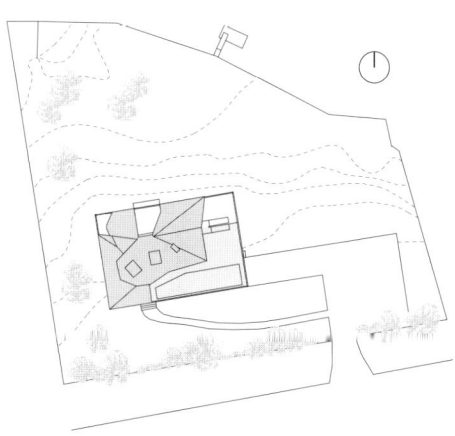

North elevation

Site plan

Living room: looking west

View toward kitchen

Kitchen

Living room: looking east

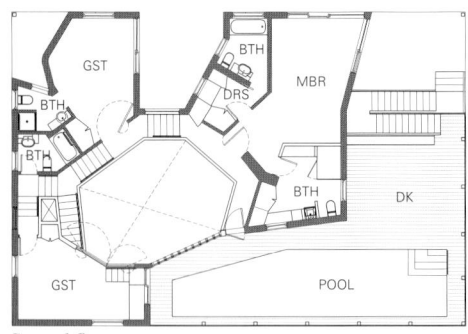

Second floor

First floor

The concept of this linear wooden beach house evolved from the inspiration of the site's close proximity to the studio of the painter Jackson Pollock. Several free-form designs were made based on the 1949 painting "Seven in Eight". Opening up the interior to the free expanse of the bay and the north view of the Atlantic Ocean required closing the south side for privacy from the street.

The final scheme brackets the internal energy into an open frame, which the sun shines through in projecting lines. The strips of white light inscribe and seasonally bend internal spaces dynamically with the cycle of the day.

The wooden balloon frame construction is comparable to the strip wood sand dune fencing along the ocean. Several guest rooms swirl around the double level living room from which one ascends to a pool suspended over the garage. From this upper pool court, the Atlantic Ocean is visible.

この線形をした木造のビーチ・ハウスのコンセプトは，敷地が画家ジャクソン・ポロックのアトリエに近いことから得た発想をもとに展開されている。いくつかの自由な形は，1949年の"セブン・イン・エイト"と題するポロックの絵に基づいてデザインした。屋内を湾と北側の大西洋の眺めに開放するためには，道路からのプライバシーを守るために，南側を閉ざすことが必要だった。

オープン・フレームのなかに内部のエネルギーを挟みこみ，射し込む陽光はストライプを描いて輝く。その白い光の縞模様は季節の推移と共に屈曲し，1日の循環に従ってダイナミックに内部空間を刻む。

木造のバルーン・フレーム構造は，海辺に沿って続く細い木片でつくられた砂丘のフェンスに似ている。ゲストルームがいくつか，2層吹抜けたリビングルームをぐるりと巡って配置され，そこからガレージの上のプールに出られる。この上階にあるプール・コートからは大西洋が見える。

Northeast corner: view toward dining room

Alberto Kalach

2004

Bross House, Santa Fe, Mexico City, Mexico

Entrance (left) and living room (right)

It is rare for an architect to receive such a level of trust from a client. Two years under construction, *Bross House* is the result of that trust.

Sunlight plays a major role inside every room of the house, as it caresses the surface of its raw materials and blends with darkness in unexpected proportion.

The different volumes that make up the house are built on the lower part of a slope, below street level. They are accessed from the garden through a bridge-like walkway, or climbed to directly from a red brick staircase.

The house seems to always give you the choice of taking a different path, providing many views on itself as well as the surrounding landscape. There are spaces intended to make a pause, at every turn. Light flows from a different direction on every room; all throughout the entire 800 square meters of construction. A house meant to be gradually experienced and discovered from every corner.

Entrance

View toward entrance from family room on level 1

Entrance hall: looking northwest

Level 2

Roof

Level 1

Level 3

Elevations, sections and plans

94

Entrance hall

View from entrance. Entrance hall on left

View toward family room on level 1: staircase to level 2 on right

Master bathroom

Master bedroom

96

Living room

建築家にとって、クライアントからこれ程までの信頼を得られることは稀だ。2年の建設期間を経た「ブロス邸」はこの信頼の成果である。

太陽の光は、各部屋において重要な役割を担う。仕上げをしていない材料の表面はなめるように照らし出され、驚くような形で、暗闇と混ざり合う。

住宅を形づくるそれぞれのヴォリュームは、道路レベルより下に位置する坂の低い部分にある。ブリッジのような歩道を抜けて、公園からも、赤いレンガ造りの階段を直接上がってもアクセスできる。

この住宅は、周辺のランドスケープと同様、それ自身によるいくつもの風景を生み出し、訪れる者に様々な順路を選ばせてくれるようだ。どの場面でも一息つけるように意図された場所がある。延べ800平方メートルにわたる建物全ての部屋には、様々な方角から光が射し込む。この住宅はあらゆる場所から、徐々に目に留まり、体験されるように考えられている。

Kitchen

Hiroyuki Arima

2004

Second Plate, Fukuoka, Japan

Overall view from street on north

Elements that structure the space are: ground plate; second plate; B-1 (office, guest room); B-2 (living room, dining room); sb-1 (bedroom); sb-2 (warehouse); sb-3 (entrance); sb-4 (utility room); stairs A/B/C. The vicinity is an area in Fukuoka City where nature is comparatively well preserved. B-1 and B-2 are placed on top of the second plate, with the terrace in between. The two are in complementary position with one another, but each has an individual set of stairs offering separate access from the outside, for independent operation. People will move about to and from this second plate, taking the stairs up and down. The terrace is equipped with a triangular water basin. Its shallow water is basically transparent, but may be tinted at choice—blue in summer, yellow in autumn, black in winter and red in spring.

At the beginning, there was a request for a parking space large enough to accommodate 5 cars. But the level difference between the ground plate and the front road was 1,600 mm, and has proved to be too short in height to house a parking space. Our choice was to create another level, the second plate, which would separate and superimpose the cars and the living spaces.

The actual manipulation consisted of: 'ensuring a planar spread with enough height for the parking space on the second plate'→'detach this plate from the ground to the maximum, with basically no contact with the ground itself'→ 'placing the open terrace and the water basin in the center, with the office (B-1) and the living/dining rooms (B-2) on left and right'→ 'then arrange the facilities (sb) that are necessary to complement the above functions'→'so that people would walk around to lead their lives.'

Ensuring the parking space while arranging side by side the distinctive functions of the living space and the office space along a loose-knit link... the presence of the second plate is the key factor providing solution to all of them.
Hiroyuki Arima

View from west

Terrace: view toward living/dining room

Second floor

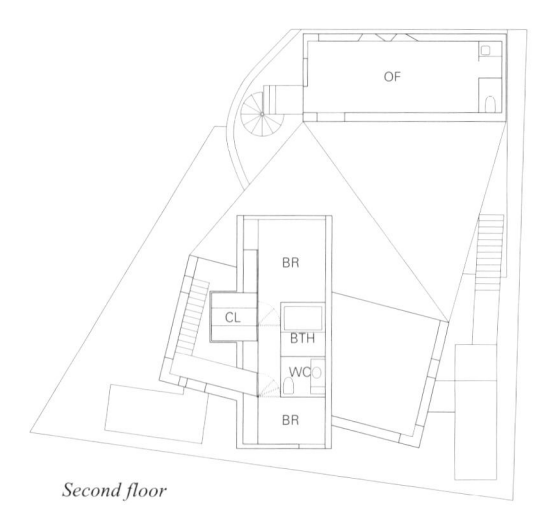

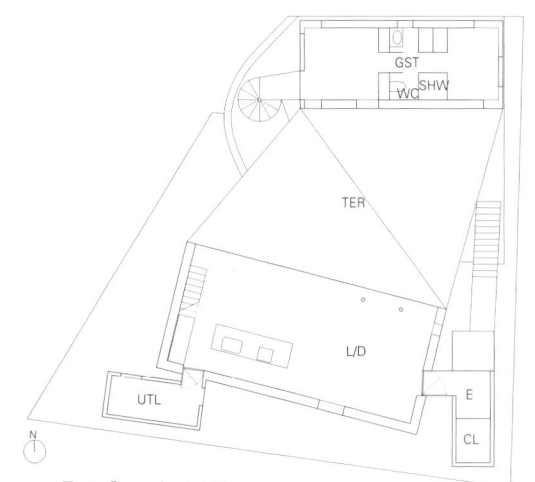

First floor S=1:300

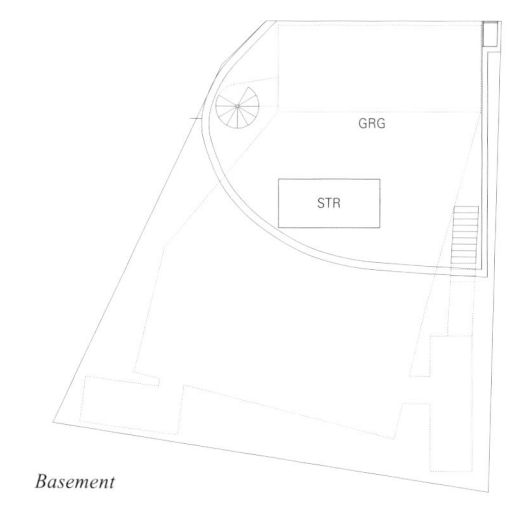

Basement

Living room (left) and terrace (right): floating box houses private space

Bathroom on second floor: view toward bedroom

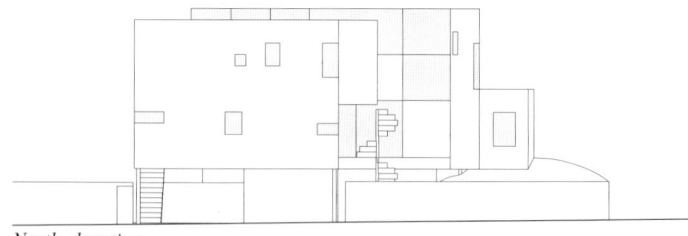

North elevation

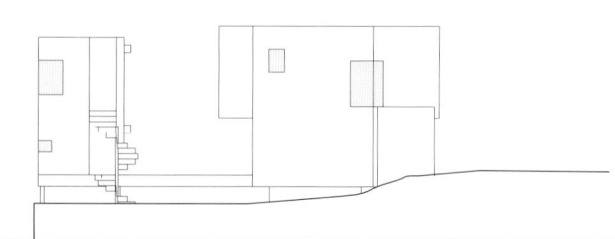

West elevation S=1:300

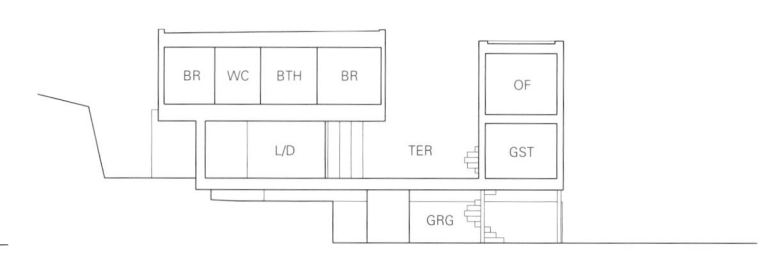

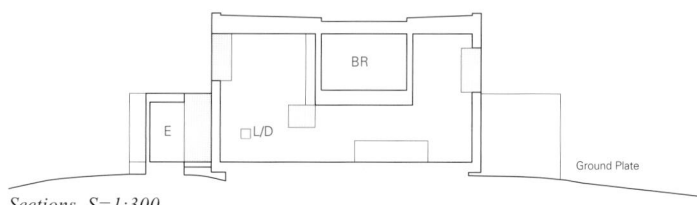

Sections S=1:300

Living room: view toward entrance

View of staircase to private space from kitchen

　空間を構成するエレメントは,「ground plate」／「second plate」／B-1（オフィス, ゲストルーム）／B-2（リビング, ダイニング）／sb-1（寝室）／sb-2（倉庫）／sb-3（エントランス）／sb-4（家事室）／階段A／B／Cである。周辺は, 福岡市の中でも比較的に自然の木々が点在しているエリアで, 隣地には市指定の保存樹があるなど, 豊かな環境が保全されている。「second plate」の上に, テラスを挟んでB-1とB-2が配置されている。それら相互は補完関係にあるものの, それぞれが独立して運営できるように各々に外部からのアプローチ階段が設置されている。人はこの「second plate」を中心に動き, 階段を上がり下りし行き交う。テラスには薄く水のはられた三角形の水盤があり, 基本的には透明だが好みの色水を溜めて楽しむことができる。夏：青, 秋：黄, 冬：黒, 春：赤という具合にである。

　車5台程を停められる広い駐車場を確保したいという要望が最初にあった。しかし一方,「ground plate」と前面道路との高低差は1,600ミリ程で, 駐車場を確保するには高さとしては足りない。新たに「second plate」レベルを設定し, 駐車と生活の場を上下に重なり合わせるという構成を選択した。

　行った操作は「second plateで必要な駐車場高さのとれる面的な広がりを確保する」→「そのplateはできる限り地面から切り離されていて, 接地部は基本的に無い」→「中心にオープンな水盤とテラスを設け, それをはさむ形でオフィス(B-1)とリビングダイニング(B-2)を並べる」→「それらをセットした後に, それを補足する必要なファシリティー(sb)を並べる」→「人々は歩き回り活動する」である。

　駐車場を確保し自宅とオフィスそれぞれの機能を並列させつつ, ゆるやかに繋ぐ……「second plate」1枚でその全てを解決している。　　　（有馬裕之）

Steven Holl

2005

Planar House, Phoenix, Arizona, U.S.A.

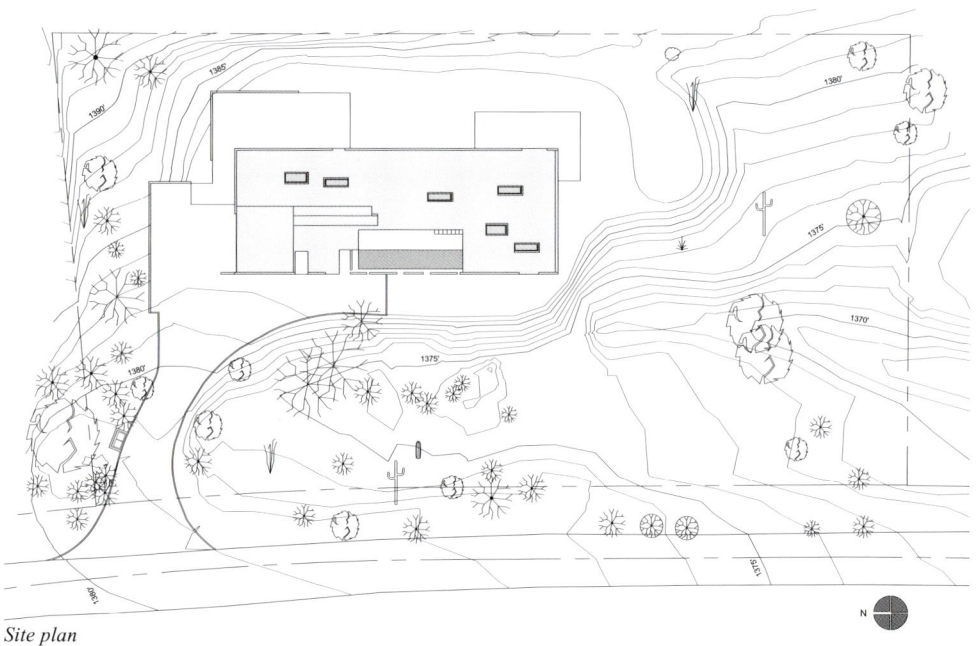

Site plan

West elevation: behind low wall on center is court with swimming pool

View from southwest : porch on south

Court: slope to rooftop on right

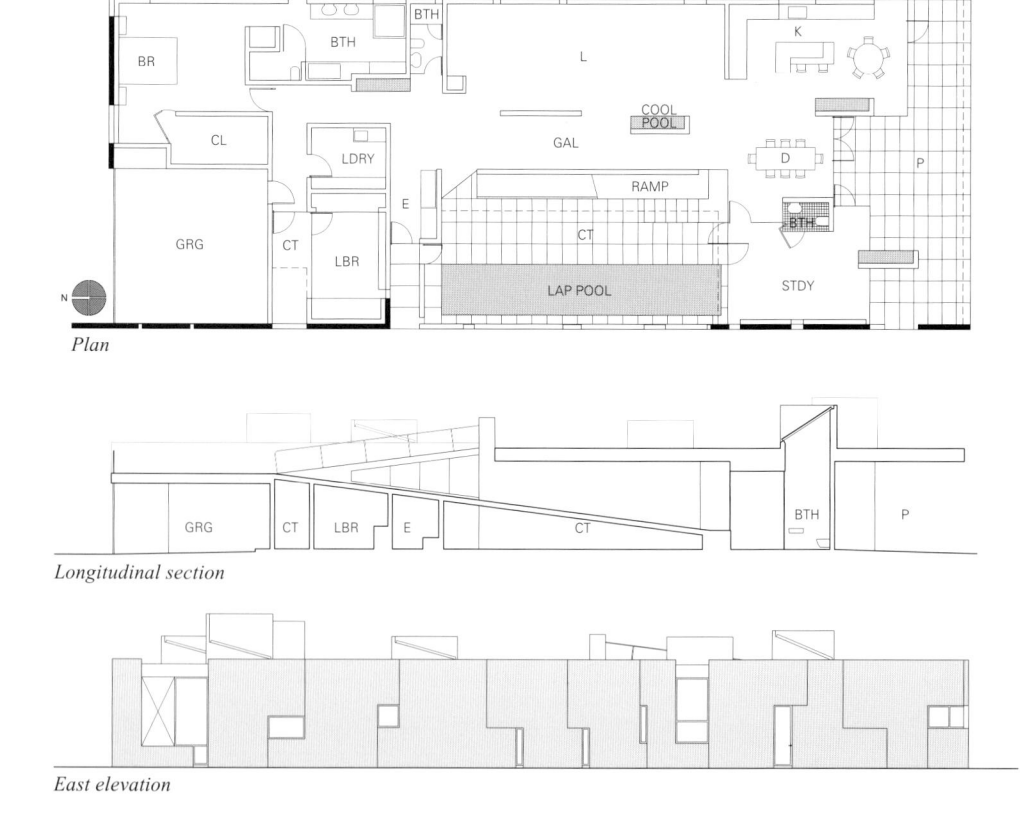

View from entrance hall toward south: living (left), gallery (center) and entrance (right)

Plan

Longitudinal section

East elevation

South elevation

West elevation

North elevation

104

Entrance

Sited in Paradise Valley with a direct vista to Camelback Mountain, this house is to be a part of, and vessel for, a large contemporary art collection. Great 20th century works by Bruce Nauman, Robert Ryman and Jannis Kounellis are part of the collection which includes important video artworks.

Constructed of tilt-up concrete walls, the nature of the walls merges with the simple orthogonal requirements of the interiors for art.

Shape extensions and light and air chimneys connected to cooling pools articulate the planar geometry. From a courtyard experienced at the entry of sequence, a ramp leads to a rooftop sculpture garden—a place of silence and reflection.

パラダイスヴァレーにある敷地からはキャメルバック山が真っ直ぐ前方に望める。膨大なコンテンポラリーアート・コレクションの一部であると共にその器となる住宅である。ブルース・ノーマン, ロバート・ライマン, ジャニス・コルネリスの素晴らしい20世紀美術が, 重要なビデオアート作品を含めたコレクションの一部を占めている。

ティルトアップ工法で建てられた壁は美術作品の展示に必要な, 四角形の簡素な内部空間に同化する。

形態の延長部, そしてクーリング・プールと結ばれた光と外気を通すチムニーが, 平坦な外形に明快な節をつける。内部空間が展開してゆく起点となる中庭から, 静かに思いに浸る場所である屋上の彫刻庭園までスロープが続いている。

Gallery

Kitchen: furniture are made of laminated bamboo board

View toward kitchen from study: porch on right

Living room: looking south

Master bedroom

Bathroom

Library

Álvaro Siza

House Armanda Passos, Porto, Portugal

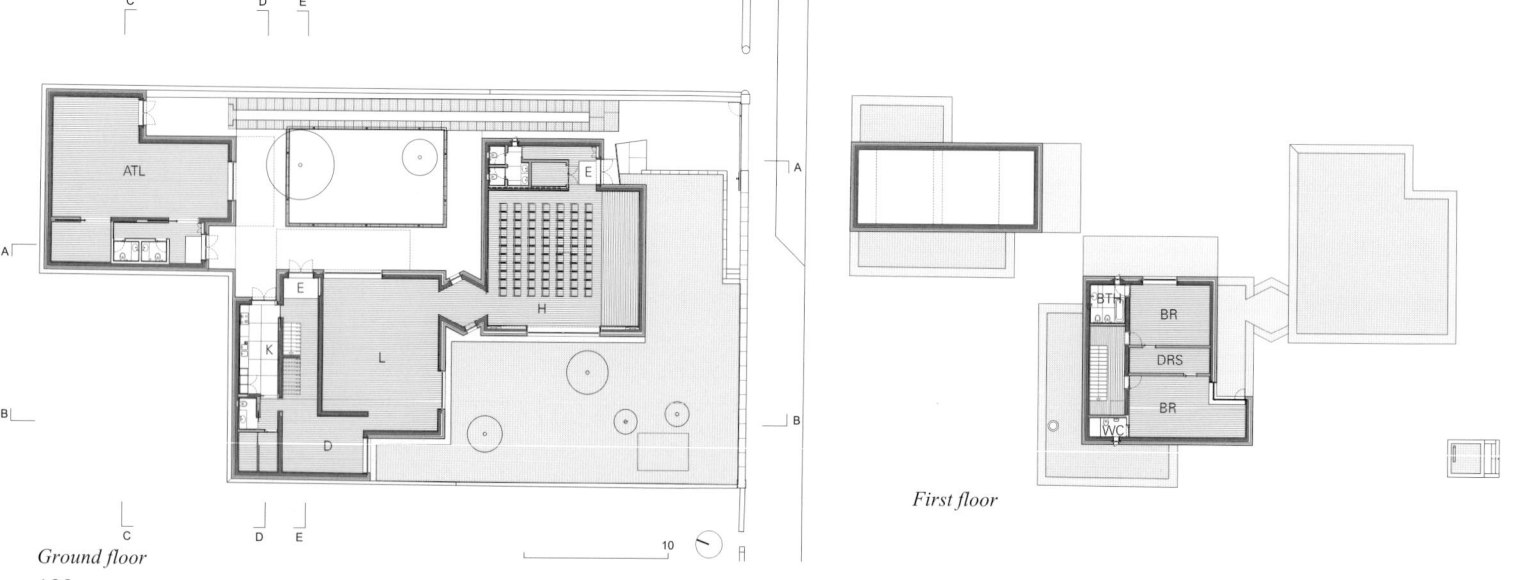

2005

Courtyard: view of atelier on center, entrance on left

Ground floor

First floor

Hall

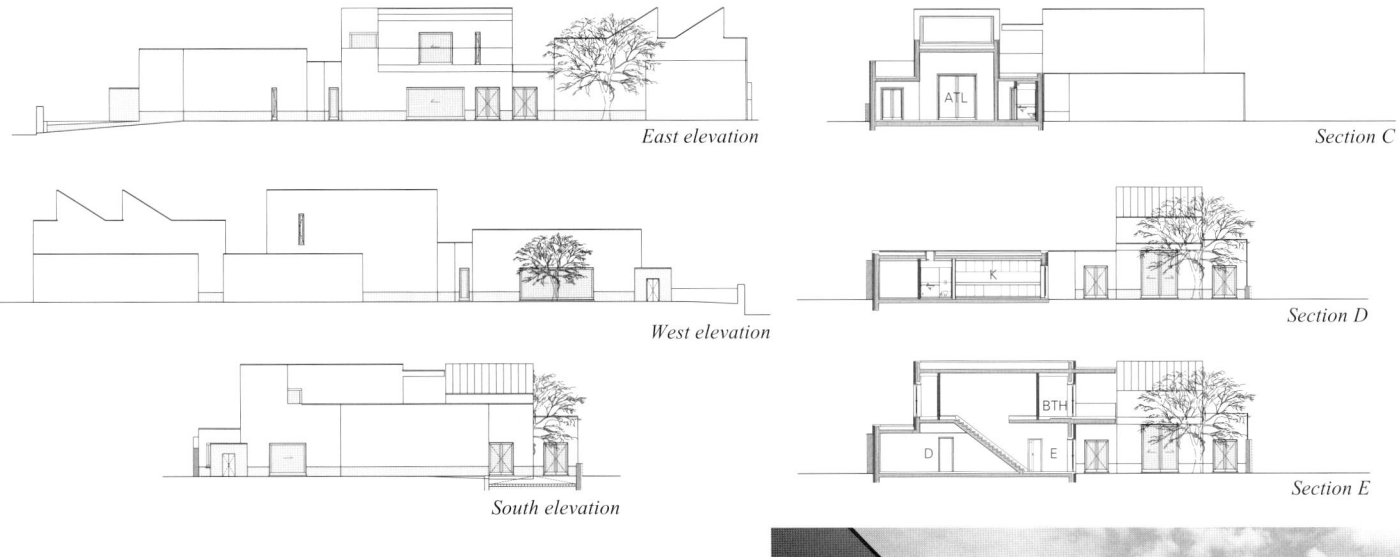

East elevation

Section C

West elevation

Section D

South elevation

Section E

Section A

Section B

Entrance: approach to atelier on right

109

This is a house of Sra. Armanda Passos, who is a Portuguese painter.

The house is designed to meet the demands of her artistic activities.

The three inter-connected bodies of the building define and articulate the landscaped patios (integrating the existing trees).

The program is distributed into three volumes: A, B, and C.
- Volume A (in two floors)
  Floor 1: hall, common living room, kitchen, closet and bathroom
  Floor 2: two bedrooms with bathrooms and closets
- Volume B (one floor with double height)
  hall, atelier, closet and bathroom.
- Volume C (one floor with double height)
  hall, multipurpose room, closet and bathroom.

A large garden and a wall separate the house from the Avenue, which runs in front of the lot.

Álvaro Siza

Living room

ポルトガルの画家，アルマンダ・パッソス女史の住宅。

この家は，彼女の芸術活動が必要とするものに合わせて設計されている。

内部で連結された三つの棟が，既存の樹木を取り込んで修景されたパティオの境界を定め，明快に区分する。

諸室はA，B，C，三つの棟に配分されている。
・A棟（2フロアから成る）
  フロア1：ホール，共有の居間，台所，クローゼット，浴室
  フロア2：浴室とクローゼットの付いた寝室二つ
・B棟（2層分の高さを持つ1フロアから成る）
  ホール，アトリエ，クローゼット，浴室
・C棟（2層分の高さを持つ1フロアから成る）
  ホール，多目的室，クローゼット，浴室

広い庭と塀が，敷地の前を通る大通りから家を引き離している。

（アルヴァロ・シザ）

Atelier

Hall: chairs designed by architect

View toward living room from hall

Atelier with skylight

Blank Studio

2005

Xeros Residence, Phoenix, Arizona, U.S.A.

View from southeast

East elevation

Courtyard: looking north

113

Studio entry: view toward courtyard

「ゼロス・プロジェクト」は50年代後期の住宅地にあり，ここはフェニックスの都市グリッドが北側に広がる，山岳保護区の有機的な地形に迫っている地域である。2本の袋小路の終点にある敷地は，北は保護区である山，南は市の中心部に顔を向けた50×250フィートの上り斜面になった2区画を占める。

建物は，低層部を占める，掘り下げられた2層のデザイン・スタジオとその上に位置する1層の住宅で構成され，住宅へは外階段だけが通じている。スタジオ階へは，メッシュ・スクリーンの後ろを通って，さらに，メッシュで囲まれた前庭のある屋外への短い階段を降りて行かねばならない。ステンレス・スティールの水路が階段にそって人を導き，リフレクティング・プールに注ぐ。前庭から，スティールで枠取られた，幅3.5フィート，高さ19.5フィートのガラス扉を抜けてスタジオに入る。住宅へは，スティールの外階段を上がり，共有スペース(居間，食堂，台所)に入る前に上階のバルコニーに出る必要がある。続いて，中央ギャラリーを抜けて，片持ちで張り出した主寝室スィート／メディア・ルームへ進む。ここは北面全体がガラス張りで，保護区である山の眺めを楽しめる。一連の動線の終着点である"ロミオ・アンド・ジュリエット"バルコニーが，山とは逆方向に片持ちで張り出し，黄色いガラスの手すり壁で囲まれ，建物の長手軸を見通したその先に市街が見晴らせる。

建物の主要な材料はコールテン鋼で(構造，被覆材，日除けとして)，天候に自然に曝され，周囲の丘の色調に溶け込む。

あらゆる解法はその環境に直接応答すべきであることの暗示として，"ゼロス"(ギリシャ語で"乾燥した"という意味)と名付けられた建物には，環境に配慮した決定がいくつもなされている。午後の強い西日に対しては不透明な面を向け，南と東側の露出度の高い面は金属繊維のメッシュが外側に重ねられて陽差しを防ぐ。細長い敷地からは，小さな建坪の，非常に背の高い建物が引き出され，植栽のための場所が最大限残された。水をやる必要の少ない植物が家の周りに配され，スクリーンによる日除け効果に加わる。敷地そのものは"リサイクル"され，フェニックスの野放図に広がってしまった地域の放置された区画に新しい生命を注入した。

The Xeros project is sited within a late 50's era neighborhood where the urban grid of Phoenix is overtaken by the organic land forms of the north phoenix mountain preserve. Located at the end of two dead-end streets, *the Xeros residence* is positioned upon the upward slope of a 50 x 250 feet double lot facing the mountain preserve to the north and the city center to the south.

The building parti includes a two-story lower level design studio that descends down into the earth with a single story residence that exists above the studio that is accessed solely by an external stair. The path to the studio level requires that the guest pass behind the mesh screen and descend a short flight of stairs into an exterior, mesh-enclosed forecourt. A stainless steel water feature leads you down the steps and terminates at a reflecting pool. A 3-1/2 foot wide by 19-1/2 tall steel-framed glass door offers entry into the studio from the courtyard. To access the residence, the visitor ascends an exterior steel staircase to an upper level balcony before entering the common room (sitting, dining, and kitchen). The visitor continues through a central gallery towards the cantilevered master suite/media room. This space is completely glazed on the north facade to enjoy the mountain preserve views. To complete the cycle of movement, a cantilevered yellow-glass framed 'Romeo and Juliet' balcony allows views back to the city and across the long axis of the building.

The primary building material is exposed steel (as structure, cladding, and shading) that is allowed to weather naturally and meld with the color of the surrounding hills.

Called 'Xeros' (from the Greek for 'dry') as a reminder that all solutions should be in a direct response to its environment—the building has several environmentally responsible decisions. The form turns an opaque face towards the intense western afternoon sun and the more exposed faces to the south and east are shielded by an external layer of woven metal shade mesh. The long, narrow lot precipitated very tall from with a petite foot print allows the maximum amount of site to be retained for vegetation. The low-water use vegetation is positioned around the residence to add to the shading effect of the screen. The site itself was 'recycled' in that new life was injected into a neglected plot in a neglected Phoenix neighborhood.

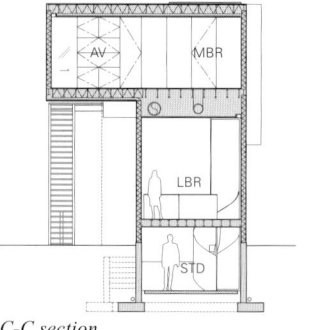

C-C section

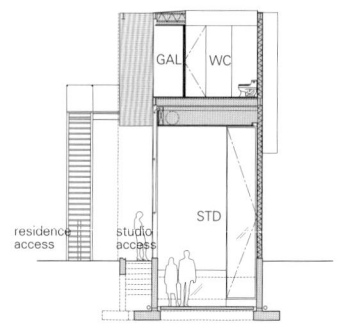

B-B section

Studio: view toward courtyard

Studio: view toward library on mezzanine

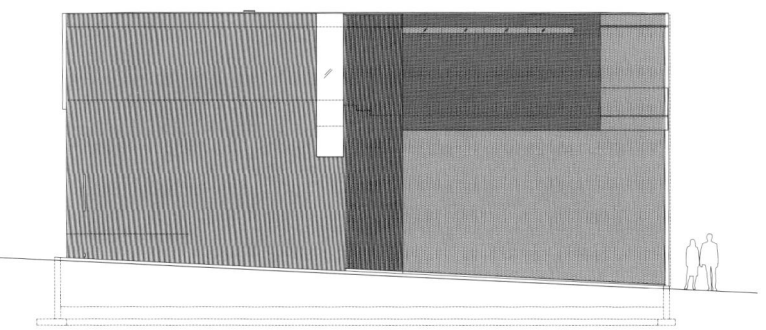

West elevation

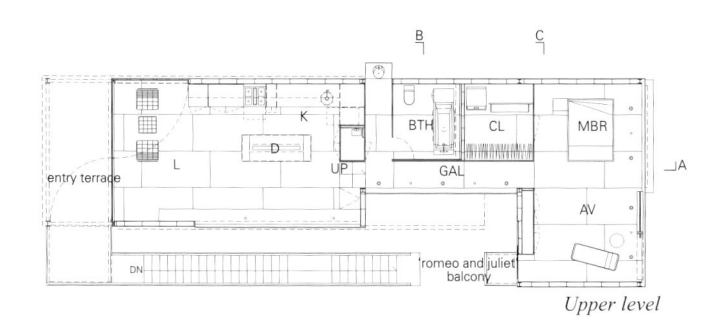

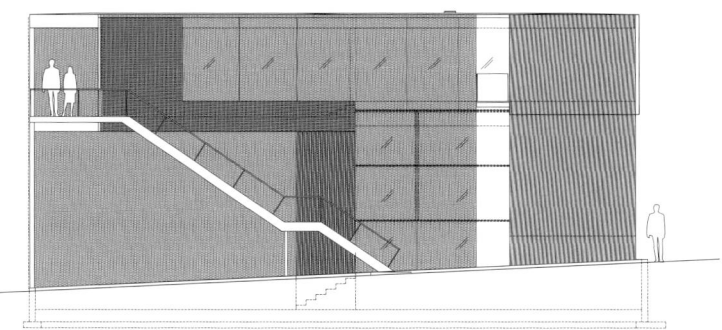

East elevation

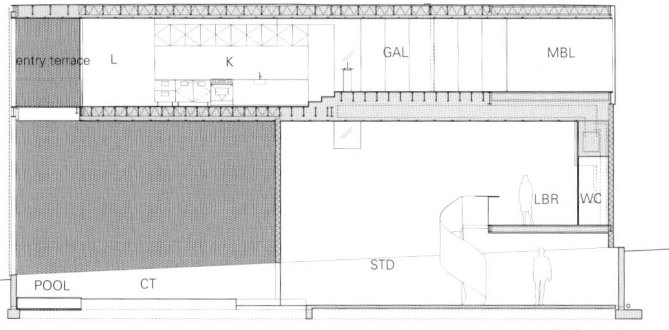

A-A section

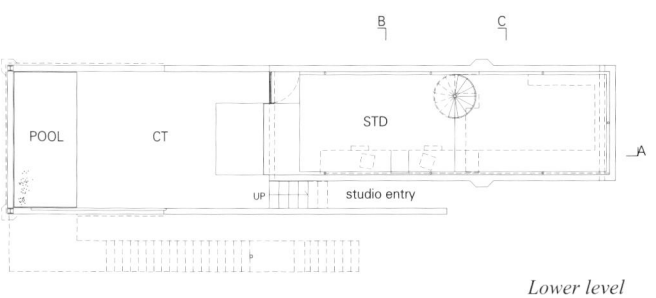

Upper level

Mezzanine

Lower level

View from living room toward dining room

View from dining room toward living room

View toward master bedroom, bathroom on left

Lavatory on upper level

Master bedroom

117

Ryue Nishizawa

2005

Moriyama House, Tokyo, Japan

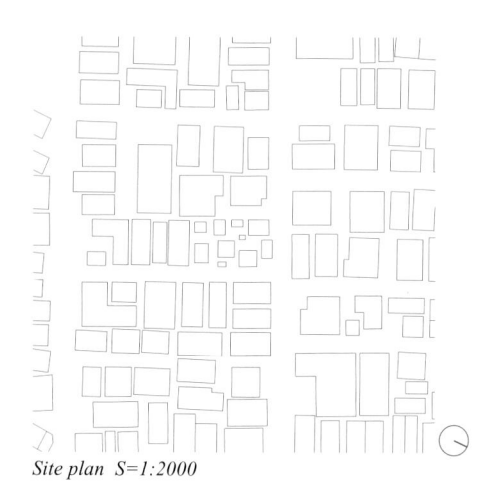

Site plan S=1:2000

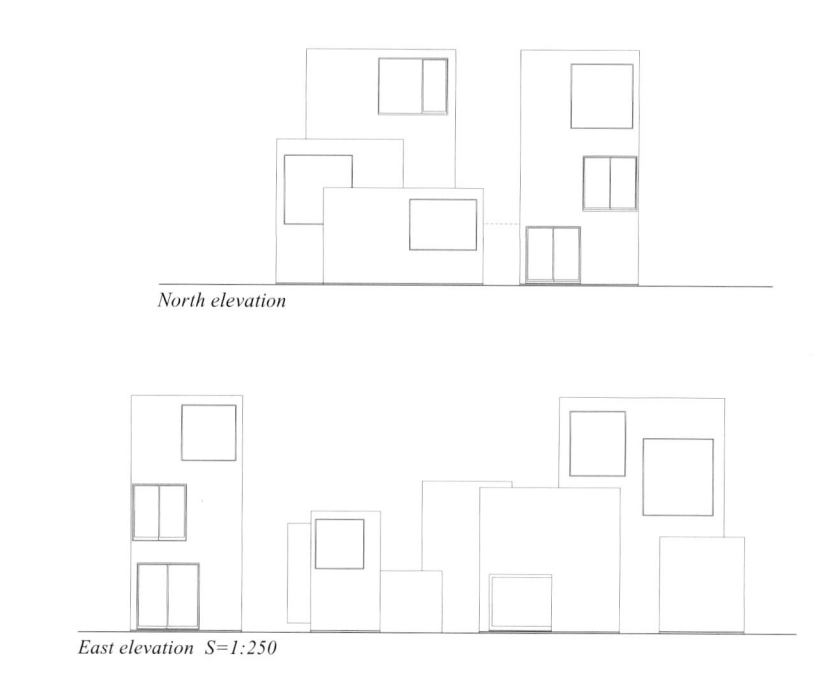

North elevation

East elevation S=1:250

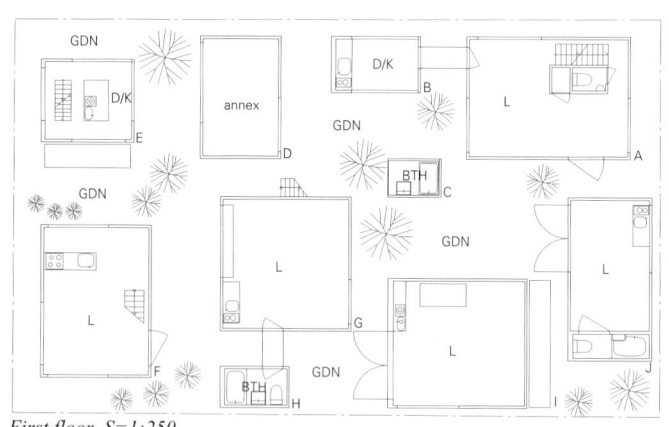

First floor S=1:250

Third floor

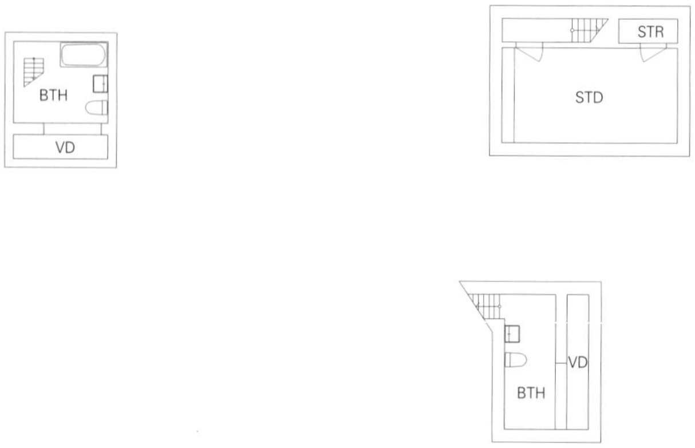

Basement

Second floor

View from south

View from north

View from east

View from west: bathroom of house C on left

View toward garden through glazed corridor of house H

Living room of house I

A project consisting of a collective housing for extremely small studios for rent called 'one-room mansions' and an independent residence built on the same site. The vicinity is a residential area that preserves the good old atmosphere of downtown Tokyo, a charming urban block where double to triple-storied, mid-scaled apartments and houses stand at small intervals in orderly rows.

Assuming that to incorporate the owner's residence into the housing complex would make the volume much too large compared to the neighboring buildings, we chose to separate the houses and arrange them independently. Our idea was that by doing so this area's urban pattern made of repeated sequence of small buildings and voids might be maintained, and each household might be provided with a tiny garden. Because the group of independent buildings has no common structure as a whole, size and shape of each building can be designed separately. As a result a variety of house types came to be created: triple-storied house; square house half buried below ground; house with extremely high ceiling; house surrounded by a garden on four sides. They are crammed into the site, generating a diversity of exterior spaces such as small gardens and alleyways. Relationship between each house with its garden is different in variation. Our attempt is to create living spaces typical of Tokyo, where life is not enclosed solely within the indoor space but continues from indoors to garden and alleyways.
Ryue Nishizawa

House F on left and bathroom of house H on right

Opening and staircase of house F

非常に小さな賃貸住戸が集まる，ワンルームマンションと呼ばれる集合住宅，それと専用住宅一つが，一つの敷地の中に建つ計画である。周辺は昔からの東京の下町の雰囲気を残す住宅地で，2，3階建ての中規模のアパートや住宅が，お互いに小さな間隔を空けて秩序だって並ぶ，魅力的な街区である。

要求されたオーナー住宅と賃貸集合住宅を一体としてつくると，ヴォリュームが周りの建物に比べて大変大きくなってしまうため，私たちは各住宅を離して，各々を独立配置することにした。そのことによって，建物と隙間が細かく反復してゆくこの地区の都市パターンを継承できるのではないかと思い，また，各住戸に小さな庭を与えることができるのではないかと考えた。独立して建つ建物群は，共通した全体構造を持たないため，各々別々に空間の大きさや形を決めることができる。そのため，3階建ての住宅，半地下の正方形の住宅，天井高が非常に高い住宅，庭に四周囲まれた住宅など，いろいろな住戸タイプが生まれた。それらはひしめき合うように敷地に並びながら，その間に小さな庭や路地のような，様々な屋外空間をつくり出している。各々の住宅は，庭との関係においてもいろいろなバリエーションを持っている。生活が屋内空間だけで閉ざされるのではなく，むしろ室内と庭・路地などに連続していくような，東京らしい住空間をつくり出そうと考えている。

(西沢立衛)

Master bedroom on third floor of house A

View toward garden from living room of house A: looking south

View toward house C (bathroom) through house B (dining room/kitchen)

View toward staircase of house A from house B

Sou Fujimoto

2005

T House, Gunma, Japan

From left to right: tatami room, piano room, study and master bedroom

This house for a family of 4 members is basically a one-room, studio-type space. The room is pinched to form a radial pattern. The distortion of space produces different degrees of depth and linkage that deliver diverse attributes such as the change of scenery that accompanies motion, spatial expanse and privacy needed in a house.

This is an 'architecture of distance perspectives'. Individual regions come into effect because they are 'slightly set back' from other spaces. The living room appears to be more spacious than it really is, due to the 'sense of distance that is continuous while being partitioned' with regard to the Japanese room on the opposite side.

The term 'distance' does not imply physical distance, but rather a 'sense of distance about relationships' created by the depth and distortion in this space. This is why diverse perspectives of distance such as 'apart and connected at the same time' 'adjacent but immensely remote' 'segmented but suddenly linked when a step is taken forward' are realized within the simplicity of this studio-like home.

Such perspectives of distance produce subtle inflections in space. These inflections present themselves as places of comfort with dramatic spatiality. A place that is almost a room and almost not a room at the same time. Consequently, it forges ties with other places, complement one another and increase diversity. Connecting all the while drawing away. In this way, a fertile relationship is created, one which can never be acquired through simple partitioning of rooms.

Bearing walls are painted white on one side, and exposing the wood sheathing on the other. One corner of the house would be a white room, and its adjacent room would be, by the nature of things, a backside, wooden room. Walls are 12 mm thick around the edges. Through this slimness, white place and wooden place alternate, clearly illustrating the adjacency of heterogeneous things and the distance between them.

This house is also a place where the client shows the pieces of modern art in possession. Art pieces decorate walls in all sorts of angles. A painting might be seen from a faraway room on the opposite side. As one takes a step forward, the painting which was within sight becomes invisible, and instead, another work of art makes its appearance. Art is closely entwined with space and action.

This 'house of inflections and distance perspectives' consisting of a single, constricted room is a suggestion about a new, and yet fundamental and primal space of living.
Sou Fujimoto

Various angled walls: contemporary art works hung on them

From left to right: study, master bedroom, living/dining room and kitchen

Overall view from east

四人家族が住むこの家は，基本的にワンルームである。そのワンルームが放射状にくびれ，空間が歪むことによって生じる奥まり方の度合い，つながり方の度合いによって，住宅に必要とされるプライバシー，広がり，移動にともなう情景の変化，などの多様な質が実現される。

　これは「距離感の建築」である。個人的な領域は，他の場所から「少し奥まっている」ことによって成立する。またリビング・スペースは，向かい合う和室との「仕切られながらも連続している距離感」によって，実際以上の広がりを獲得している。

　ここでいう距離とは，物理的な距離のことではない。むしろこの空間の歪みと奥まりによって生まれる「関係性の距離感」である。だからこのシンプルなワンルームの中に「離れていて同時につながっている」「隣り合っているけれど限りなく隔たっている」「分節されているが一歩踏み出すことで突然連結する」というような，多様な距離感が実現するのである。

　これらの距離感は，空間にかすかな抑揚を生む。それらの抑揚は居心地のよい居場所であり，同時に劇的な広がりとなる。半分部屋で，半分部屋でないような場所。それゆえに他の場所と関係を持ち，相互に補完し，多様さを増す。つながりつつ離れることで，単に部屋として仕切ることでは得られない豊かな関係が生まれる。

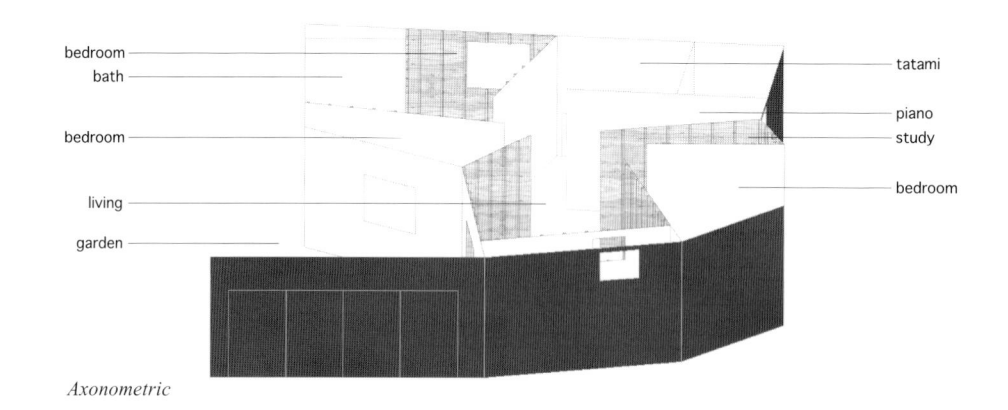

　一面を白ペイント，裏面を木下地表わしとした構造壁。ある場所は白い部屋であり，その隣の部屋は，必然的に裏側の木の部屋となる。壁は端部で12ミリの厚さであり，その薄さを介して白い場所と木の場所とが繰り返すことで，異質なものの隣接性とその間の隔たりを鮮明に映し出す。

　この家は施主が持つ現代アートを展示する場所でもある。さまざまな角度の壁にアートが飾られる。ある絵は，遠く離れた向かいの部屋から見ることができる。一歩踏み出すと今まで見えていた絵が隠れ，替わりに別の作品が視界に入ってくる。アートが，空間と行為とに密接に絡み合っている。

　くびれたワンルームによる「抑揚と距離感の住宅」は，新しく，同時に根源的，原初的な住空間の提案である。

（藤本壮介）

Axonometric

Looking southwest: bedroom on center

Piano room and study

View from south: surrounding black wall and white wall facing courtyard

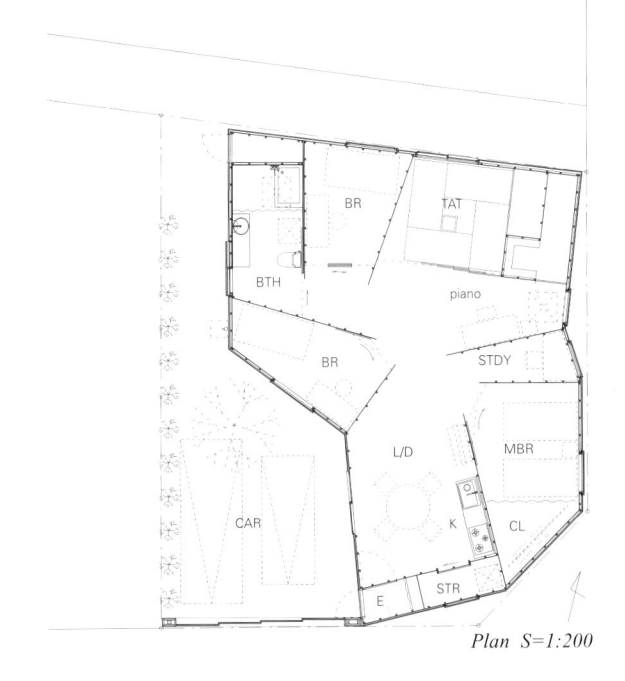

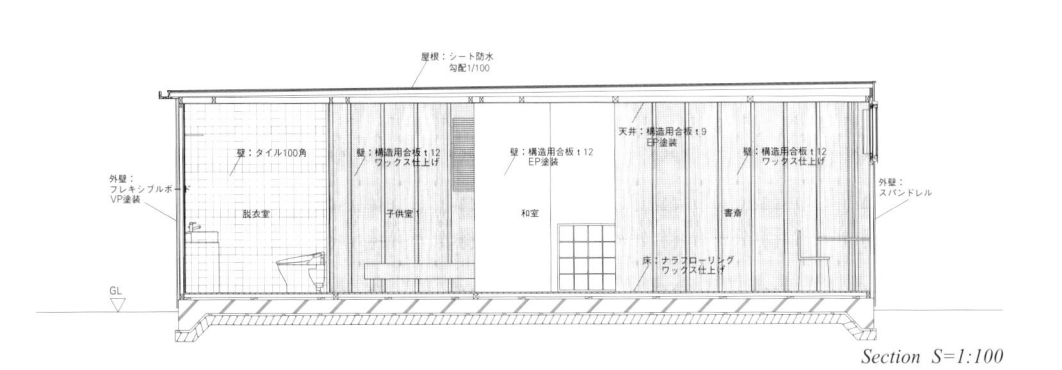

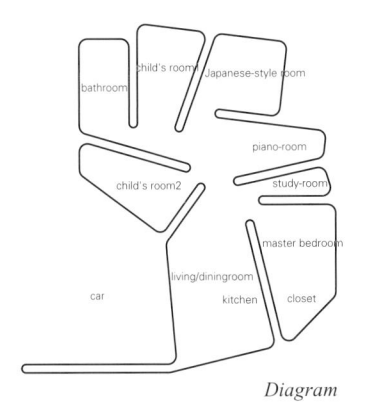

Plan S=1:200

Section S=1:100

Diagram

View toward living/dining room from tatami room

127

Hiroshi Sambuichi

2005

Stone House, Shimane, Japan

Overall view from southeast

View toward court

West elevation: entrance on second floor

Entrance on south

129

Living/dining room: looking north

Living/dining room: looking south

View toward study from terrace on second floor

Downward view of living room

Personally, I am interested in picturing the Earth's details through architecture.

The client is a family of four, and has requested for a main house that can be used at times of snowfall, and a guesthouse annex with a large terrace. The site is situated on the border between Hiroshima, Yamaguchi and Shimane prefectures in a region of heavy snow where ski resorts freckle the range of mountains as much as 1,000 meter-high. Surrounded by rice fields, it is fully exposed to the north wind during winter, and is subject to high temperatures and high humidity during summer.

Under such harsh climatic conditions, there was a need to adjust the balance between the surface condition and the exposure status of non-architectural zone and the surface of above-ground part of the building, and minimize the amount of superficial area exposed to outside air. The building is buried among crushed stones instead of burying in leveled ground surrounded by rice fields for better response to humidity. In wintertime, it is protected against cold air. After snowfall, air space similar to snow cave is formed among the crushed stones. In summertime, ventilation through these crushed stones softly cools off the inside by geothermal power. The plan proposed consists of a single building in order to minimize the total area of the roof. Each room function was laid out onto the floor plan and arranged cross-sectionally in terms of the rate of utilization per hour, ventilation, natural lighting and thermal change. The guesthouse with its lower utilization rate is placed on the upper level, catering to various purposes and client's ideas such as the solarium during winter, clothes-drying space in rainy seasons and shady party terrace during summer. It also serves as an air space and provides cross-sectional ventilation together with the garden so that the main living space on lower level maintains a stable comfort throughout the year. Roof surface is covered with glass for adhesive properties to snow and durability. Its slant faces south out of consideration for the remaining snow. The roof structure composed of layers of air and wood that also work as insulation coordinates light, heat and convection along the slant.

Today, planning based on total energy balance including demolition and waste is required in architecture, regardless of how harsh the given climatic conditions may be. We have come to a stage in which we have to pursue an intellectual relationship with the environment by means of interaction with the form of the architecture itself that would minimize the use of oil products hard to recycle such as waterproof agent and insulation material, and maximize the material's potential.

Hiroshi Sambuichi

Tatami room (left) and living room (right)

Dining room

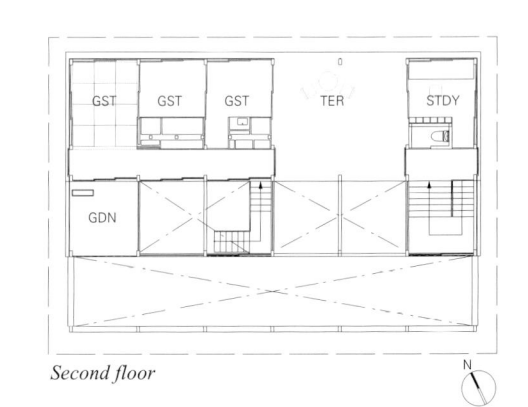

First floor S=1:300

Second floor

North elevation

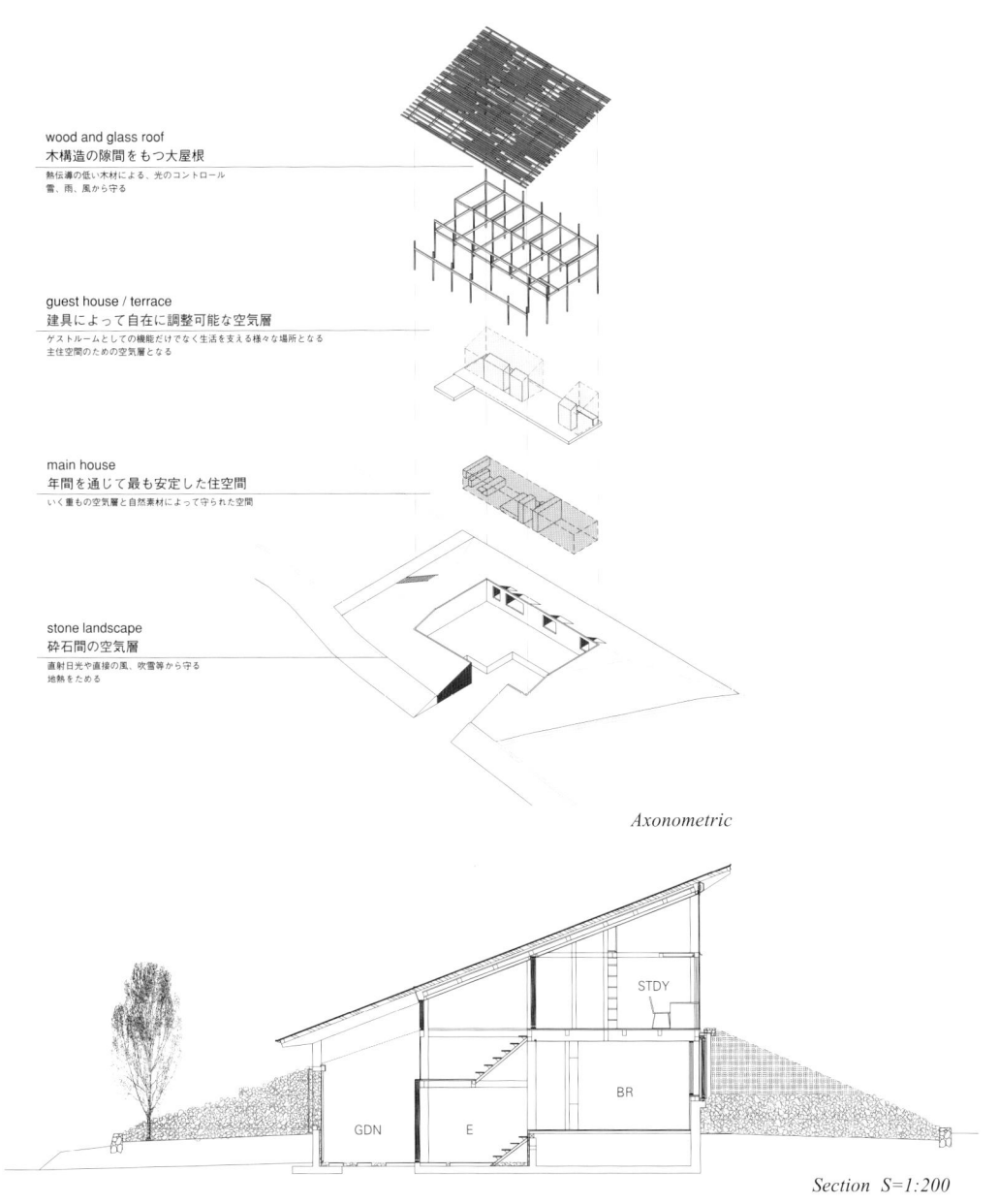

wood and glass roof
木構造の隙間をもつ大屋根
熱伝導の低い木材による，光のコントロール
雪，雨，風から守る

guest house / terrace
建具によって自在に調整可能な空気層
ゲストルームとしての機能だけでなく生活を支える様々な場所となる
主住空間のための空気層となる

main house
年間を通じて最も安定した住空間
いく重もの空気層と自然素材によって守られた空間

stone landscape
砕石間の空気層
直射日光や直接の風，吹雪等から守る
地熱をためる

Axonometric

Section S=1:200

　私は建築を通して地球のディテールを考えることに興味がある。

　クライアントは四人家族で，積雪時に対応した母屋棟と，さらに広いテラスを持つゲストハウスとなる離れを望まれていた。敷地周辺は，広島と山口，島根の県境で1,000メートル級の中国山地が連なり，多くのスキー場を有する多雪地域にある。周囲を水田に囲まれているため，冬は北風を遮るものが何もなく，夏は高温で多湿な環境にある。

　このような過酷な気候条件の中では，非建築部分と建築地上部分表面の露出状況と表面状態とのバランスを調整し，外気に接する面積をできるだけ少なくする必要があった。水田地で土に埋めると湿度に対応しにくいため，砕石に埋め，冬場は冷気から守りながら積雪後はかまくらのような空気層を砕石の隙間で形成し，夏場は砕石の隙間で地熱の効果で緩やかに涼しい通気ができるように考えた。さらに全体の屋根面積を少なくするため母屋とゲストハウスを一棟とし，各室機能は時間的利用率と，通風，日照，熱変化を考慮しながら平面，断面的に整理していった。結果，上層には利用率の低いゲストハウス機能を設け，冬場のサンルームや雨期のドライスペース，夏場の日陰のパーティテラス等，施主の発想とさまざまな利用に対応する。また庭部分と一体となった断面的な通風や空気の層とすることにより，下層の主住空間は年間を通じて安定した居住性を確保することとなる。屋根表面状態は雪の滑性と持続性を考慮してガラスとし，勾配は残雪に対応する南向きとした。断熱材を兼ねた木と空気の層から成る屋根構造は同時に勾配に沿った空気の対流と熱や光を調整する。

　今，建築は気候や風土など過酷な与条件下においても，解体廃棄までを視野に入れた総合エネルギー収支に基づく計画の必要性が求められている。防水剤や断熱材などの再生しにくい化石燃料系素材の使用を最小限にとどめ，自然素材の可能性を最大限に引き出すような建築自体の姿形との相互作用により，環境との知的な関係を模索していきたいと考えている。

（三分一博志）

Kengo Kuma

2005

Lotus House, Japan

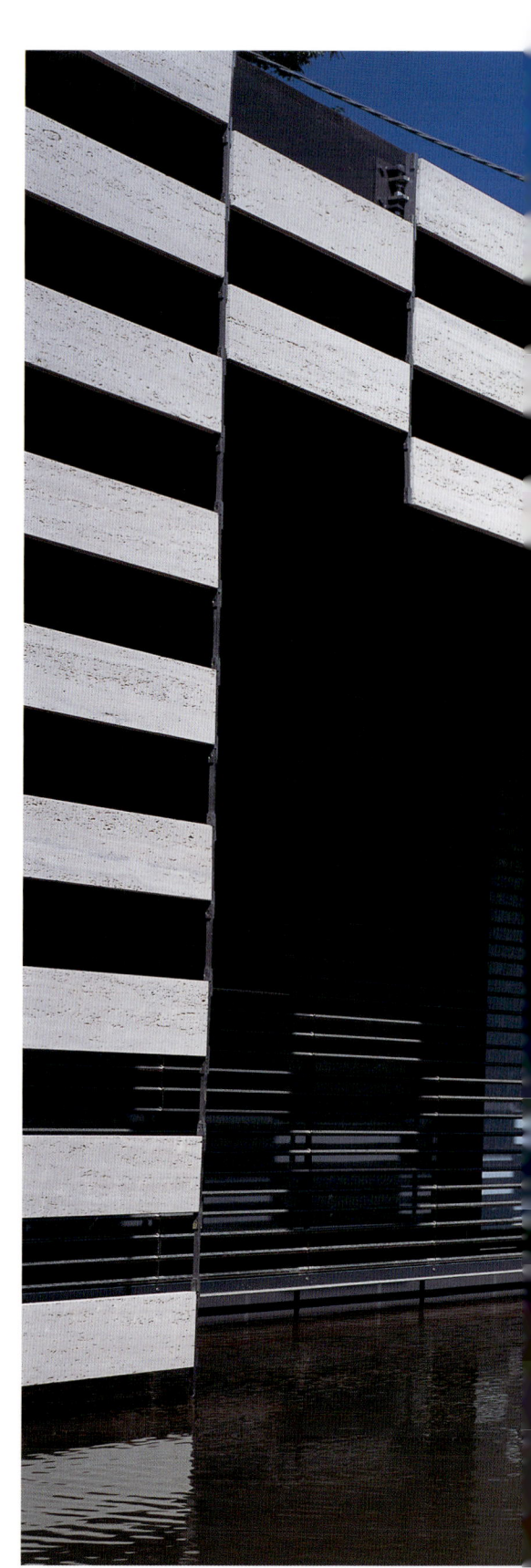

Second floor

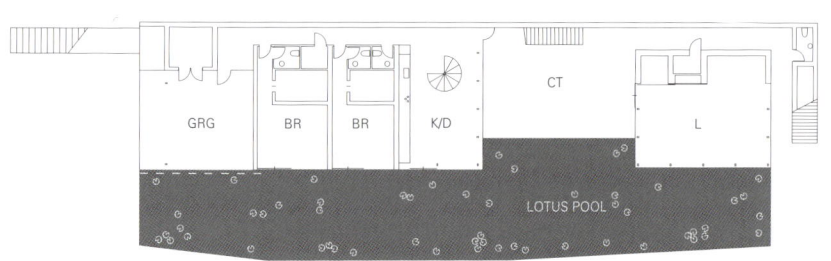

First floor S=1:500

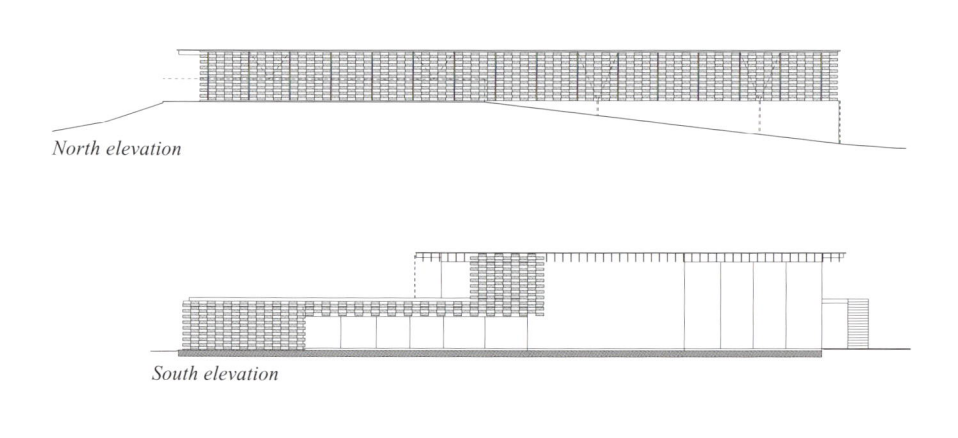

North elevation

South elevation

Section S=1:500

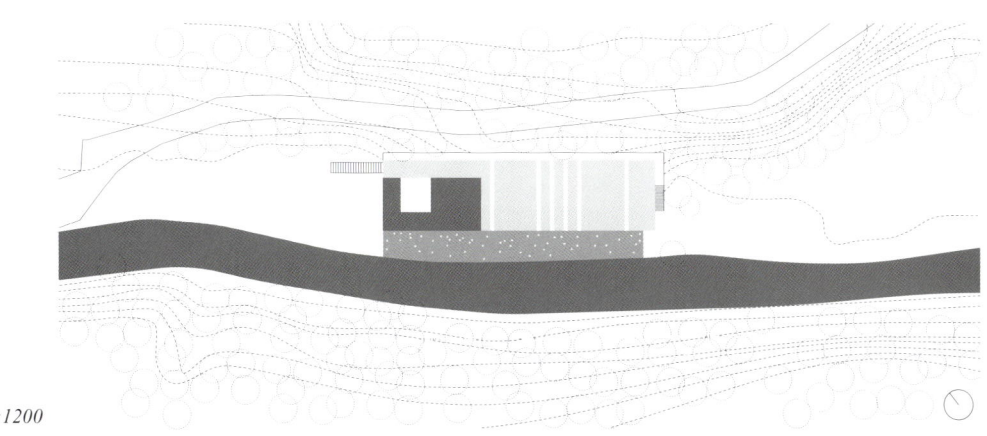

Site plan S=1:1200

View from west

Entrance court on second floor

Court: view toward dining room on west

A house by a quiet river, deep in the mountains. I have thought of filling water between the river and the house and planting lotus so that the dwelling would be conveyed by the lotus to the river and continue into the woods on the other side of the river.

The architecture itself is basically composed of holes. It is divided into two wings, with the hole-shaped terrace in between serving to connect the woods in the back of the house with the woods on the opposite bank.

Wall surfaces are also designed as countless holes. I have wished to create ethereal walls that the wind would sweep through, using the massive material that is the stone. I have come up with the details of the 'hole': thin travertine plates sized 20 x 60 cm and 30 mm thick would be suspended from stainless steel flat bar 6 x 16 mm to constitute a porous checkerboard pattern. The light, porous wall surface that takes advantage of the stone texture is an approach I have taken once in the past with *Stone Museum* (2000). This time, an even lighter detail was made possible by combining stainless steel flat bars.

An expression of lightness of lotus petals using stone.
Kengo Kuma

View toward court from second floor

深い山の中の静かな川岸に，計画された住宅。

川と住宅との間には水をはり，蓮を植え，住まいが蓮池を媒介にして川へ，そして対岸の森へと連続していく状態をつくろうと考えた。

建築自体の構成は孔を基本としている。建築は2棟に分割され，その間に生じた孔の形状をしたテラスが，裏側の森と対岸の森とをつなぐ役割を果たしている。

壁面もまた無数の孔としてデザインされている。石という重量感のある素材を用いながら，風の吹き抜けるような軽やかな壁面をつくりたいと考えた。「孔」のディテールを考案した。具体的には20×60センチ，厚さ30ミリの薄いトラバーチンの板を6×16ミリのフラットバーに吊るし，チェッカーボード状のポーラスなパターンを構成するディテールとした。石の質感をいかしながら，軽くポーラスな壁面をつくる作業は「石の博物館」(2000年)で一度試みた。今回はステンレスフラットバーを併用する事で，さらに軽いディテールが可能となった。

蓮の花びらの軽やかさを，石を用いて表現したいと考えたのである。　　　　　　　　（隈研吾）

Dining room

Court: living room (right) and dining room (left)

View toward living room on east

Looking south: lotus pool

Living room: book shelves

Living room: looking west

139

Gurjit Singh Matharoo   2006

Patel Residence, Ahmedabad, India

View from northeast

Located in the fast growing suburbs of Ahmedabad, a prosperous city in the state of Gujarat in the west of India, the house is designed for a family consisting of a very social couple, their teenage son and frequently visiting parents and relatives.

This house on the one hand looks for inspiration at the inward looking traditional 'Pol' houses of Ahmedabad memories of which are still fresh in minds of the owners of this house, while on the other hand it looks at the post-independence 'open plot dwelling' best exemplified by Le Corbusier's *Shodhan House*, also in Ahmedabad.

Two blocks, of bedrooms in the north and services towards the south, are placed longitudinally on the site creating a central void, which is enclosed by raised compound walls on the shorter sides. The house shuts off the road and the anonymous neighborhood, and draws in nature: breeze, rain, sun and sky deep into the interiors through varying degrees of openness.

The rear walls of the house, cast in concrete and replete with windows and cabinets, pivot out mechanically, claiming the rear margin and turning it into a room with the sky as the roof. This, coupled with sliding doors along the verandah in the middle of the house, make the entire length of the house a unified private living domain. This space is then graded with open, enclosed and covered sequences of hierarchy. The notional center of the house, defined by four exaggerated round columns and natural yellow stone flooring creates an open living space and tries to re-establish the lost connection to nature.

Built in the aftermath of devastating earthquake of 2000, the structure of the dwelling became an overriding concern, making concrete a rational choice, which combines the enclosing surfaces and structural surfaces into one. The use of concrete as material reduces the space usage and makes the resultant structure clear, delicate and extremely light. Moreover as against 11-12% of plinth area used by the usual brick and concrete frame construction the RCC uses only 5% of plinth area resulting in saving of 18-20 square meters of precious land and built up area, which would otherwise have been lost in constructed dead space.

Another direct outcome of thin building elements is in the fine scales achieved, which makes the house intimate and human. The columns, walls, beams thus appear to be woven into an intricate lattice which comes alive with the strong sunlight falling on it. An example of this filigree is a 50 mm thick stair entirely cantilevered on its risers and composed as a square helix.

The other materials used are natural black stone for flooring and Aluminium for doors and windows. The stone flooring is cool, ideal for barefoot use and all the furniture is in natural teakwood to provide the requisite warmth. The material theme is continued in the bedrooms and toilets as well. These are the only two natural materials used in an otherwise industrially produced material ambience. These materials are rendered by the ever-changing natural light brought in through various crevices and openings.

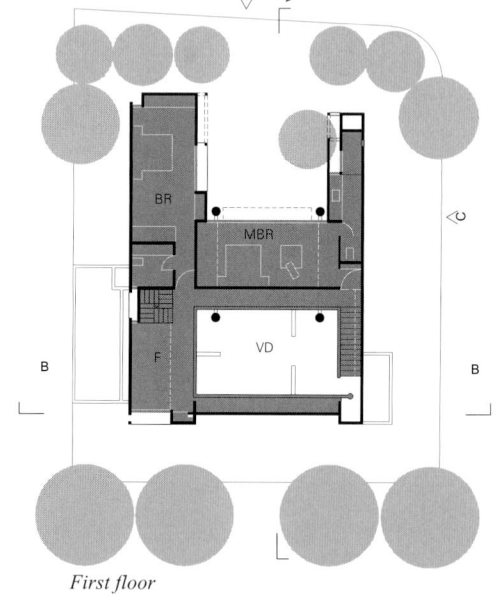

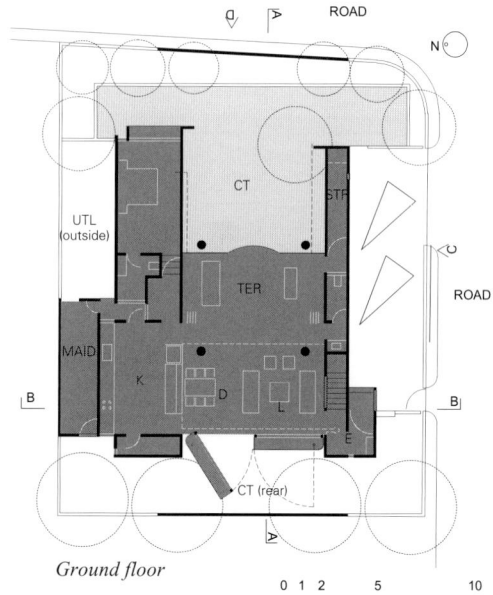

First floor

Ground floor

View of courtyard from east

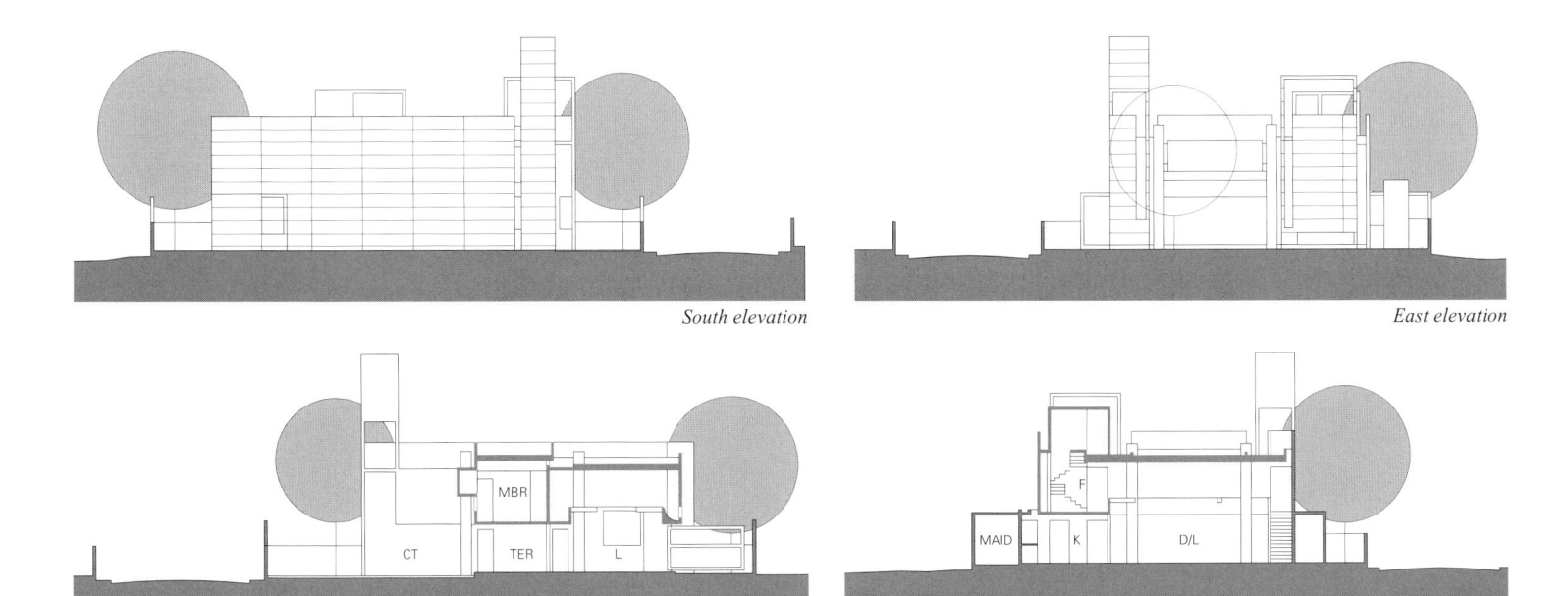

South elevation

East elevation

Section AA

Section BB

141

Courtyard

Dining/living room: fully-opend to courtyards on both side

インド西部グジャラート州の豊かな都市，アーメダバードの急速に発展している郊外に位置して，この住宅は，非常に社交的な生活を送っている夫婦とその10代の息子，頻繁に訪れる両親と親戚で構成される，ある家族のために設計されている。

この住宅は，オーナー夫妻の心の中で今なお鮮やかなアーメダバードの記憶である．内側に向いた伝統的な植民地の「為政者」の住宅にインスピレーションを求めている。同時に，もう一方では，これもまたアーメダバードのル・コルビュジエによる「ショーダン邸」が最良の範例となっている，インド独立後の「オープン・プロット住居」を考察している。

北側に寝室があり，南側に向かうサービスがある二つのブロックは，短手方向が持ち上げられた屋敷塀で閉ざされている中心的なヴォイドを形成しながら，敷地に対して長手方向に位置している。この住宅は，誰とも知れぬ近隣住民と道路を遮断し，そよ風，雨，太陽，空といった自然を，多様な度合いの開口部を通じて，屋内深くに引き込んでいる。

窓と棚を十分に備えている背面のコンクリート打放しの壁は，背部の余地を獲得しつつ，その余地を空が屋根となっている部屋へと変えながら，電動で回転する。さらに，住宅の中ほどでベランダに沿って引き戸を備えることにより，住宅の全長を統一感のあるプライベートなリビング領域にしている。その結果，この空間には，屋根のない空間，四方を取り囲まれた空間，屋根のある空間と，連続する空間のヒエラルキーが，段階的に配列されている。4本の誇張された円柱と，黄色い天然石の床で規定されているこの住宅の概念上の中心は，広々としたリビングスペースを創造し，かつ，失われてしまった自然との関係を復興しようと試みている。

2000年の壊滅的な地震の余波の中で建設されたため，居住施設の構造は最重要の懸案事項となり，外観と構造的な表現を一体化する選択肢として，コンクリートが合理的であるとされた。材料としてコンクリートを使用することは，使用される空間の量を削減し，また，結果として，構造体を非常に軽く優美で自由なものにしている。加えて，通常のレンガを使用した場合の柱脚面積が11〜12パーセントであるのに対して，ローラ転圧コンクリート(RCC)を用いたコンクリート・フレーム構造では，柱脚面積が5パーセントでしかない。他の方法では，建設過程においてデッドスペースと化して浪費されてしまう高価な土地と建築面積が，結果的に，18〜20平米節約されることとなる。

さらに，薄い建築のエレメントを微細なスケールにおいて使用することによって，この住宅は，人間らしく，寛げるものとなった。したがって，円柱，壁，梁は，織り込まれた複雑な格子のように見え，強い太陽光が当たることによって生き生きとする。この精巧なすかし細工のようなデザインの一例は，蹴上板が完全にキャンティレバー構造で，四角い螺旋で構成されている，50ミリ厚の階段である。

使用されているその他の材料は，床の黒い天然石と，ドアと窓のアルミである。石張りの床は涼しく，素足で過ごすには理想的である。また，全ての家具は，天然チーク材で，必要不可欠なぬくもりをもたらしている。この材料上のテーマは，同様に，ベッドルームとトイレにも続いている。これらの天然石とチーク材という2種類の天然の材料以外は，この建築において使用されている材料は，すべて工業製品である。これらの材料は，変化に富んだ間隙と開口部を通って降り注ぐ，絶え間なく変化する自然光によって，多様な表情を見せている。

Furniture-like wall can be fully opened to courtyard

Cantilevered staircase with thin steps to roof terrace

Master bedroom

selgascano

2006

House in the Florida, La Florida, Madrid, Spain

This is an allotment on a gentle slope covered by evergreen oak, elm, ash, acacia, prunes and plane trees, all seeded spontaneously by birds from the surrounding plots. All of these trees and their canopy perimeters were measured and drawn on to plan. Le Corbusier said he wanted the empty *La Tourette* courtyard to be populated naturally with vegetation, by birds and the wind. Le Corbusier left a void in his architecture to be populated by nature. We think this project has arisen in opposition to that idea. Nature has left us a gap and here, only here, can we populate it with something that is architecture, because it is rational. We agree with *La Tourette*, however, that neither camouflage nor integration nor what is called 'organic architecture' have ever really been sought. The house adapts by pure opposition. In Italy, some of the motorway bridges are painted sky blue. An innocent, sweet camouflage that only works as expected on a few days and at certain moments, yet we find it most beautiful on the days when you can actually see the trick. The ultimate purpose is (it would be an exaggeration to say 'always') whatever is admired.

This allotment is already choked with something that should be preserved, and the only choice left to us is to fill in the remaining interfaces, only the areas that are possible, remnants, between the trees, which we have no intention of touching at all. Respect, but to a manic extent. The house is set beneath two platforms that strive to arise our gaze above the natural setting towards the eastern sky. The views of the house look at the base of the natural environment. The project consists of these two platforms. The house is an addition underneath them. These two platforms are comfortable, with soft pavements, for living inside most of the time. Each one has a different colour an a different level to facilitate access. Each one corresponds to an interior time of the house, and each one is nothing without the other. The only thing we can say about the interior space is that it goes unnoticed. It arises as a remainder from the reaction of the only space being worked here. Outdoor space. This is a project that is only related to the exterior. Two horizontal platforms cultivate it in generic proximity but a metaphoric distance. Distance in which we speak of inanimate nature, reproduced or abstract, also a reflection of an earth and a sky, which becomes involved with both but belongs to neither. The resemblances in its zoomorphic or anthropomorphic silhouette that seem to belong of similarities, the coincidences of the situation of the spherical lightwells/lookouts with eyes and the other skylights with backbones, are just coincidences.

周囲の敷地から小鳥たちが偶然に運んできた種から成長した，常緑のカシ，ニレ，トネリコ，アカシア，スモモ，スズカケの木々が繁る緩やかな斜面に広がる小区画の敷地である。これらの木々のすべてとその枝葉がつくりだす天蓋の周囲は計測され平面図の上に描かれた。ル・コルビュジエは，小鳥や風によって運ばれた植物が自然にその場所を覆って行くように「ラ・トゥーレット」の中庭を空っぽにしておきたいと述べている。ル・コルビュジエは彼の建築の中に，自然が入り込めるようにヴォイドを残した。このプロジェクトはそのアイディアと逆方向に考えることから生まれている。自然は私たちに空白を残し，ここが，この空白のみが建築のようなもので占拠することができるのではないだろうか。何故ならそれが理にかなっているからである。けれども，私たちは，自然の偽装でも，統合でも，また，"有機的建築"と呼ばれるものが実際に探求してきたものでもない点で「ラ・トゥーレット」と同じである。この家は純粋な対峙によって場所に順応する。イタリアでは，高速道路にかかる橋のいくつかはスカイブルーに塗られている。ある数日間，ある瞬間だけ効果を発揮する，無邪気で魅力的な偽装ではあるが，そのトリックを実際に見ることができるその日，橋が最も美しいことを発見する。一義的な目的がどうあろうと，("常に"と言うのは言い過ぎかもしれないが）それは素晴らしい眺めと賞賛される。

この敷地には，既に保存すべきものがぎっしり詰まっており，私たちに残されている選択は残存するインターフェイス，唯一可能であるエリア，少しだけ残された，全く手を触れるつもりのない木立の間の領域を満たすことである。周囲への過剰なまでの配慮。家は，私たちの視線を自然風景を越えて東の空に向けさせる二つのプラットフォームの下に配置される。家からの視線は自然環境の足下に向かう。二つのプラットフォームでこの家は構成されている。家はプラットフォームの真下への付加である。二つのプラットフォームは，滑らかな舗床と共に，ほとんどの時間を屋内で快適に過ごさせてくれる。それぞれが異なった色彩をまとい，アクセスを簡単にするために高さも異なる。それぞれが，家の内部で過ごす時間に対応し，それぞれが他方なしでは意味をもたない。内部空間について言える唯一のことは，目立たずに存在することである。内部空間は，ここで少しずつ変転している唯一のスペース — 戸外空間 — の反作用からの残余として生まれる。これは外部にのみ関係づけられたプロジェクトである。二つの水平に広がるプラットフォームは外部を，全面的に近接させながら，しかしメタフォリカルな距離をとってつくりあげる。距離とは，再現されたあるいは抽象的な，静的な自然を指し，そしてまた地と空の反影であり，両者に関わりながら，しかしどちらにも所属しないものとなる。プラットフォームの輪郭の，動物あるいは人の形との類似，球状の光井／望楼に感じられる両眼との符号，細長いスカイライトの背骨との符号は，単なる偶然の一致に過ぎない。

View from street

Entrance: 1.0 meter lowered from ground level

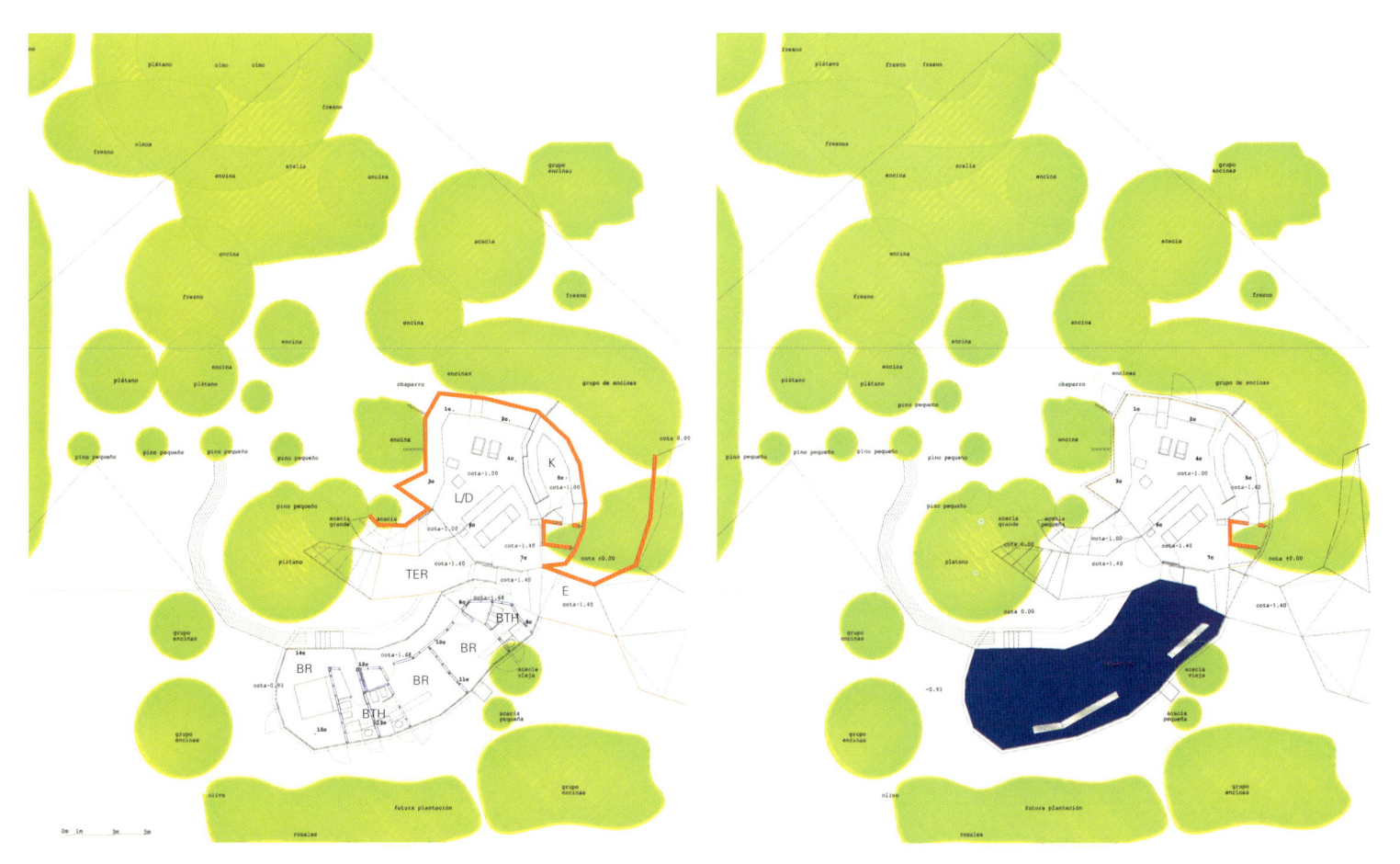

Level -0.90 *Level +1.00*

145

View toward living/dining room wing from roof of bedroom wing

Terrace: view toward entrance

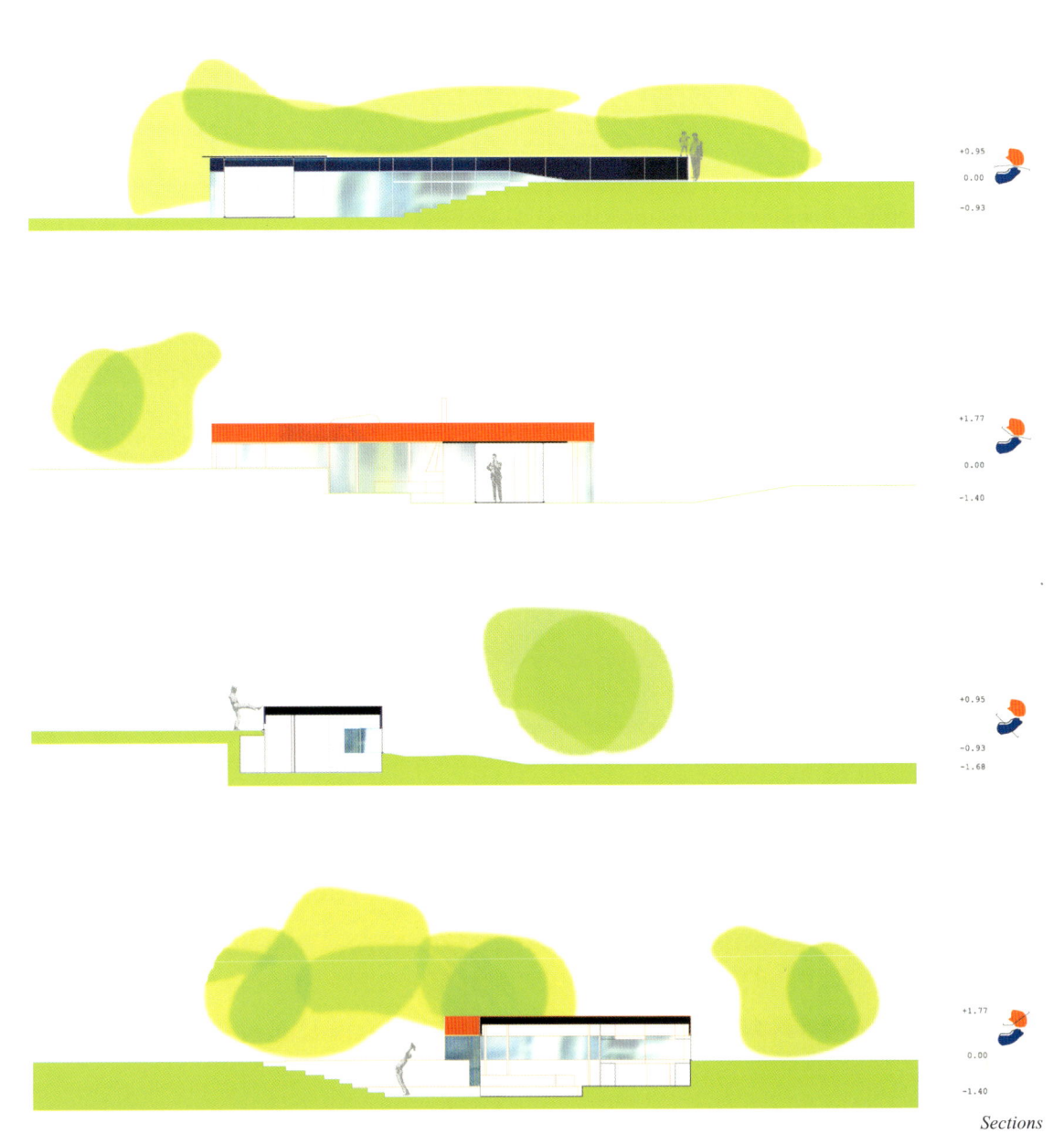

Sections

View toward terrace from dining room

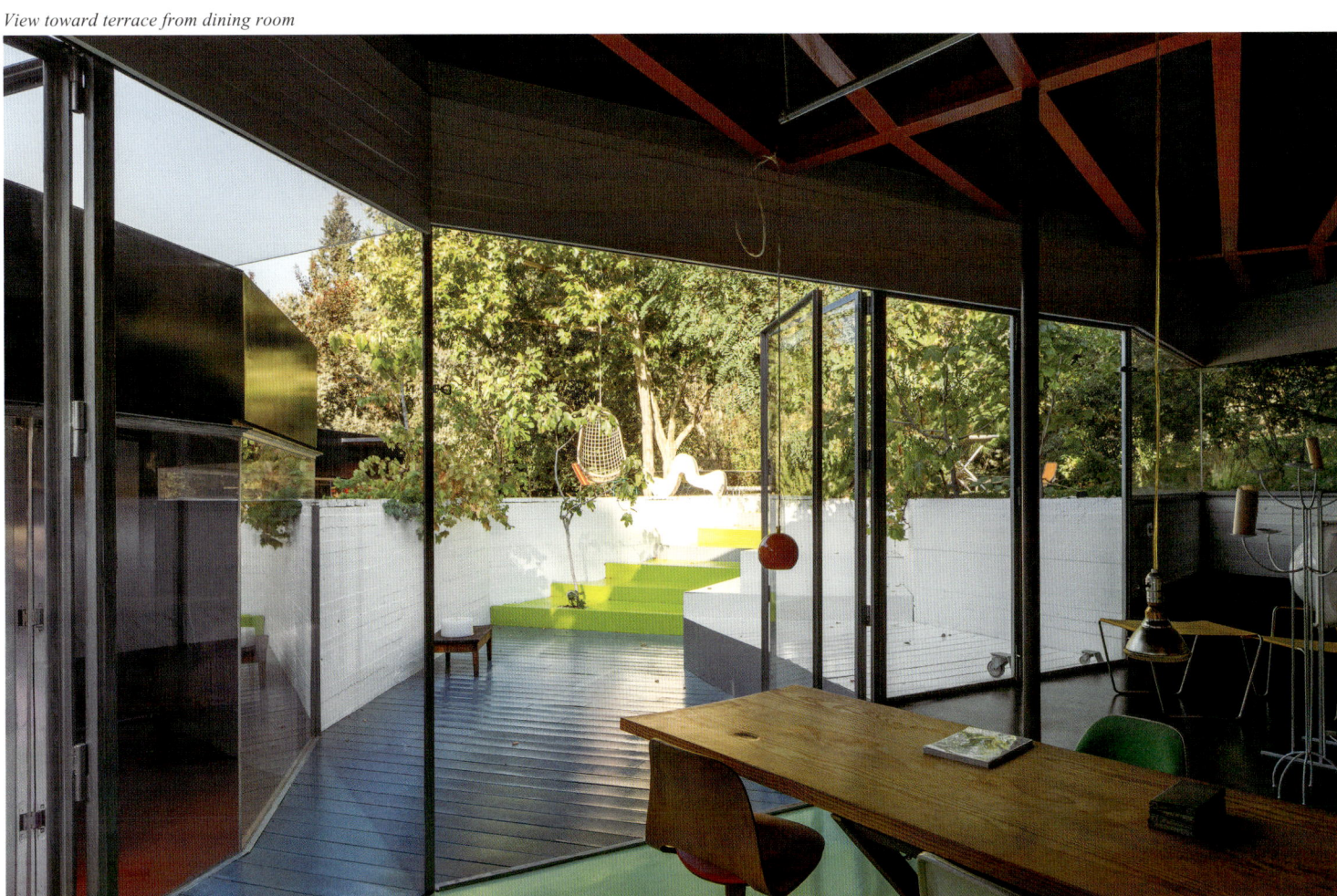

View of living/dining room from garden

Dining room

148

Living room

Bedroom: folding wooden panels on walls as sun shade

Kitchen

Will Bruder

2006

Feigin Residence, Reno, Nevada, U.S.A.

Overall view from southeast

Site plan

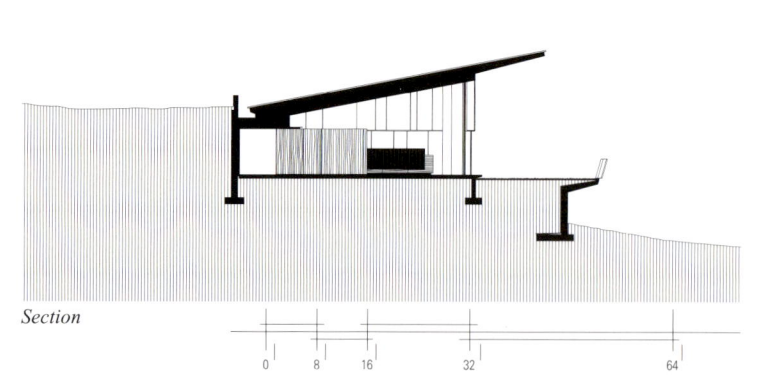

Section

Northwest view: entry court on left

Bamboo garden on right

151

Flowing along the topographic contours of the arid rock strewn landscape above Reno, Nevada, *the Feigin Residence* is an essay of fluid form and movement, celebrating the nuances of perception stretched and measured along a single contour of its hillside site. Along the soft line of the house, plan and sectional geometry mediate functional needs with episodic courtyards and gardens inspired by ideas and landscapes, both imported and local.

Approached from below along an S-shaped English Drive, the house appears once in the distant landscape and then disappears again. At the top of the drive, a canyon cleaves the landscape between the weathered steel plate retaining wall of the site and the silky anodized aluminum plate 'squiggle' of the house. Bearing semblance to entering Richard Serra's "Snake" sculpture, both horizon and vista recede from your awareness, bringing the intensely dramatic and dynamic sky into focus.

The house is entered through a glowing constriction between the canyon walls, opening to a 220 degree glazed view of the east mountain horizon beyond. With Reno and the airport's landing pattern running parallel below, a kinetic juxtaposition of the natural and manmade is revealed through the scrim-like layers of the house: shear fabric curtains, frit and vision glass, and perforated steel rails. Within this living pavilion, living, dining, and library functions are unified under the gentle curve of the warped shed roof. The single volume is anchored by the open kitchen, a 'slippery egg' form placed askew to the radial geometry which orders the plan.

A single-loaded passage sweeping south along the house's up-slope boundary links the master bedroom to the living pavilion, separated by the bamboo garden which affords it privacy. The personal and modest scale of the bedroom is expanded by a sunken water court carved into the landscape and lined in weathered steel plate. Floating over the steel edge of the water court is the view to the mountains of the Carson Range surrounding Lake Tahoe.

Exterior spaces are conceived as an extension of the interior. Courtyard gardens, like pearls on a string, meter the serpentine passage with light and air. The dramatic, down-slope, floating lawn tray projects from the living pavilion as it reaches for the horizon. The secret garden, accessed by a hidden stair provides a 360 degree view of the surrounding landscape.

The house's materiality grounds it in the landscape as a mysterious dark shadow by day and as a luminous glowing aperture into the earth at night. Weathered steel plate walls define the entire form and weathered dark patina copper standing seam roof skins the sculptural roof of the living pavilion. Anodized aluminum plate cladding reveals the refinement to the interior. Polished white plaster walls line the courtyard garden alcoves within the shell of the weathered steel.

Inside polished concrete floors, white Venetian plastered and black plate steel walls complement planes of clear, frit, and translucent glass. The simple elegance of the house is reinforced by minimally detailed colored resin doors and cabinets of silvery aniline died primavera veneer and stainless steel. Architect selected furnishings, fabrics, and art complete a seamless experience.

As a quiet canvas for the carefully choreographed dance of movement and light, the sculptural form gives rhythm to the owner's life—a statement of quality and quiet away from the chaos of the world below.

Gallery

Entrance hall: door on left

ネバダ州リノを見晴らす丘の上，岩が一面に散乱する荒涼とした風景の中，地形に沿って広がる「フェイジン邸」は，流体の形と動きについてのエッセイであり，斜面を構成する敷地の等高線の1本に沿って伸びる，綿密に計画された，知覚の微妙な差異の表現である。建物の柔らかな線に沿った平面と断面の構成は，外国や地元からアイディアや景観のヒントを得た挿話的なコートヤードや庭によって機能的ニーズを調停する。

S形の英国式ドライヴに沿って下から近づくと，家は遠くに一度姿を現し，再び視界から消える。ドライヴを上がり詰めたところで，キャニオンが，耐候性鋼板でつくられた敷地の擁壁と，建物を包む，「短く不規則に曲がる」滑らかな酸化皮膜アルミ板の間にランドスケープを切り開いて進む。リチャード・セラの「蛇」の彫刻に入って行くかのように，地平線や眺めが意識から後退し，強烈でダイナミックな空に焦点が向かう。

東の地平線に連なる山並みが220度に渡ってガラス越しに望める，峡谷の狭間につくられた壁面に沿ってリビング・パヴィリオンに入る。リノ市街と空港の平行して走る滑走路を眼下に，自然と人工物の動的な並置が，軽い半透明の布地のカーテン，フリット・ガラス，ビジョン・ガラス，有孔鋼板の手摺など，紗幕のような効果を持つレイヤーを通して現れる。ひずんだ片流れ屋根の緩やかなカーブの下に居間・食堂・書斎が続く。平面を規定している放射状の幾何学構成に対し，斜めに置かれた"つるつるしたタマゴ型"のオープン・キッチンがこの一室空間を繋ぎ留める。

上り勾配になった家の境界に沿って南に広がる1本の通路が，プライバシーを確保する竹の庭で隔てられた主寝室をリビング・パヴィリオンに結ぶ。寝室のパーソナルで簡素なスケールは風景のなかに刻み込まれ，耐候性鋼板で内側を被覆した水のサンクンコートが広がりを与える。鋼板の縁から水が溢れ落ちるコートは，タホー湖を囲むカーソン山脈の山々の見立てである。

戸外空間は内部の延長であり，コートヤード・ガーデンが，紐に通された真珠のように，蛇行する通路に光と空気を供給する。ドラマチックな下り斜面に向かって，地平線に手を伸ばすように芝生貼りのトレーがリビング・パヴィリオンから浮かぶように突き出す。隠れた階段を上がって出るシークレットガーデンからは周囲の風景を360度見晴らせる。

この家は，風景のなかで，日中は神秘的な暗い影，夜は大地に嵌め込まれた輝く開口のように見える。耐候性鋼板の外壁が全体の輪郭を描き，濃い緑青を帯びた銅の立てはぜ継ぎが，リビング・パヴィリオンの彫刻的な屋根を覆う。酸化皮膜アルミ板の被覆は屋内の洗練された雰囲気を伝え，艶のある白いプラスター仕上げの壁は，耐候性鋼板のシェルの中にあるコートヤードガーデンの輪郭を描く。

屋内は，磨き仕上げのコンクリート床，白いベネチア風プラスターを塗装した壁と黒い鋼板の壁が，透明ガラス，フリット・ガラス，半透明ガラスの面を引き立てる。この家の簡素な優美さは，最小限のディテールを施し，カラーレジンで仕上げた扉，銀色に輝くアニリン染めのホワイト・マホガニーの薄板やステンレス鋼のキャビネットでさらに強調される。家具，布地，アートも設計者が選び，混然一体とした空間体験を仕上げている。

細心に演出された動きと光の舞踊のための静謐なキャンバスとして，彫刻的な形態は住む人の生活にリズムを与える。下界の混沌から遠く離れた，質の高さと静けさの表現が，この家の主題となっている。

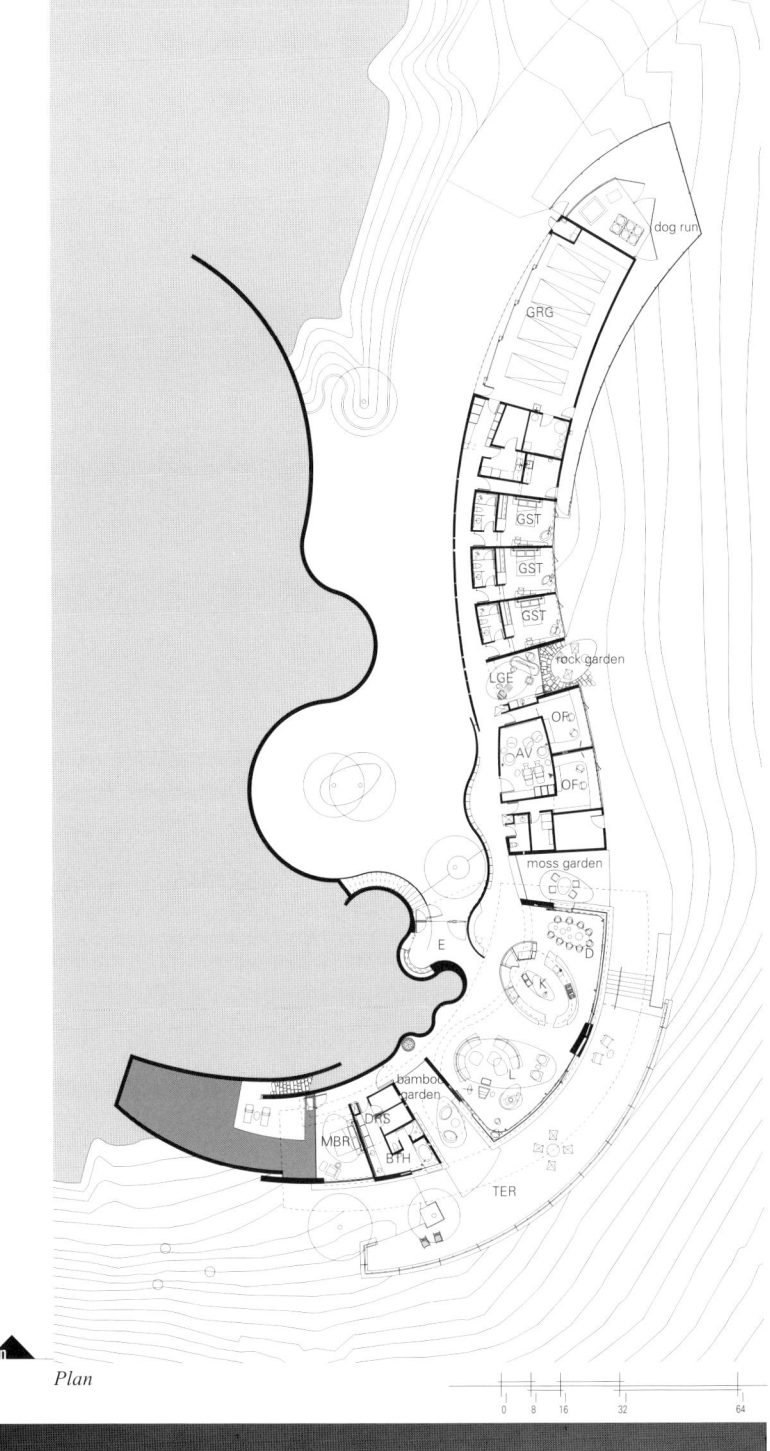

Plan

Kitchen

Living room: view toward kitchen/dining room

Living room

Fireplace

Steel curved wall: view toward master bedroom

Galley with slits: guest sitting on right

Downward view of master bedroom

Master bedroom

155

Ryue Nishizawa

2006

House A, Tokyo, Japan

View from northwest on street: guest room box

View from south

A house standing in a residential area lined with old wooden houses. The client's requests included a space large enough to hold parties and a guest room. The oblong site stretches south to north, bounded by wooden houses in close proximity on east and west. My impression was that the environment was somewhat dark. Counting on the sunshine from the south, I strung the rooms like beads in zigzag. Starting from the street on north—the guest room, entrance foyer with shoe storage room, sun parlor/laundry room, dining kitchen, and dressing room—various rooms are aligned in zigzag along the site's topography. In this manner, gaps are created here and there, bringing sunlight into the building. The result is a well-lit space filled with sunshine.

The structural planning, in order to achieve a transparent, open structure, features the use of steel H-beams 100 x 100 mm. I expected to create a bright environment, something that looks like a garden rather than an interior, a garden dotted with furniture and plants, or a lawn party under a simple roof. The sun parlor/laundry room in the middle may be used for parties, but serves to dry laundry or watering plants on daily basis. It is a space that most resembles a garden in the entire building in terms of both usage and spatial impression. However, every other place in the house was intended to be also bright and transparent, as if there were no difference between indoors and outdoors, as if the whole building were a garden. I wish that this house became a peaceful, comfortable living space always filled with springlike transparent light and fresh breeze sweeping through the rooms.
Ryue Nishizawa

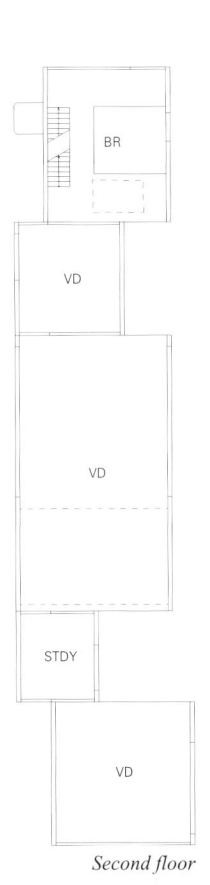

Second floor

View toward sunroom through foyer: entrance on left, guest room on right

Elevation

First floor S=1:200

Section S=1:200

157

Sunroom: view toward bath living, dining/kitchen and bedroom

Sunroom: view toward guest room

Guest room   *View toward dining/kitchen from bath living*   *Bath living*

Downward view: each room aligned in zigzag along site's topography

〈庭のような家〉
古い木造住宅が建ち並ぶ住宅地に建つ住宅である。パーティが開けるような大きな場所をどこかに設けたいということ，ゲストルームを併設すること，などが望まれた。敷地は，南北方向に長い形をしており，東西の隣地側はすぐそこまで木造家屋が迫って建つようなところであった。環境としては若干暗めと感じた。そこで，ぼくは南からの日照を期待して，各部屋をずらしながら数珠繋ぎ状につなげていった。北道路側から順に，ゲストハウス，玄関ホワイエ＋靴部屋，サンルーム＋洗濯室，ダイニングキッチン，ドレッシングルーム，と言った諸室が，左右にずれながら，敷地形状に沿って並んでゆく。これによっていろんなところに隙間が生まれ，あちこちから建物内に光が入り込み，建物の隅々まで光に満ちた，たいへん明るい空間となった。

構造計画としては，透明で開放的な構造体を目指して，全体を100×100ミリのＨ形鋼材で組むことを考えた。室内というよりは，なにか庭のような，庭に家具や植物がぱらぱらと並んでいるような，もしくは原っぱのパーティに簡単な覆いを架けただけというような，明るい状態がつくり出せるのではないかと考えた。真ん中のサンルーム兼洗濯室は，パーティに使ったり，通常は洗濯物を干したり乾かしたり，もしくは植物に水をやったりと，使い方としても空間の印象としても，この建物の中でもっとも庭に近い空間として考えられているが，ここに限らずどの場所も，気持ちとしては中も外もないような，全体が庭であるような，明るく透明な空間を目指した。春のように透明な光と空気がつねにそこにあり，爽やかな風が室内を通りすぎていくような，穏やかで快適な住空間になればと思っている。

（西沢立衛）

View toward north from bedroom

View toward bath living from dining/kitchen: bedroom above

Randy Brown

Laboratory, Omaha, Nebraska, U.S.A.

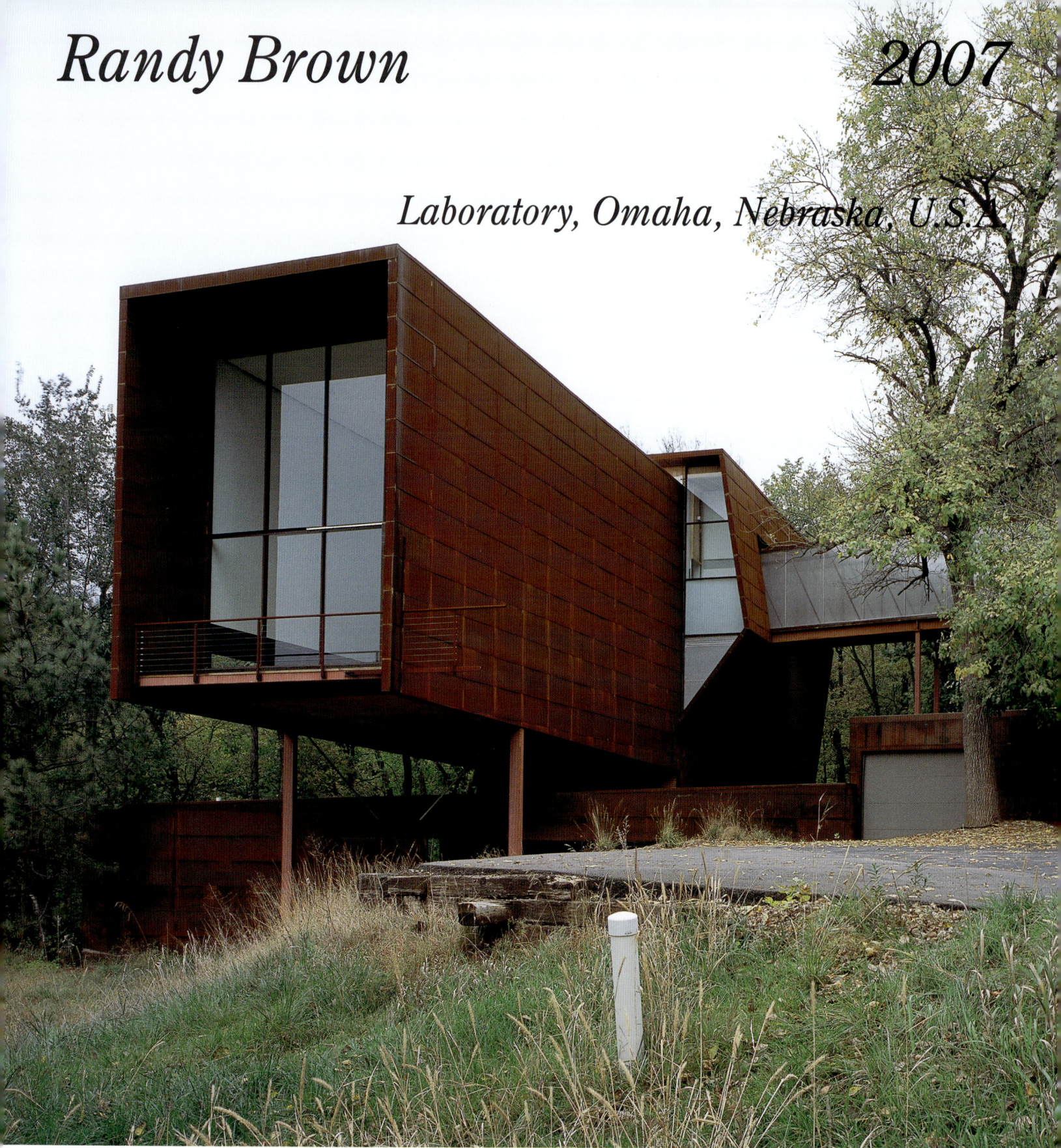

2007

View from south. New wing (left) and existing wing (right)

The architect purchased this property and decided to move into the existing house while phasing construction projects. The intention is for the project to be a laboratory for architectural experiments.

The site is in the country in a wooded area with rolling hills. The views are to the west and south. The existing house is located on the highest ground of the site on the edge of where the trees meet the native prairie grass meadow.

Ideas that informed the project:
1) The project has been built by the architect with his own hands. Each of the last 4 summers, college architecture students have been hired to assist with the design and construction. Each piece of the project was designed and then constructed, which allowed the design to continue to evolve as it was being constructed. Everything was custom designed and built on site: Panelization of walls, fabrication of custom hurricane clips, hybrid wood and steel wall structures, 5 staircase designs, 3 custom window frames, doors, floors, ceilings, and custom millwork.

2) The project is intended to continue for the rest of the architect's life. It is a "work in progress" with many areas unfinished today, opportunities for tomorrow.

3) Green building techniques were integrated into the architecture: passive solar, natural ventilation insulated concrete forms, R-45 roof insulation, renewable materials, radiant flooring, heat pumps, and a green roof system.

4) The design explores ways to intertwine what is man-made with what is natural. The intention is to create a house that is so interconnected

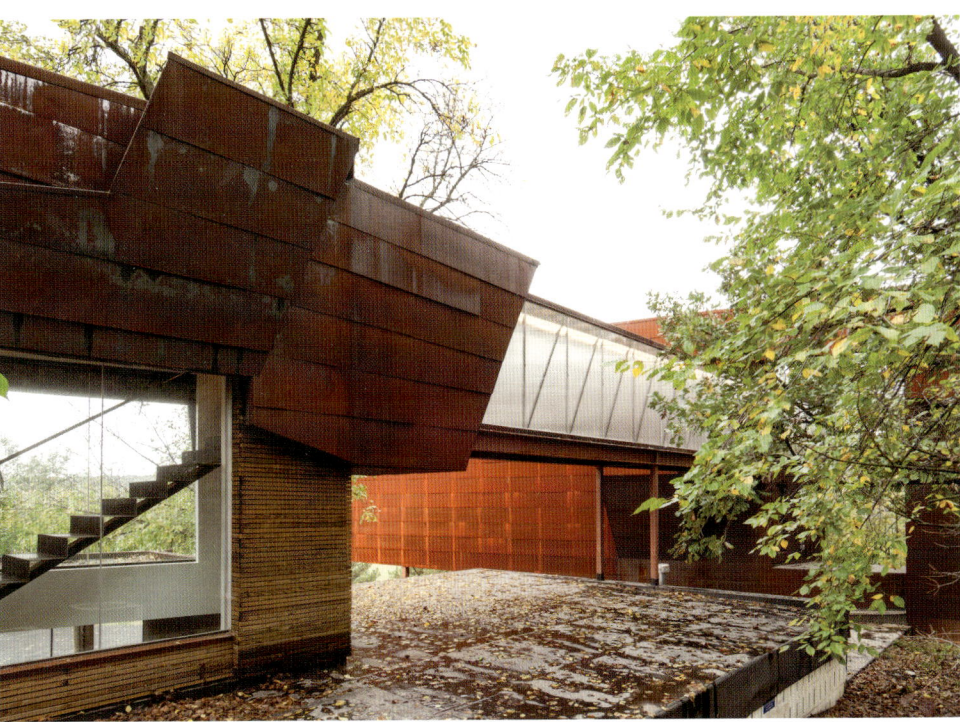

View toward bridge connecting existing wing (left) and new wing (right)

Staircase to bridge from existing wing

Bridge

with the land that it is simultaneously natural and man-made. Much like abandoned tractors and farm machinery rusting away in the rural landscape.
5) The intent was to create open dynamic spaces that are defined and still feel connected to the larger whole. This was done by canting walls, pulling floors away from walls, creating mezzanine spaces, large window walls and stairs that seem to fly.

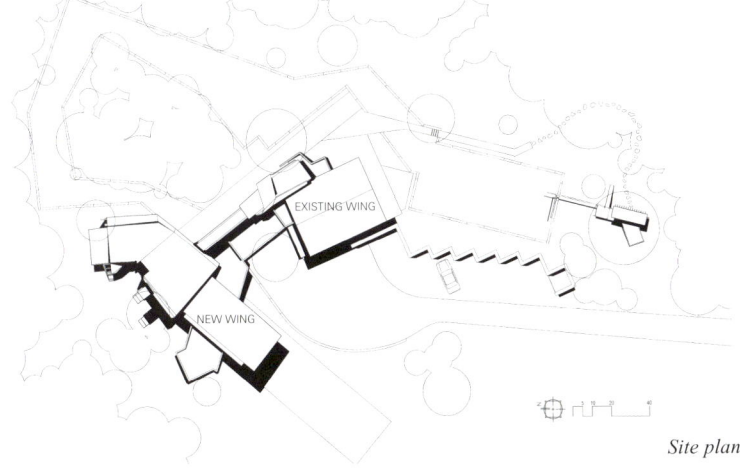

Site plan

Evening view: living room above

Living room: looking southwest over glazed wall

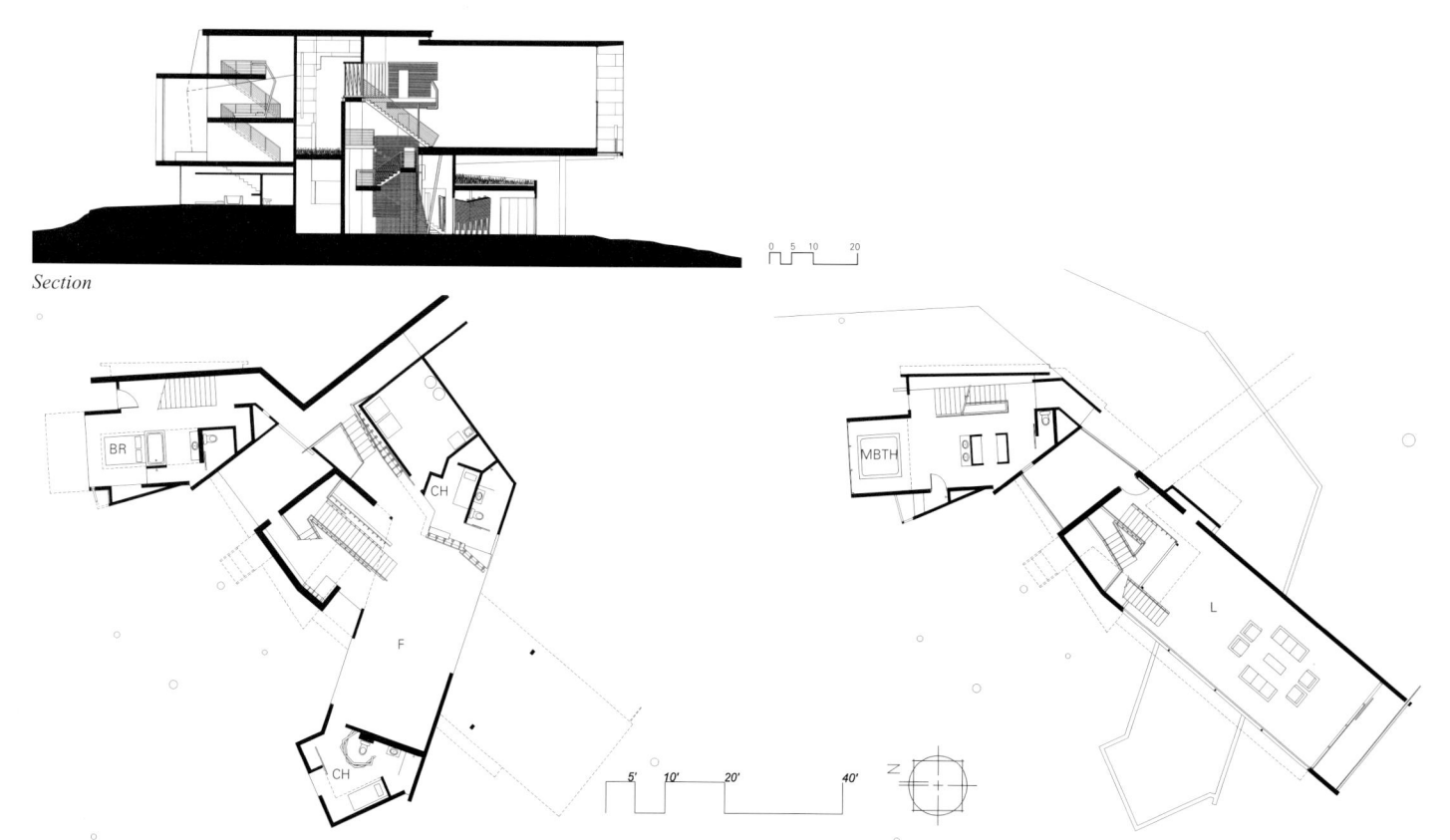

Section

First floor

Second floor

164

建築家はこの地所を購入し，そして段階的な建設プロジェクトの間，既存の住宅に引っ越すことを決意した。プロジェクトの意図するところは，作品自体が建築的な実験のための研究室となることである。

敷地は郊外の丘が連なる雑木林の中にある。視界は，西と南に開けている。既存の住宅は，その敷地の一番高い場所で，木々が自然のプレイリー・グラスの牧草地に接する端部に位置している。

プロジェクトを特徴付けるアイディアは，次の5点である。

1）プロジェクトは，建築家自身の手で遂行されつつある。過去4度の夏には，設計と建設を手伝うために，建築専攻の大学生が雇われていた。プロジェクトのそれぞれの部分は，デザインされては施工されていった。よって，建設されていく間に，デザインが展開し続けていくことが可能となった。現場では，あらゆるものが特注デザインであり，特注製造だった。壁のプレハブ化，特注ハリケーン・クリップの製造，木材とスティールのハイブリッド壁構造，5種類の階段室のデザイン，3種類の特注の窓枠，ドア，床，天井，そして，特注の木造作部である。

2）それは"進行中の作品"で，現在は未完成な部分が多々あり，未来にその可能性を託すものである。

3）環境負荷の低い「グリーン」な工法が建築に組み込まれている。太陽熱利用，断熱コンクリートブロックの自然換気，R-45屋根断熱，再生可能な材料，蓄熱床暖房，冷暖房装置，そして，屋上緑化である。

4）デザインは，人工的造形と自然の造形とを，深く結びつけるための手法を探求する。狙いは，敷地と非常に強く結び付き合っているため，自然でかつ人工的でもある住宅を創造することである。それは，田園風景の中で錆びていく，打ち捨てられたトラクターや農業機械そっくりなものとなろう。

5）設計意図は明確に区分されていて，なおかつ，より大きな全体につながっていると感じられるような，広がりのあるダイナミックな空間を創造することにある。これは，傾斜している壁，床を壁から引き離すこと，中2階スペースをつくること，飛ぶかのように見える大きなウィンドウ・ウォールと階段によって，実現した。

Living room: wood millwork next to staircase

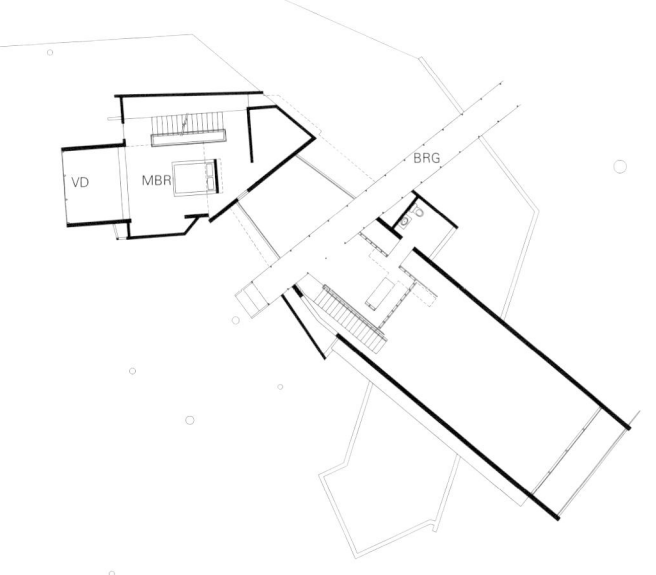

Third floor

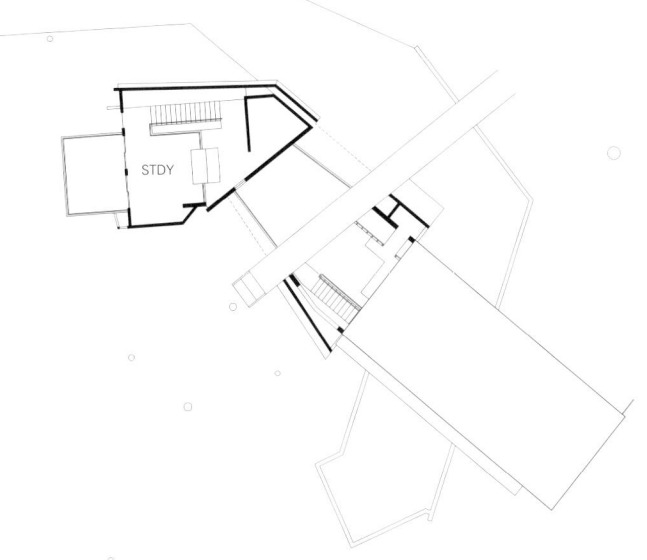

Fourth floor

Family room on first floor: looking west

Looking east at family room: staircase to second floor

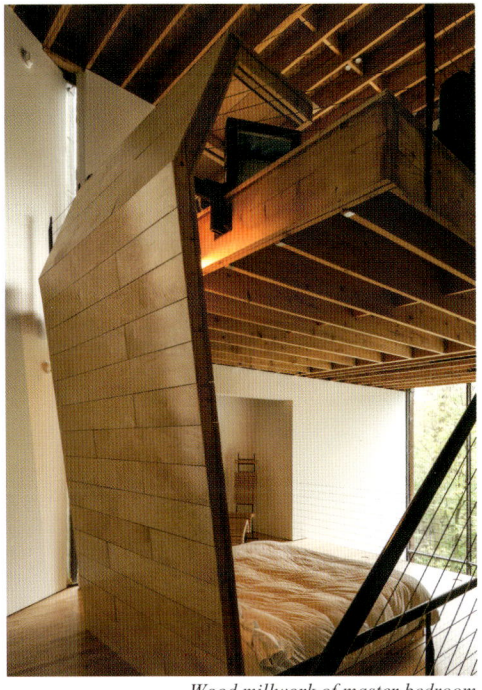

Wood millwork of master bedroom

Bedroom wing

Master bathroom on second floor

Master bedroom on third floor

◁△ *Bedroom on first floor*

Peter Stutchbury 2007

Avalon House, Avalon, New South Wales, Australia

Walkway to entrance

West elevation

Downward view of living/dining room on middle level

169

Upper level

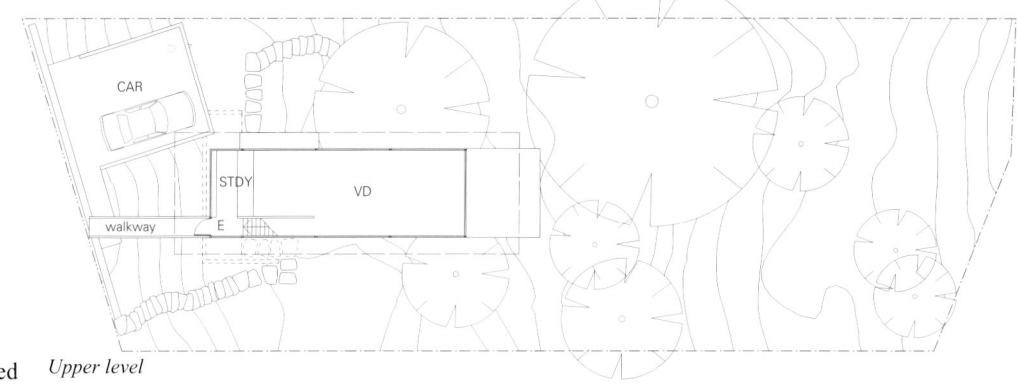

Spending her childhood in an architect designed family house our client and her husband were determined to provide the same for their own young family.

Steep east facing land on the Northern Beaches of Sydney, the site was difficult to access and prone to slip.

We saw the project as an opportunity to produce a low cost building that would satisfy the client's faith in a work of architecture being an educative tool.

Our approach was to initiate a prefabricated building using steel as the primary structure. Extreme care then selected sympathetic components both primary and secondary such that the Meccano set of parts took two days to assemble with a unification of finishes that sat wholly within the discipline of the frame. The elegance of such resolution is evident, what is not obvious is the time it takes to design an integrated façade and structure. North and south were treated with obvious function, industrial (thus economical) fixtures and fittings were employed throughout and finishes were direct and low cost.

A skillion roof connected the building with site and highlight glazing gave the roof a lightness that sits at ease with the surrounding canopy. The entry space is deliberately grand and communicates both the site beyond (context) and the life within. Location of the office at the entry restricts business to the edge of the home. The main space is designed, using standardised components, to flow to open views rather than adjacent neighbours. The scale of this primary space plays a significant role in the architecture. Downstairs, bedrooms and bathrooms are quietened by major shifts in scale and reductions in light. The outcome is a palate of varied experiences using a minimum of architectural tools.

The difficulty of the site and associated costs (including significant carport piling) would suggest a high cost building. As the project budget indicates, the built outcome is extremely economical and has provided a reference for ongoing prefabrication work.

The opportunity to produce low cost architecture is discussed as an ideal but rarely engaged as it requires an appropriate project and a willingness to invent and refine based upon cost. Our initial product was almost double the cost of the house produced. The process of cost cutting was educated and drove us to further research materials, precise floor space, repetition, tradition and systems.

With this in mind, we adjusted the building's built order to accommodate site. It was this adjustment that gave the building unique personalised qualities, and the discipline of prefabricated order that produced a style of architecture.

It is our ambition as an office to produce a wide range of work to embrace a wide range of clients and budgets, this way architecture becomes inclusive.

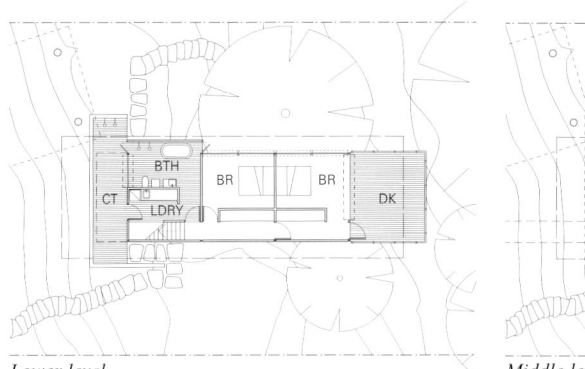

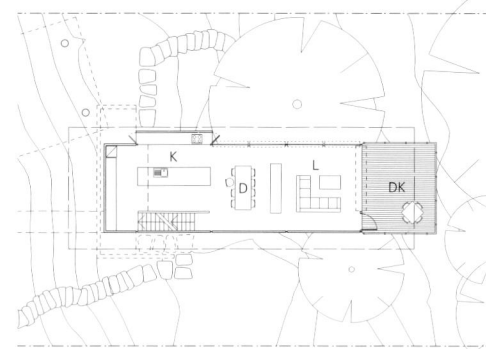

Lower level *Middle level*

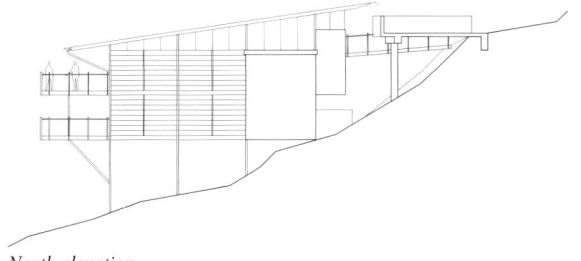

North elevation *East elevation*

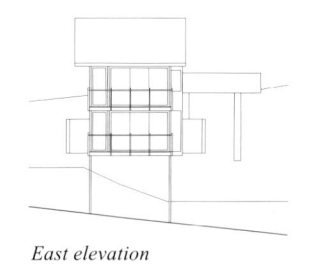

この住宅の施主は子供時代を建築家が設計した住宅で過ごしたので，彼女とその夫は子供たちにも同じ住環境を与えることにした。

シドニーのノーザン・ビーチの，東面した急勾配の土地にある敷地は，アクセスしにくく滑りやすい場所だった。

我々は，このプロジェクトを，建築が教育に役立つ手段にしたいという施主の信念に添った，低コスト建築を実現する機会として捉えた。

その取り組みは，スティールを主構造に用いたプレハブ建築から始まった。次に，細心の注意を払って，主要な部品と補助的な部品の両方に同質の部品を選択した。その構成部品は，架構の秩序内に全体がおさまっている，統一感ある仕上げの，パーツ一式を組み立てるのに２日かかるイギリス製玩具メカノのような部品であった。このような解法の正確さは明白だが，ファサードと構造をデザインとしてまとめるのにかかる時間は不明である。北側と南側は，はっきりとした機能的な処理がなされ，工業的（それゆえに経済的）な建具と什器が完全に取り入れられて，仕上げは直仕上げで低コストなものになった。

差し掛け屋根は，建築を敷地に結びつけ，目を引くはめ込みガラスは，周囲のキャノピーにくつろいで座っているような優美さを屋根に与えた。玄関のスペースは，意図的に広壮なものとし，敷地を越えた外部（コンテクスト）と建築内部での生活との両方に通じている。玄関にあるオフィスの位置は，仕事を，家庭の端部に限定している。主要スペースは，規格化された部品を用いて，近隣よりも広々とした眺望へと流れていくようにデザインされている。この主要なエリアのスケールは，この作品において，重要な役割を果たしている。

階下では，寝室と浴室が，スケールを大きくし，明るさを減らすことによって，落ち着いたものとなっている。その結果，最低限の建築ツールを用いて，変化に富む空間体験を味わうことができる。

敷地の持つ困難さと関連コスト（大きな車庫の杭打ち工事を含む）は，高コストの建築を示唆していた。プロジェクトの予算が限られていたので，結果として非常に経済的なものとなり，現在進行中のプレハブ

Living/dining room

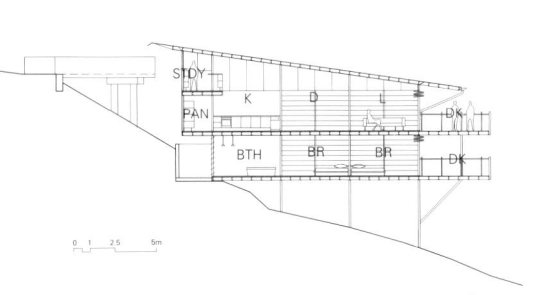

Section

Study on upper level

工事に参考資料を提供する成果を生んだ。

　ロー・コスト建築を実現する機会は，コストに基づいて創意工夫を凝らす意欲と適切なプロジェクトが必要なので，理想に過ぎず滅多に実現できるものではない，と言われている。我々の初期の提案は，最終的に実現した住宅に比べて，ほぼ倍のコストが掛かっていた。コスト削減の過程は，経験に基づいたものであり，我々を，材料，的確な床面積，反復，伝統，システムのさらなる探求へと駆り立てた。

　このように考慮することで，この作品の建築オーダーが敷地に適応するように調節した。この適応こそがまさに，ここにしかない，この施主に特化された質をこの建築に与えたのであり，そして，まさにこのプレハブ・オーダーの秩序こそが，一つの建築様式を実現したのだった。

　様々な施主と予算に対応できる幅広い作品を実現することは，我々の事務所としての念願であり，このようにして，建築が総括的なものとなるのである。

Master bedroom with deck

Terunobu Fujimori + Keiichi Kawakami

2007

Yakisugi House, Nagano, Japan

View from south

Downward view of garden from tea room, "Shou-ken" on second floor

Standing in the middle of a vast suburban residential area east of Nagano Station, this house, owned by the original proprietor of the neighborhood, still retains its lush homestead woodland with a view over an expanse of land and green all for itself.

Yakisugi House is a rehabilitation project of the old house that the present landowner has been refurbishing over the years to the point that further remodeling and expansion will no longer suffice. It was Keiichi Kawakami's idea to preserve and restore the crumbling mud-walled warehouse in the garden. A right choice indeed.

The theme here is a cave. I have had this belief that a cave is the very origin of a house from way back prior to my start in architecture design at age 45. In my career as an architect, I have always been conscious about cave-like qualities: the main living room in *Tampopo House* and the bedroom in *Leek House* both have upper part of walls inclined inward. There are two basic criteria for a cave: round-shaped space and a single type of finishing material for all floor, wall and ceiling. Point is, the same finish all over that surrounds and embraces those who sit inside.

What inspired me to decide to fully develop this cave theme that I have been thinking and partially implementing was a trip to Perigord region in southern France two years ago. Along my visits to cave paintings such as Lascaux, I stopped by a cave where prehistoric men had actually dwelled. Cavemen had separate caves for dwelling and paintings. And that left me with strong impressions.

Up until then my imagery of cave dwelling was a closed space with small entrance like a cellar, from what I have seen in China and Turkey. Whereas in the case of Perigord the cave's entrance is large, open to the outside. As one sits in the back of the cave and glance outside, a landscape of water, greenery and blue sky of Perigordian valleys rolls out beyond the generous curve of an arched earthen frame. An extrovert cave—a covered space that is fully open at one end—was the actual dwelling of prehistoric men and women. The cellar-type structure with piles of bricks that close the entrance is probably a newer invention.

When dealing with opening and closing spaces in a house, people tend to create subtly controlled apertures that make a space 'open while being closed', so to say. But what we really need is to simply open one end to the full and close the others to obtain a sense of loose- bottomed release that is hard to find in architecture today.

Terunobu Fujimori

Main entrance on north

View from northeast

View toward tea room from northwest

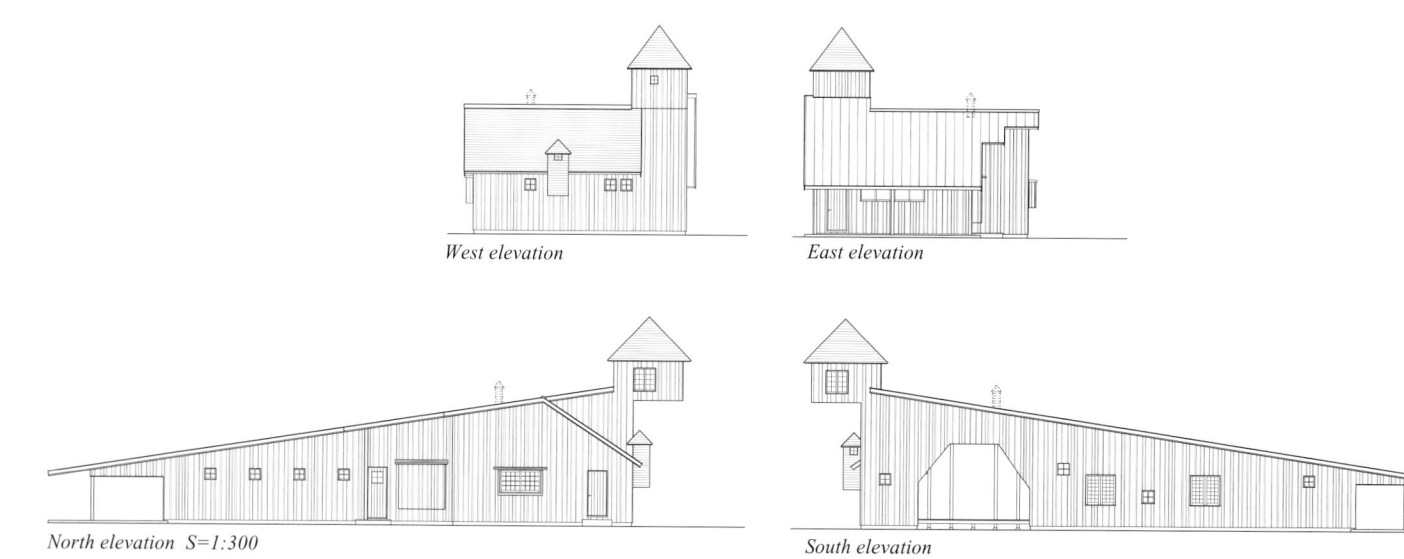

Site plan S=1:1000

West elevation

East elevation

North elevation S=1:300

South elevation

Ladder to tea room

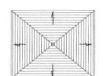

Second floor and roof

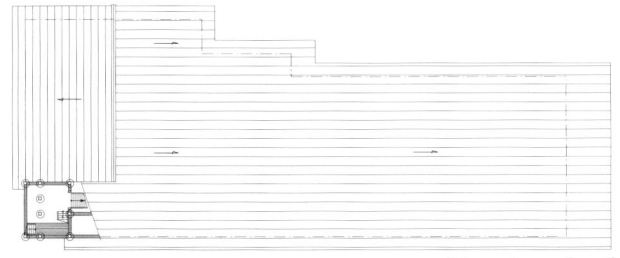

Second floor: tea room, "Shou-ken"

Mezzanine and roof

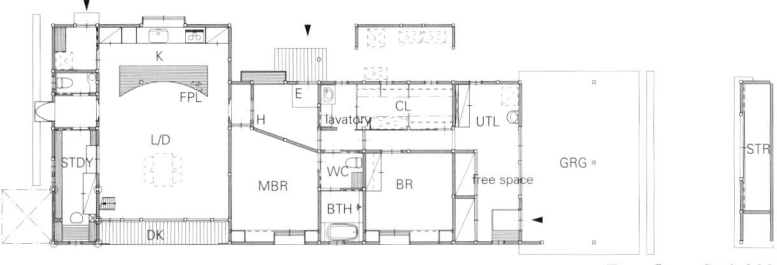

First floor S=1:300

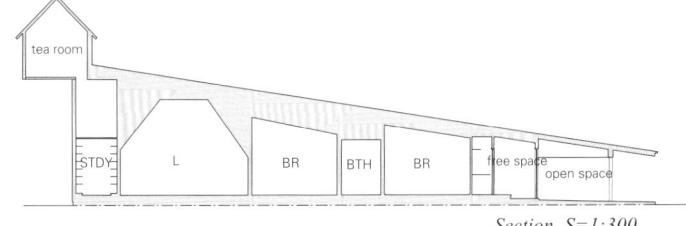

Section S=1:300

175

Living/dining room: view toward garden. Ladder to tea room on right

Living/dining room: view toward kitchen  *Kitchen*

　長野駅の東に広がる郊外住宅地のただ中にあるが、当家はこの地の草分け地主だけのことはあって、今も豊かな屋敷林を保ち、眼前には自前の土と緑が広がる。

　「焼杉ハウス」は、現当主がこれまで増改築してきた古い家を、いよいよ増改築ではすまなくなって、全面建てかえにいたったものだが、庭先の崩れかけた土蔵は共同設計者の川上恵一の提案で、残して手を入れた。残してよかった。

　テーマは洞窟である。洞窟こそ住宅の原点という思いは、45歳で設計を手がけるずっと前からあったが、設計をするようになってからは、「タンポポハウス」の主室や「ニラハウス」の寝室でも、洞窟ふうの納まりを意識し、壁の上部を少し内倒ししている。洞窟の基本条件は、空間が丸みをおびることと、床・壁・天井の仕上げが同一材によることの二つ。ようするに同じ仕上げがグルリと回り、中に座す人を包み込めればいい。

　長い間、思い、部分的に実現してきた洞窟をテーマとして全面展開しようと決めたのは、一昨年、フランス南部のペリゴール地方を訪れた時だった。ラスコーはじめ洞窟絵画を見に行ったのだが、その時、旧石器時代の絵のある洞窟のついでに、人類が実際に住みつづけた洞窟を見学した。旧石器時代人は、住む洞窟と絵を描く洞窟を分けていた。そして、感銘を受けた。

　それまでの私の洞窟住居のイメージは、中国やトルコで見た例から、入口は閉鎖的につくられた穴蔵的空間であったが、ペリゴールの例はちがい、穴の入口はドーンと外に向かって開けているのである。穴の奥に座って外側に目をやると、ほぼアーチ状にのびやかにカーブする土の額縁の向こうに、ペリゴール渓谷の水と緑と青空の光景が広がる。解放性洞窟。一端だけ外に開けきった自閉空間、それが石器時代の人類の本当の住まいだった。入口にレンガなぞ積んで穴蔵化するのは後のことだろう。

　住宅の内外の閉鎖と開放については、"閉じつつ開く"とかいって、微妙に調整された開口部を設けたりするが、もっと単純に、一端をドーンと開き、あとは閉じてしまえばいい。建物には珍しい底の抜けたような解放感が味わえる。

（藤森照信）

Master bedroom

177

Antón García-Abril 2008

Hemeroscopium House, Las Rozas, Madrid, Spain

For the Greek, Hemeroscopium is the place where the sun sets. An allusion to a place that exists only in our mind, in our senses, that is ever-changing and mutable, but is nonetheless real. It is delimited by the references of the horizon, by the physical limits, defined by light, and it happens in time.

Hemeroscopium House traps, a domestic space, and a distant horizon. And it does so playing a game with structures placed in an apparently unstable balance, that enclose the living spaces allowing the vision to escape. With heavy structures and big actions, disposed in a way to provoke gravity to move the space. And this way it defines the place.

The order in which these structures are piled up generates a helix that sets out from a stable support, the mother beam, and develops upwards in a sequence of elements that become lighter as the structure grows, closing on a point that culminates the system of equilibrium. Seven elements in total. The design of their joints respond to their constructive nature, to their forces; and their stresses express the structural condition they have. By the way this structure is set, the house becomes aerial, light, transparent, and the space kept inside flows with life. The apparent simplicity of the structure's joints requires in fact the development of complex calculations, due to the reinforcement, and the prestress and post-tension of the steel rods that sew the web of the beams.

It took us a year to engineer but only seven days to build the structure, thanks to a total prefabrication of the different elements and a perfectly coordinated rhythm of assembly. All of our effort oriented to develop the technique that would allow to create a very specific space. And thus, a new astonishing language is invented, where form disappears giving way to the naked space. *Hemeroscopium House* materializes the peak of its equilibrium with what in Ensamble Studio we ironically call the "G point", a twenty ton granite stone, expression of the force of gravity and a physical counterweight to the whole structure.
Antón García-Abril/Ensamble Studio

View of terrace over pool

Overall view from southeast

South view: lap pool on center

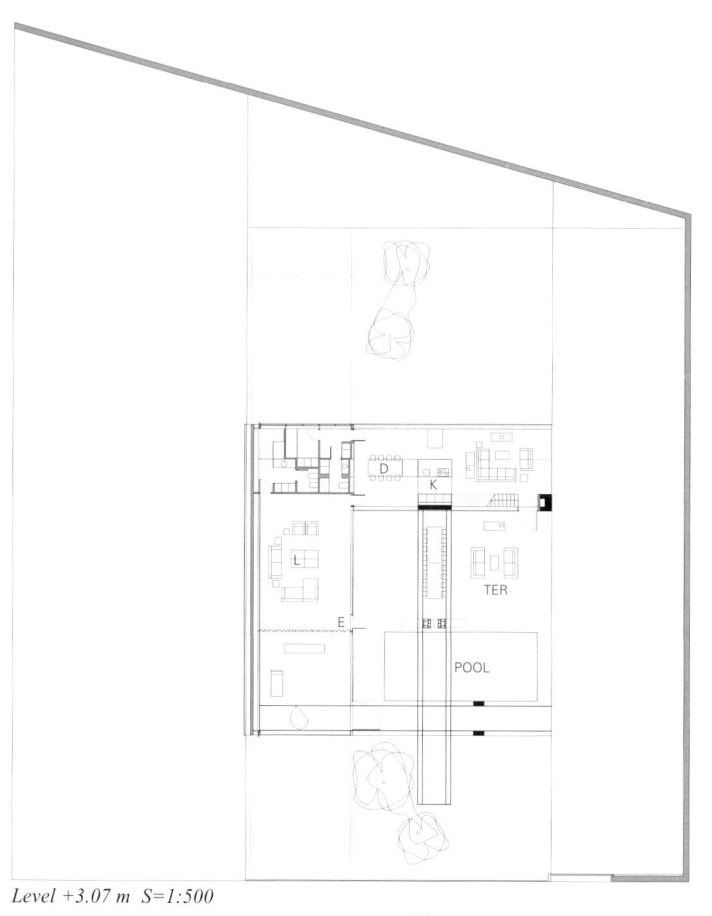

Level +3.07 m S=1:500

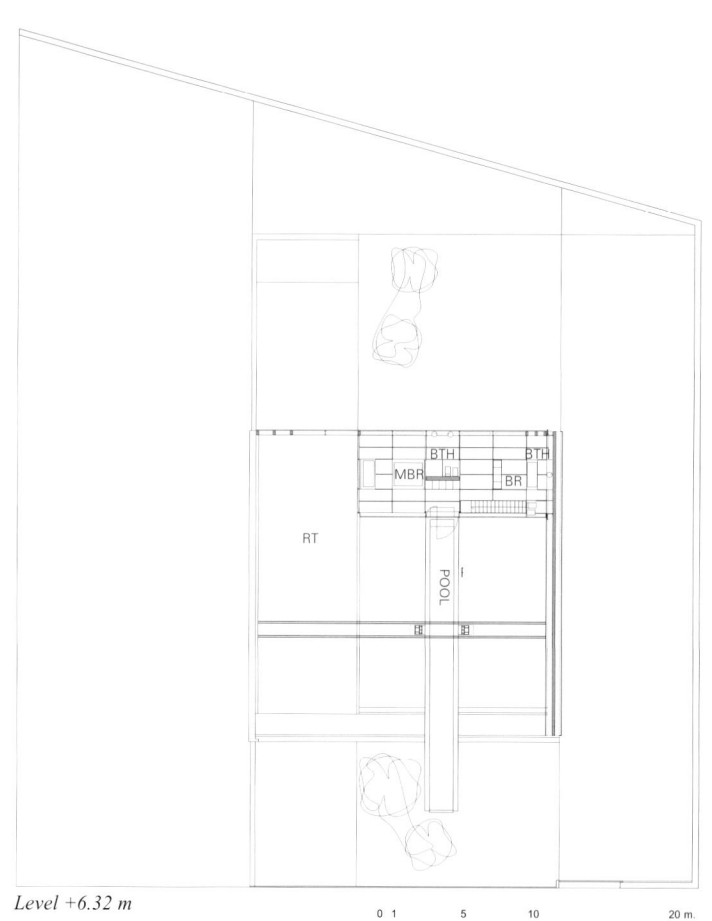

Level +6.32 m

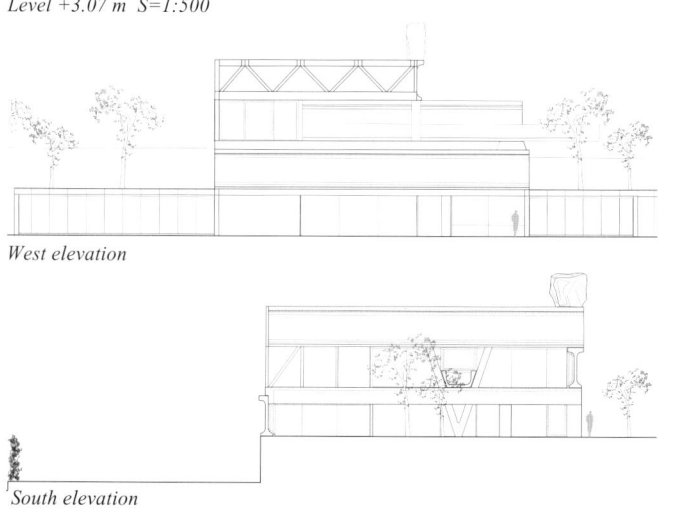

West elevation

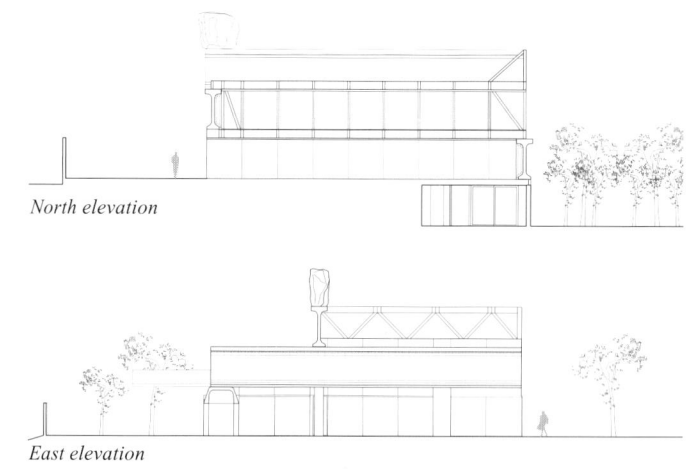

North elevation

South elevation

East elevation

Living room

180

ギリシャ人にとって，ヘメロスコピウムとは太陽の沈む場所を指す。我々の心や感覚の中だけに存在する場への示唆。それは，変わり続けるものであり移ろいやすいものだが，それでも真実のものである。それは，地平線を参照しており，物理的な制約によって境界が定められ，光によって定義されるのだ。そして，それは定期的に起こる。

「ヘメロスコピウム・ハウス」は，身近な空間と遠くにある地平線を同時に捉えている。明らかに不安定なバランスにある構造を，まるでもてあそぶかのようにして，その構造は眺望のための抜けを残しながらこの住まいの場を取り囲んでいる。重量のある構造と大胆な操作によって，重力を活かして空間に動きを与える方法が採られている。このようにして，この場がつくり出されるのである。

これらの構造が組み立てられていく中で，ある螺旋状の流れが生じる。それは，安定した支持材や一連の要素の中でさらに展開し，構成が突き詰められるにつれて一層軽やかになり，均衡の取れたシステムの頂点へと近づくのである。ここでは全部で七つの要素がある。それらの接合部は，構造的な原理，つまりそれぞれの力の状態に基づいて考えられている。応力がそれらの持つ構造上の状態を表現しているわけだ。ところで，このような構成方法によって，住宅は軽快で明るく透明感を帯びたものになり，内包している空間は活き活きとしたものになる。実際には，接合部の明解なシンプルさは，梁のウェブをつなぐスティール・ロッドのプレストレスやポストテンション，あるいは補強材によって，複雑な解析方法の開発を必要としている。

我々は設計するのに1年を費やしたが，異なる要素をまとめてプレハブ部品として製造し，組み立てを完全に調整の行き届いた日程で行うことにより，建設に要したのは7日間だけだった。私達の苦労の全ては，技術力の向上を目的とするもので，それにより極めて個性的な空間が創造できるようになった。こうして，ありのままの空間をつくるために形態を消すところから，驚くべき新言語が考え出された。「ヘメロスコピウム・ハウス」は，我々アンサンブル・スタジオが皮肉を込めて"Gポイント"と呼ぶもの（ここでは，20トンの御影石。すなわち重力という外力を表現したものであり，建築全体を物理的に釣り合わせるおもり）との均衡の頂点を具体化するものである。
（アントン・ガルシア＝アブリル／アンサンブル・スタジオ）

Lap pool on upper floor

Kitchen and dining room

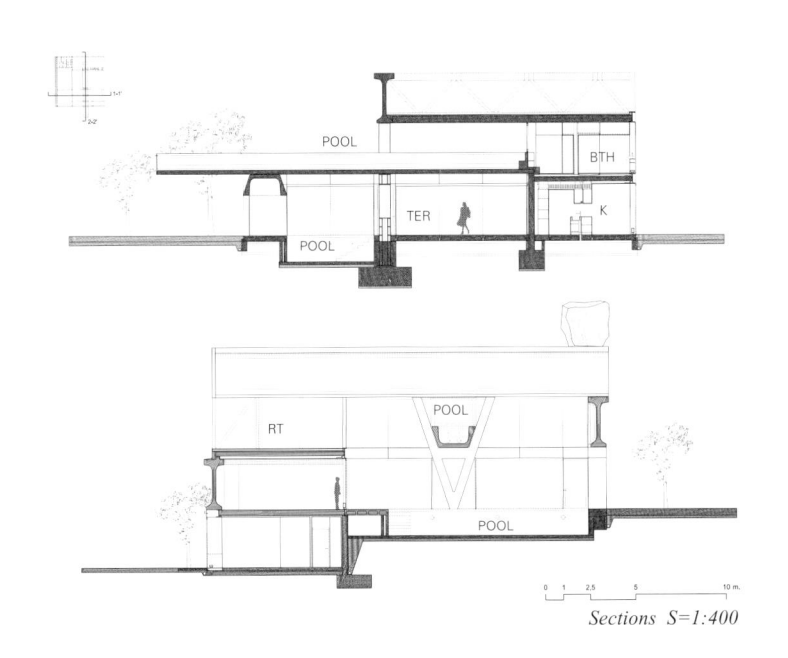

Sections S=1:400

Lap pools on each floor

181

Enric Miralles Benedetta Tagliabue   2006

House in Barcelona, Barcelona, Spain

Living/dining room

Living room

Living/dining room: existing wall of medieval era

The task involved cleaning, approaching and discovering
　The intensity of the utility of construction….
Always the same walls…
　　…and the floors,
　　　　Used and reused from the Gothic done to the present…

Learning to live with a given,
　And second hand structure,
like rummaging throught the pockets of an old coat,
setting the things one finds one a clean surface…

This house works like a chessboard.
　The pieces move according to the rules of each object… They must
always return to the starting point to
　　　　　　　　　　restart the game…

Hence the floor,
　Which set the existing items back in front of the windows,
　　…or the paints on the walls, which
Reveals the discovered fragments,
　are the rules of the game…

Amongst them, moving in an orderly fashion, are
　　　　　　　　　　　tables,
　　　　　　　　　　　　　books,
　　　　　　　　　　　　　　　others…

Enric Miralles

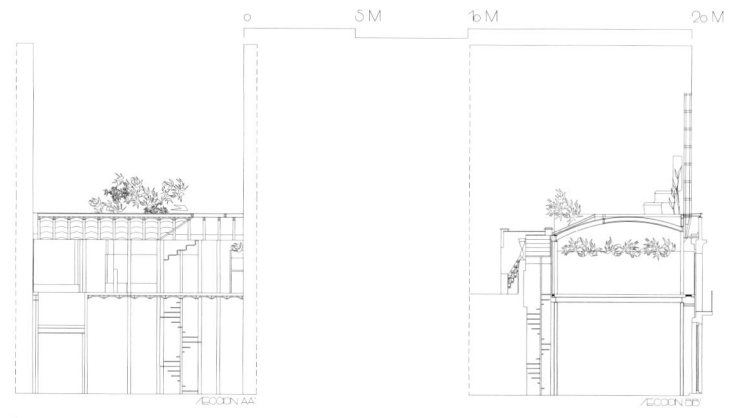

Plan

Sections

この作業には，余分なものを取り除き，対象に近づき，発見することが必然的に伴う
建造物の実用性が持つ強度……
常に同じ壁……
……そして床
このゴシック様式の建物がつくられたときから現在まで
使われ，再利用されてきた……

与えられたものと共に住むことを学ぶこと
使い古された建物
古いコートのポケットのなかを，何かを見つけ出そうと隈無く探すように
一つひとつ白紙の面を見つけながら物を配置する……

この家はチェスボードのように働く
一つひとつの駒は，それぞれのルールに従って動き……
ゲームを再開するため
常に出発点に戻らねばならない……

それゆえに
既存のアイテムを窓の前に戻してはめこんだ床……
あるいは発見された断片を表出させた壁の彩色は
このゲームのルールである……

それらの中で整然とした流儀で運び込まれるのは
テーブル，本，その他のもの……

（エンリック・ミラージェス）

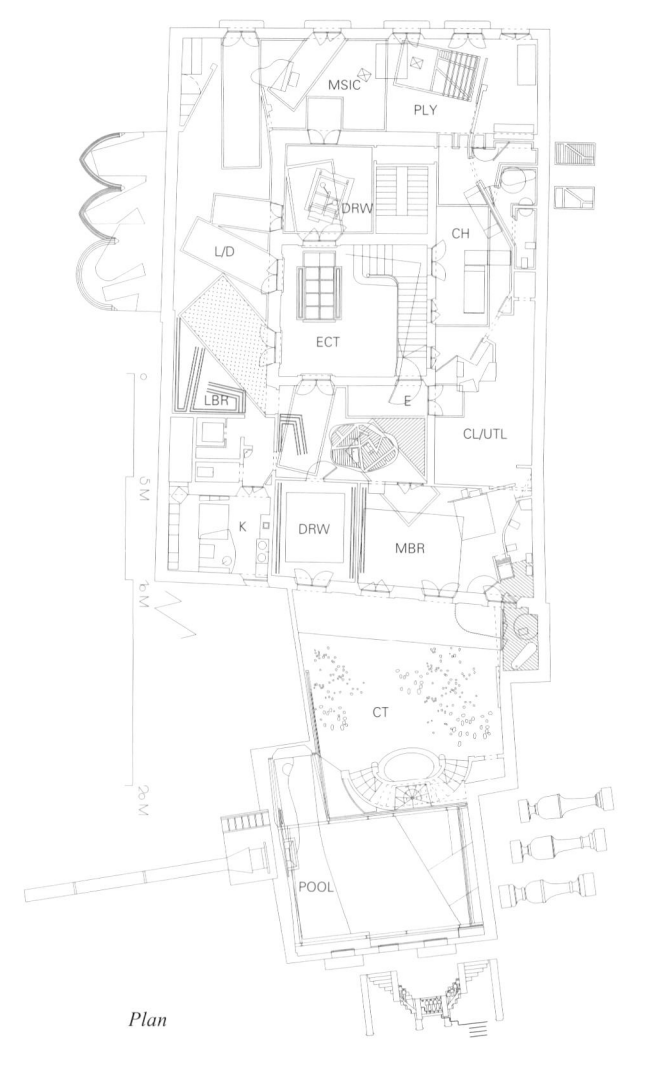

Entrance court

Foyer

Music room

Pool area covered by arched roof with brick plate

Master bedroom

Bed: wooden fixture designed by architects

Pool area

Studio Mumbai

2008

Belavali House, Belavali, Maharashtra, India

View from north: large roof

Designed for an extended family, *Belavali House* occupies a five acre rice plantation in the district of Alibag, a forty minute boat journey from Mumbai city.

Conceived as a pavilion in the garden, the house is positioned between the forest to the east and the terraced rice fields to the west.

The project is entered from the east down a broad flight of stairs that opens onto a large verandah straddled between the building. The long narrow structure framed in steel supports a large roof that moves through a series of mango trees. Walls and floor are rendered seamlessly in pigmented cement plaster that define spaces and follow the terraced levels of the paddy fields, leading onto a large stone deck, a pool and view of the mountains.

Masonry walls, glass, wood and timber louvers form the enclosure of the house. The operable facades can be tuned to provide privacy or exposure to changing weather conditions, and control views of the surrounding landscape.

Two small outhouse buildings are set slightly apart from the main house; provide additional living and sleeping spaces for the extended family and guests.

The colonized footprint of the project is controlled and minimized in order to maintain the cultivation of rice. Stone retaining walls used for plantation terracing have been restored, and a network of footpaths paved with reclaimed stone traverses the site and integrates the natural and built environment as they have done for generations.

Site plan/ground floor S=1:500

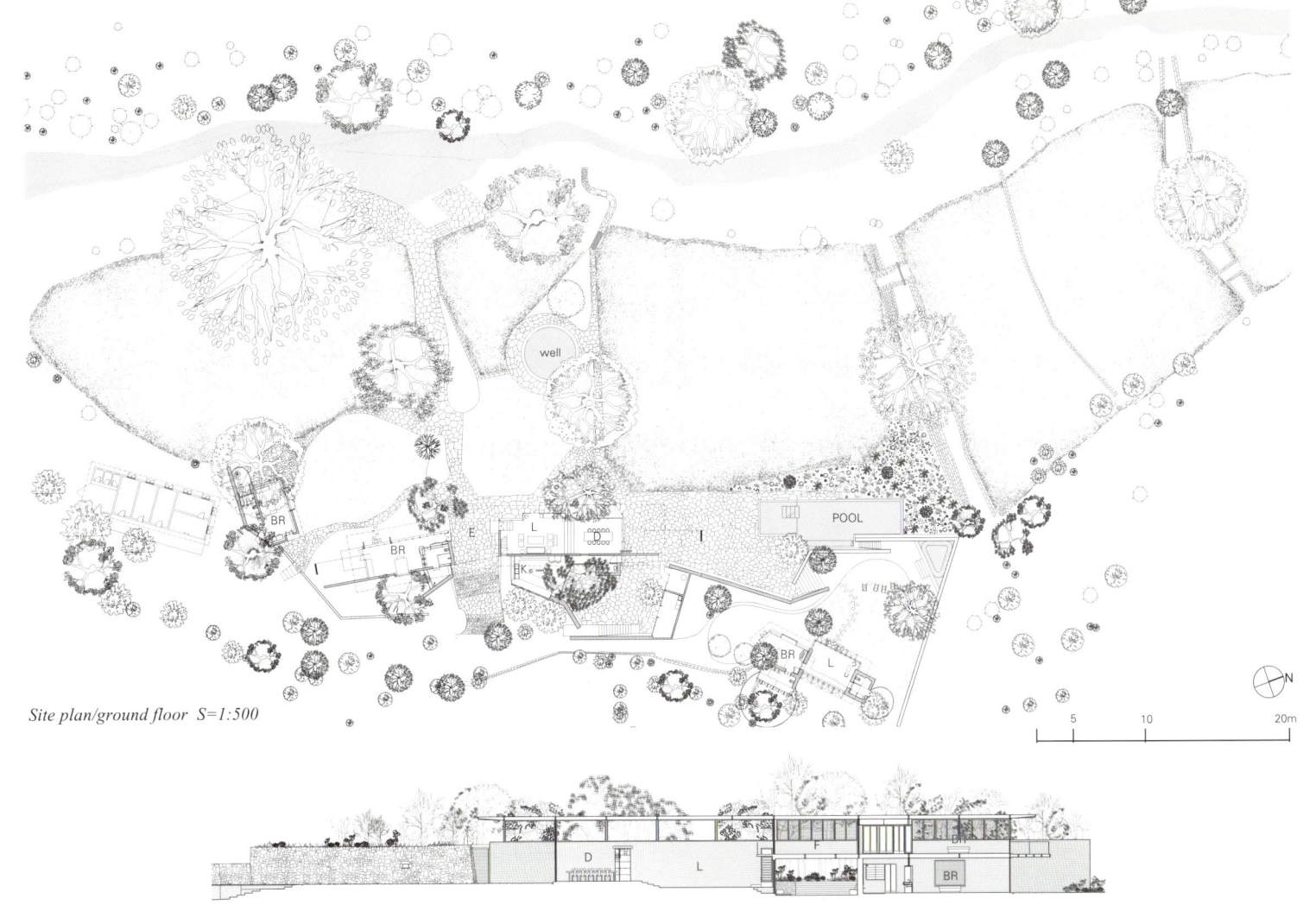

Longitudinal section S=1:500

Entrance: view toward living room

Glazed wall of living room

Living room: looking south

Dining room: looking north

大家族のために設計されたこの住宅は，ムンバイ市からボートで40分，アリバグ地区の米作農園5エーカー分を占めている。

庭の中のパヴィリオンとして計画されており，東側は森に，西側は棚田に挟まれている。

建物の合間に据えられた大きなベランダへと繋がるひと続きの広い階段を下り，東側から家屋に入る。マンゴーの木々の連なりに沿って伸びる大屋根を，細長いスティール製フレーム構造が支えている。壁と床は，空間に輪郭を与えると同時に棚田ともよく馴染む色彩の漆喰で継ぎ目なく塗られ，その先にある大きな石造りのデッキ，プール，さらには山岳風景へと導いてくれる。

石壁，ガラス，木材，木製ルーバーがこの家の壁面を形成している。可動式ファサードは開閉の調節が可能なため，時にプライバシーを，時に気候の変化との触れ合いをもたらし，さらに周囲の景色の眺めをコントロールすることもできる。

二つの小さな離れが母屋からわずかに離れて配置されており，親戚やゲストのための付加的な居間や寝室を提供している。

米の栽培を維持するために，建物の土地占有面積は最小限に抑えられている。棚田の造成に使われていた石積み擁壁は復元され，再生石で舗装された歩道網が敷地を横切り，彼らが先祖代々やってきたように，自然と一体化した環境がつくられている。

Living/dining room

Bedroom wing on south

Family room on first floor: looking south

Bedroom on first floor: looking north

Outhouse on south

Bedroom in outhouse on south

Kitchen

Tadao Ando

House in Sri Lanka, Mirissa, Sri Lanka

2008

Distant view from south

This house is located at the top of a sheer cliff facing a small gulf in the Indian Ocean, on the southern end of Sri Lanka. The client is a Belgian couple, he established a local manufacturing company and developed it into a global corporation, and his wife is an artist whose works are inspired by Sri Lankan culture. They spend most of their time in Sri Lanka and they are deeply attached to the climate, the culture and the people. The commission was from him. He wanted to build a substantial house and a studio as a gift for his wife, with whom he has shared a challenging life for many years.

The first request was in early 2004 and there were some preliminary meetings with a local architect, but later that year there was the Sumatra Earthquake and the Asian Tsunami struck Sri Lanka. Many people were washed away and many buildings and ports were damaged around the site. At this point, it seemed impossible to continue the project. However half a year later, there was a request to re-start the project from the client who had set up his own relief effort to assist in the reconstruction.

We completed the detailed design within several months and a local construction company once with financial ties to a Japanese company was selected to construct this house. However they had no experience with building in exposed concrete and also the general standards of construction in Sri Lanka are not so high. It was decided to send two Japanese technicians who had experienced our projects to the site. Though they were both around retiring age, they were still fit and wanted to put their experience to good use in this society. They struggled with the different culture and customs but they went to the site in turns to instruct and to enhance the construction accuracy.

The building consists of the residence, guest rooms and studio. These functions are laid out to form a zigzag volume, and the voids in this form an intermediate space to be in dialogue with the nature of Sri Lanka. To accommodate the Sri Lankan perpetual summer climate, we designed a breezy house like most Sri Lankan residences by creating several partially exterior spaces. At the client's request, there is a pool on

Site plan S=1:6000

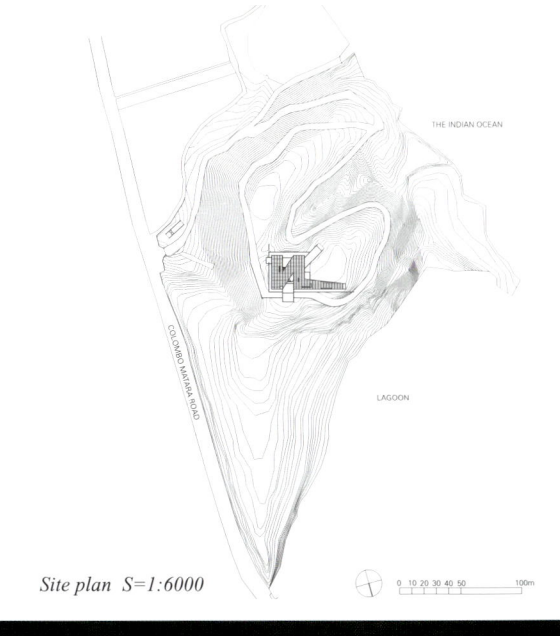

View from swimming pool

the second floor terrace which is visually connected with the Indian Ocean. Many local materials and construction methods are used for the finishes and the building is designed to be surrounded by a local style masonry wall. The metal joinery is from Belgium.

Overcoming difficulties through cooperation between the local and Japanese teams and also people from several other countries, I believe that an exemplary work of quality modern architecture, which could be a kind of new model for this paradise floating on the Indian Ocean, has been achieved.
Tadao Ando

View toward swimming pool

View from west: studio on left

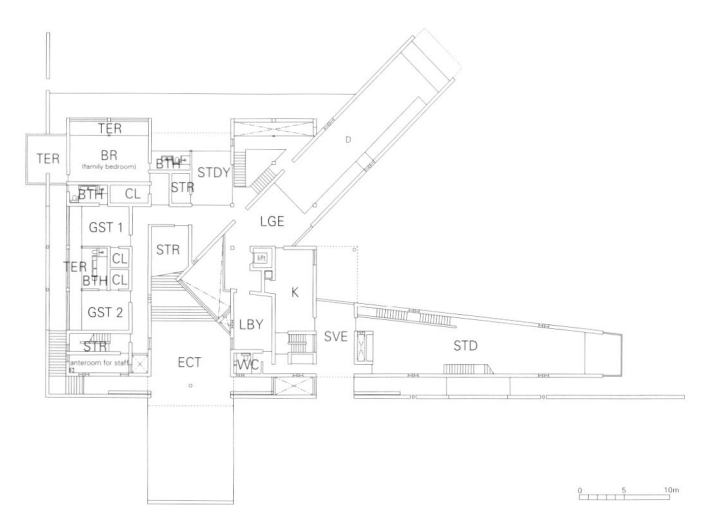

First floor S=1:800

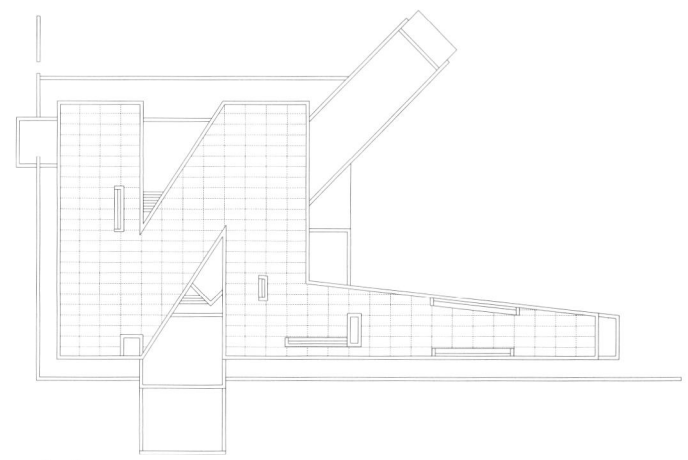

Roof

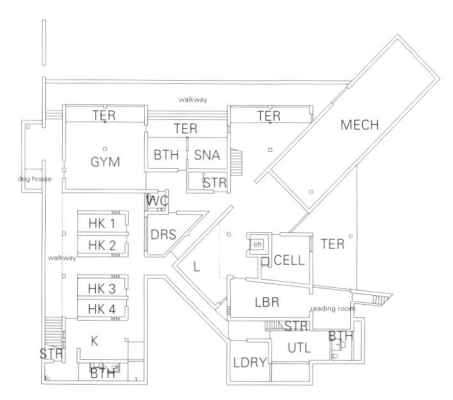

Basement

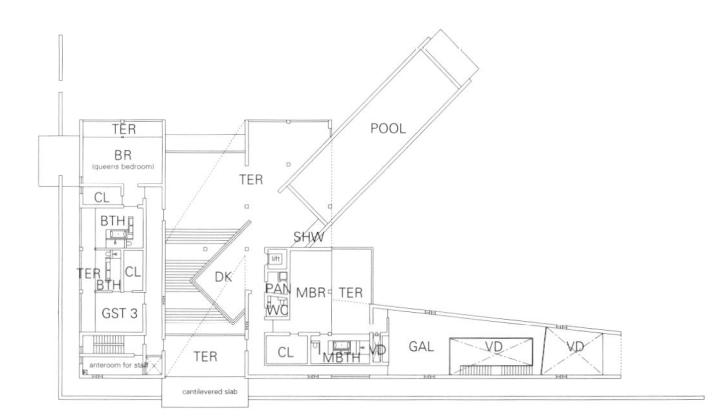

Second floor

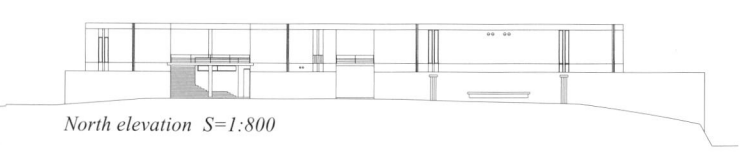

North elevation S=1:800

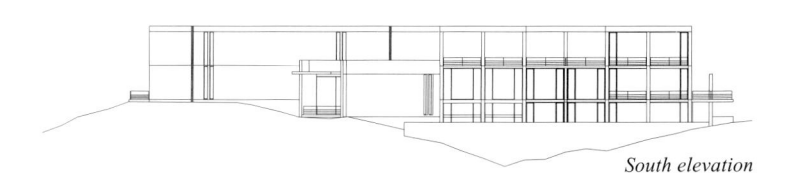

South elevation

Entrance court: staircase to terrace and swimming pool on second floor

Terrace on second floor: staircase to entrance

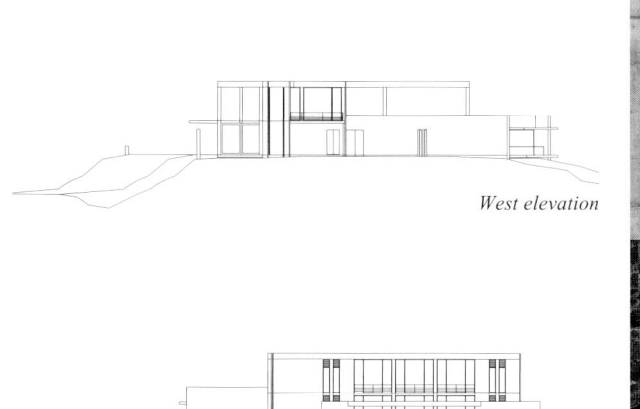

West elevation

East elevation

Entrance on north

Dining room on first floor

Lounge: view toward dining room

Studio on first floor

Master bedroom on second floor

Master bathroom

Terrace of master bedroom

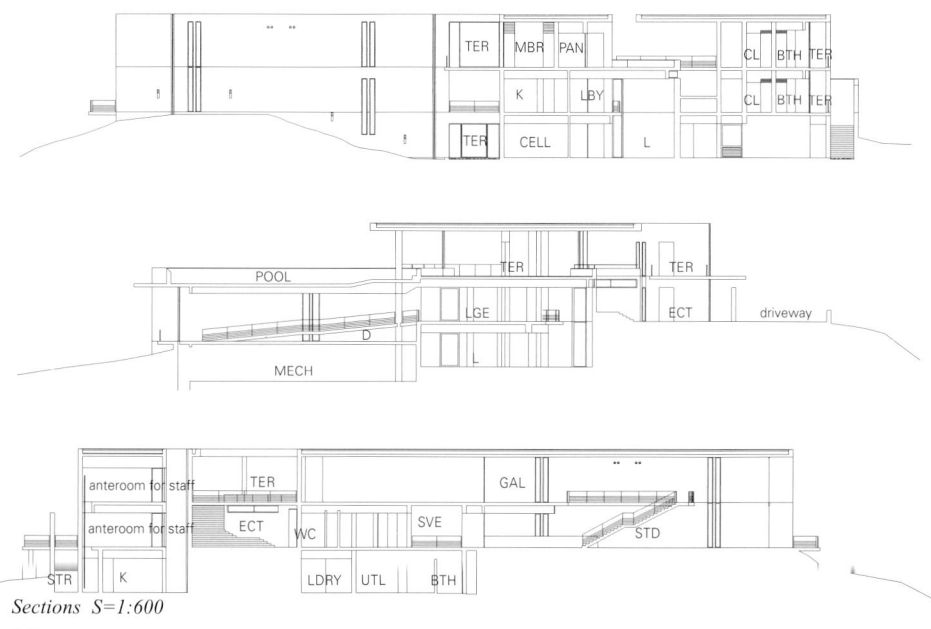

Sections S=1:600

インド洋に浮かぶ島国スリランカの南端の，小さな湾に面した切り立った崖の頂上に建つ住宅である。クライアントは，現地で製造業の会社を興しグローバルな企業へと発展させた会社社長である夫と，スリランカの風土にインスパイアされた作品をつくり続けている画家である妻の，ベルギー人夫婦である。一年の多くをスリランカで過ごし，その風土と文化，人々をこよなく愛している。ここに，苦労をともにした妻へのプレゼントとして，終の棲家としての住宅と，妻のアトリエをつくりたいという夫の依頼であった。

2004年の初旬に依頼を受け，現地建築家を交えて設計の打合わせを進めていたが，その暮れにスマトラ沖の大地震が起こり，津波がスリランカをも襲った。敷地の周辺でも，多くの人が波にさらわれ，建物や港が破壊された。そのような情勢の中で，いったんはプロジェクトの続行が不可能かと思われたが，自ら組織を立ち上げて復興支援事業を行っていたクライアントから，津波から半年後に住宅の設計を再開してほしいとの連絡があった。

それから数ヶ月後に実施設計は完了し，かつて日本の建設会社と資本関係のあった現地の建設会社が施工を担当することに決まったが，彼らには打放しコンクリートの実績はなく，またスリランカの一般的な施工水準は決して高いとはいえなかった。そこで，施主の希望もあって，かつて我々と共に仕事

Reading room next to library on basement

したことのある二人の日本人技術者が送り込まれることになった。二人とも，定年前後の年齢であったが，まだまだ元気で自分の力を社会のために生かしたいという方たちだった。この二人が，異なる文化・習慣に悪戦苦闘しながら，交代で現地に指導に行くことで施工精度を高めることができた。

建物は，クライアントの住宅，ゲストルーム，夫人のアトリエからなる。それらの機能をジグザグに蛇行するヴォリュームの中に配し，その間にできたすき間を，スリランカの自然との対話の場としての中間領域となるように計画した。常夏のスリランカの気候に合うように，半屋外の空間を多く設け，現地の住宅の多くがそうであるように風通しのよい建築になるように心がけた。クライアントの要望で，2階のテラスには，インド洋と視覚的につながるプールが設けられている。仕上げには現地に産する素材や工法を多く用いるようにし，建物の外周を，現地風の石積壁で包むようにした。金属製建具はクライアントの祖国ベルギー製である。

さまざまな困難を乗り越えて，現地チームと日本人チーム，そしてその他の多くの国々の人々が力を合わせることで，インド洋に浮かぶ楽園に，この国の建築のひとつの規範となりうるような，良質な近代建築が実現できたのではないかと思う。

（安藤忠雄）

Living room on basement

Gym on basement

Sou Fujimoto

2008

House N, Oita, Japan

Overall view from southeast

A home for two plus a dog. The house itself is comprised of three shells of progressive size nested inside one another. The outermost shell covers the entire premises, creating a covered, semi-indoor garden. Second shell encloses a limited space inside the covered outdoor space. Third shell is a small house within a house.

I have always had doubts about a house being separated from the streets by a single wall, and wondered that a rich gradation of domain defined by various distances between streets and houses might be a possibility, such as: a place inside the house that is fairly near the street; a place that is a bit far from the street; and a place far off the street, in secure privacy.

That is why life in this house resembles to living among the clouds. A distinct boundary is nowhere to be found, but spaces generated by faint shades of relationships. One might say that an ideal architecture is an outdoor space that feels like the indoors and an indoor space that feels like the outdoors. In a nested structure, the inside is invariably the outside, and vice versa. It is not about space nor about form, but simply about expressing the riches of what are 'between' the house and the streets.

Three nested shells eventually mean infinite nesting because the whole world is made up of infinite nesting. And here are only three of them that are given barely visible shape. I imagined that the city and the house are no different from one another, but different expressions of the same thing—an undulation of a primordial space for human dwelling. This is a presentation of a house in which everything from the origins of the world to a specific house is conceived together under a single method.
Sou Fujimoto

Garden

Dining/living room: kitchen on right, garden on left

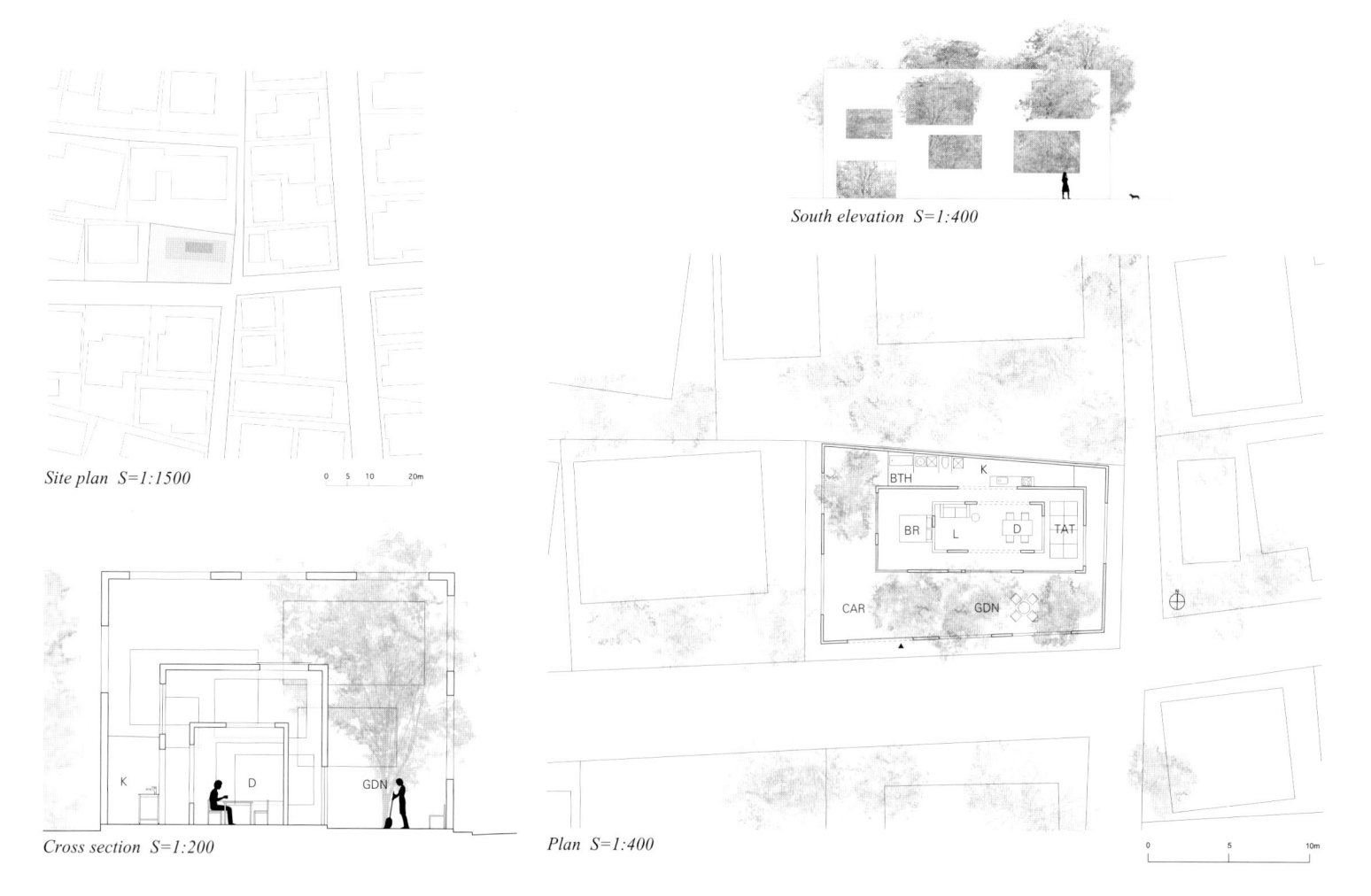

Site plan S=1:1500

South elevation S=1:400

Cross section S=1:200

Plan S=1:400

View toward garden from dining/living room

Tatami room: looking dining room through holes on wall

Bedroom/study: looking south

　家族二人と犬のための3重入れ子の住宅。一番外側の殻は敷地全体を覆っており，半ば室内のように覆われた庭をつくり出す。2番目の殻はその囲まれた外部空間の中にさらに限定された場所を囲いとる。3番目の殻は，家の中の小さな家である。

　街と家とが，壁1枚で隔てられているということに疑問を感じていた。むしろ，家だけれどもだいぶ街に近い場所，街から少し遠ざかった場所，街からすごく遠くなって，プライバシーも守られた場所，のように，街と家とのあいだには，いくつもの距離感を伴った豊かな領域のグラデーションがありえるのではないだろうか。

　この住宅は，雲の中に住むことに似ている。どこまで行っても明確な境界が存在せず，かすかな関係の濃淡によって場が生まれる。理想の建築とは，内部のような外部空間であり，外部のような内部空間であると言えるのではないだろうか。そして入れ子においては，内部は常に外部であり，外部は常に内部である。空間ではなく，形態ではなく，ただ，家と街との「あいだ」の豊かさを顕在化する。

　3重の入れ子とは，つまり無限の入れ子である。世界が無限の入れ子でできていて，その間のほんの三つが，かすかに目に見える形を与えられている。都市と住宅とは，けっして別々のものではなく，人が住むための根源的な空間の起伏の濃淡という意味で，同じものの違った現れである。世界の成り立ちから1軒の家までを，一つの方法によって同時に構想した住宅の提案。

（藤本壮介）

Keisuke Maeda

2009

Atelier-Bisque Doll, Minoh, Osaka, Japan

View from northwest

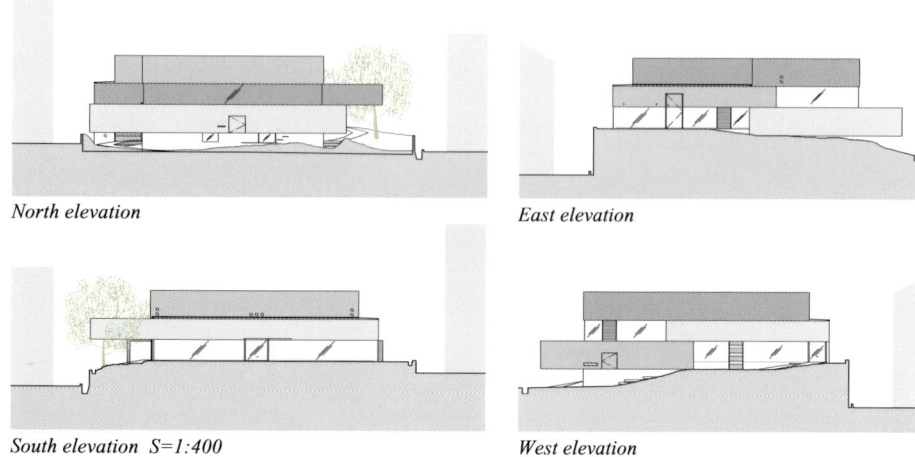

North elevation

East elevation

South elevation S=1:400

West elevation

Requests and Characteristics of Site
This is an atelier for a doll artist and a residence of the couple. The request was an atelier that can be used as a gallery at the same time functioning as a doll-making studio. Additionally, it should be a space where her friends, who are often invited, can be gathered around pleasantly. In the residential environment the atelier and the house are wished to be open, while reserving some privacy from the neighborhood.

When I first visited Minoh City in Osaka Prefecture, I remember the place was plenty of green. It is because the season was spring, but also the city was ordained by vegetation standard, which order more than 10% of the site to plant tall, middle and low trees in urban districts

View from corridor toward approach to house

Approach on northeast

Corridor between atelier (left) and house (right)

with lower than 60% of building coverage ratio.

Form without Territory

In order to secure privacy, we thought if it is possible to do so with more people's involvement rather than building walls or fences on site boundaries and capturing the whole from inside.

That is to create the whole from outside by choosing the neighbor's greenery as outdoor space and not producing necessary functions from inside. Not something like walls, hanging walls or fences but waist-high walls that are freed from gravity or floating belts surround the entire site. This is a theory to create architecture that is interior-like extending from outdoor, opposed to substantial in/out territory.

Floating Belt

Specifically, we expected that territory, which does not regulate in/out terrain, be made by a spatial diversity that is derived from floating belt, which is accumulated double or triple in rectangle taking balance, and the belt itself.

Employing 1.2 meters level difference in the site, two functions are allocated to where floating belts overlap. Atelier is put on the lower part facing north-looking front street and the residential piece on the upper south side. An approach was built as a slope as if walking on the slanted topography. By putting a small box that stores necessary functions such as a closet in the atelier and the house, it becomes a space like a street-facing piazza that has no region. The two functions become one room space by triple pile of belts.

A simple operation of overlapping belts that have directionality obscures site boundaries and formulates a relationship of the site and the neighborhood that contain new extent. That is to say, the entire site becomes a gallery without body-sensed territory and that is connected to creating variety of places that the client requires.

In this occasion, we think we could realize a space that has new link to a city by rethinking notion of walls and fences that obstruct boundaries and treating architecture, structure and landscape equivalently.

Keisuke Maeda

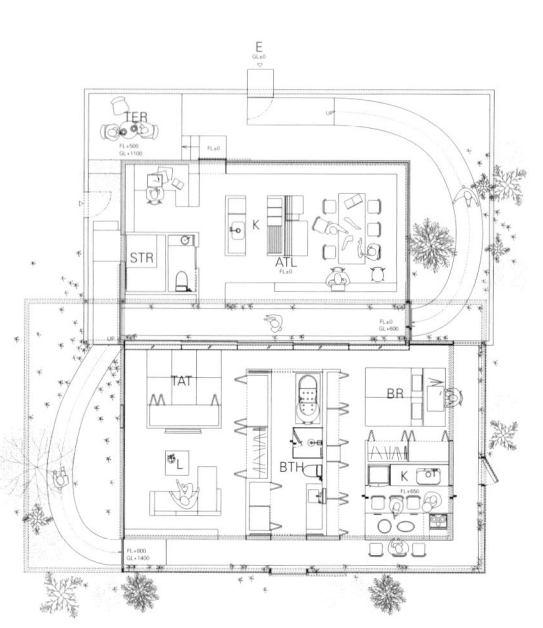

Plan S=1:250

Atelier

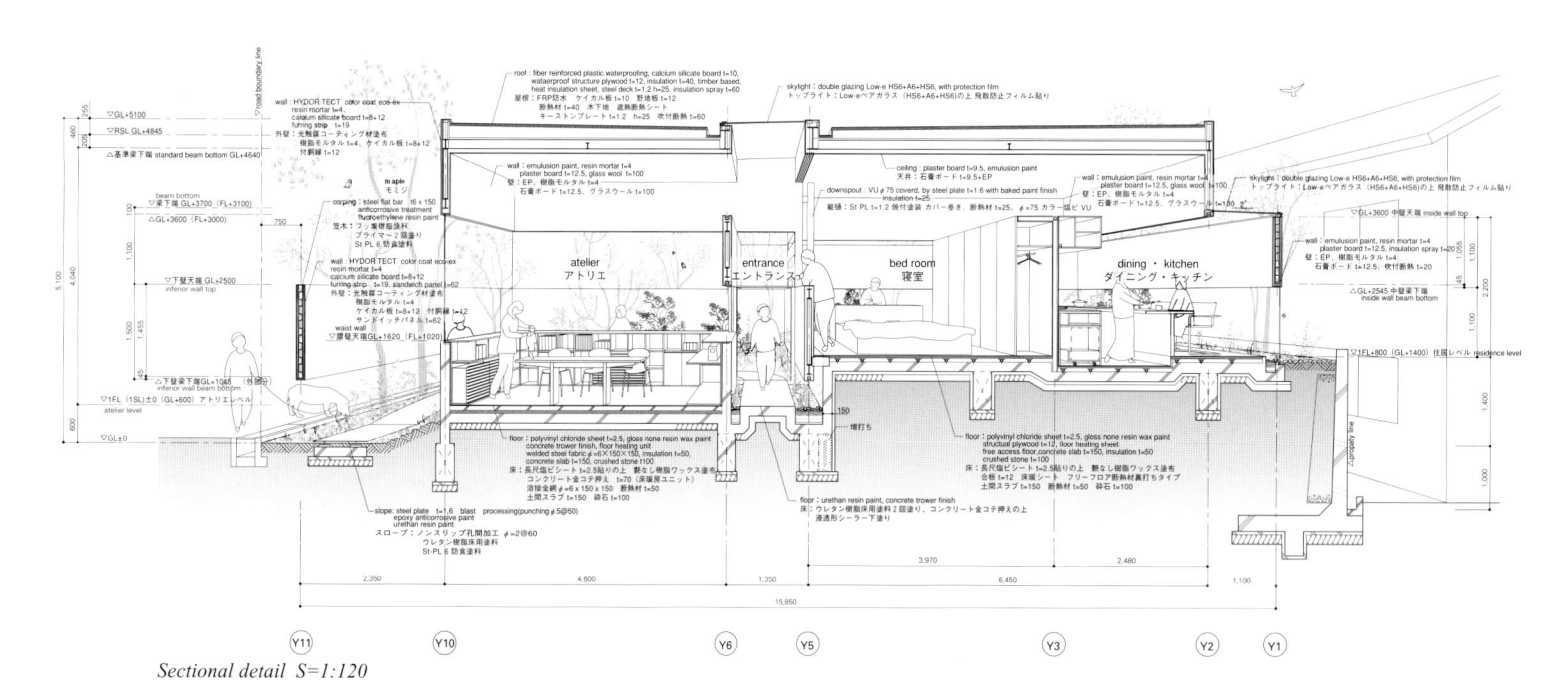

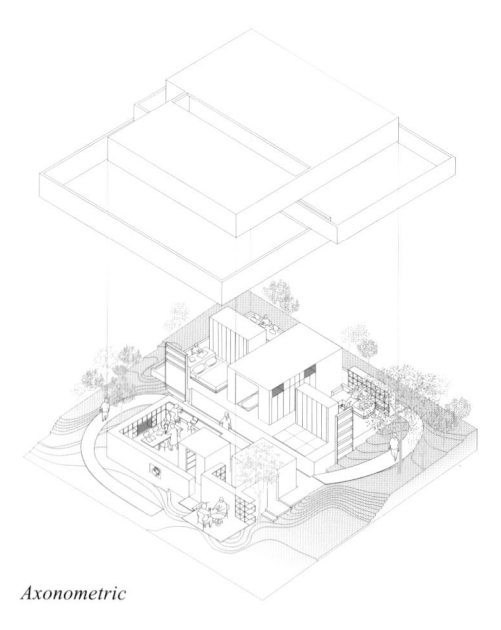

Sectional detail S=1:120

Axonometric

〈要望と敷地の特性〉
人形作家の奥様のアトリエと，ご夫婦の住宅である。要望は人形制作の工房としながらギャラリーとしても機能できるアトリエであること。また，友人などをよく招くので，楽しく集えるような空間であることだった。住宅に囲まれた敷地環境なので，近隣からのプライバシーをある程度確保しながらも開かれたアトリエと住宅にしたいということであった。

敷地がある大阪府箕面市に初めて訪れた時の印象は，緑豊かな場所として記憶された。それは新緑の春に訪れた印象もあるが，まちづくり推進条例によって，建ぺい率60パーセント以下の市街化区域では，敷地の10パーセント以上の高木・中木・低木とする緑化基準が設定された，緑溢れる街から感じたことであった。

〈領域のない形式〉
プライバシーを確保するために，塀や壁なるものによって敷地の境界を取巻く，内側から全体を捉えていく形式ではなく，もう少し人が関わりをもつ範囲を広げながらそのような与件を満たす形式で捉えることができないかと考えた。

それは必要とされる機能を内部からつくりだしていくのではなく，近隣の緑地帯をも外部空間として見立てることで全体を捉えていくような，外側からつくり出していく形式である。壁・垂れ壁・塀などではない，重力から開放された腰壁＝浮遊する帯によって敷地全体を取巻くようなもの。それは実体としての内／外部領域ではなく外部の延長としての内部のような建築をつくりだす原理である。

〈浮遊する帯〉
具体的には互いにバランスを保ちながら2重3重と直交しながら積層した浮遊する帯によって生まれる空間の多様性と，この帯によって内／外部の範囲を規定しない領域が生成されることを期待した。

敷地内1.2メートルの高低差を利用し，浮遊する帯が重複する部分に二つの機能を配する。アトリエは前面道路側北向きの低層部へ，住居部分は段上の南面へ。そして，地形の斜面を歩くようなスロープで

Night view of living room

View toward dining room/kitchen from living room

Living room

アプローチする。アトリエと住宅の空間の中に，収納など必要な機能を収める小さなハコを置くことで，街区に接している広場のような領域のない居室空間となり，3重に直交する帯によって，二つの機能はワンルーム空間にもなっている。

　方向性を持った帯が積層する単純な操作によって，敷地境界が曖昧となり，敷地／隣地の新たな広がりのある関係性を生成する。それは敷地全体が身体感覚として領域のないギャラリーとなり，施主の求める多様な場を創出することに繋がっている。

　今回，境界を遮るものとしての塀や壁という概念を少し捉え直し，建築・構造・造園を等価に扱うことで，新しい都市との繋がりが生まれる空間を実現できたのではないかと思っている。

（前田圭介）

Dining room/kitchen

Makoto Takei + Chie Nabeshima/TNA — 2009

Square House, Karuizawa, Nagano, Japan

Overall view from southeast

View from dining room toward northwest. 76 pillars are steel pipes (75 mm x 75 mm)

Evening view from north

Evening view

Plan S=1:300

Section S=1:300

This is a weekend house in Karuizawa. The site is narrow and located on along the ridge of the mountain and surrounded by bamboo and thin trunk trees. On this green sloped land, we were asked to design the house for a couple and two dogs.

We considered the building as floating in the forest and allowing people to experience various distances between natures. The site is located at the edge of a cottage land area. There is a height difference between the facing street and the site, as well as many trees surrounds the site, causing resident to not feel the existence of other people from the street. Just as a forest does not have a start or an end, we tried making the environment lose its sense of inside to outside, from one room to another.

By the slope of the land, density of trees, and graduation of the scenery, we have controlled to set various spaces inside. The factors creating each spaces are vertical columns. The position and density of the columns are defined by the daybed, the dining table, the kitchen counter, the bathtub, the furniture and the human interaction between those objects. The arrangement of the columns serve as openings to circulate people and pets, and allows invisible substances such as air, light, sound and scents to filter through. Those columns can be treated as walls depending on the angle of views. These serve as a support for the square roof and hold the distance from the ground at the same time, casting the interior plan to the ground too. Although the columns are thin, they serve multiple roles such as structural foundations, walls, and pipe shafts for utilities. We considered this as a thick and dense boundary, allowing for new relationships in adjoining boundaries.
Makoto Takei + Chie Nabeshima/TNA

View from bedroom toward bathroom

Bathroom

軽井沢に建つ週末住宅である。尾根に沿った細長い敷地には，熊笹が群生し，周辺には比較的幹の細い木々が生えている。緑豊かな，繊細な森の傾斜地に，夫婦二人と2匹の犬のための建物を計画することになった。

森の木々の中に浮かんでいるかのような，自然とのさまざまな距離を体験する建物である。別荘地の縁に位置する敷地は，前面道路からの高低差がある斜面であること，生い茂る木々に囲まれていることで通行者や隣家の気配はほとんど感じられない。そこで，森に始まりや終わりがないように，どこまでが内部でどこからが外部なのか，どこからが部屋でどこまでが部屋なのか，そんな環境をつくりだせないかと考えた。

地面の勾配，木々の疎密，そして景色の濃淡といった，風景のグラデーションを手掛かりに，室内に発生する「間」の取り方で建築をつくる。それぞれの間をつくり出しているのは，垂直部材の「柱」であり，その間隔の粗密と配列は，デイベッド，ダイニングテーブル，キッチンカウンター，浴槽といった，家具や什器との取り合いと，それに伴う行為によって規定されている。柱列は人間やペットが通過することのできる開口であり，空気や音，光や匂いといった不可視な物質のみが通過する間仕切りであり，見る角度によっては壁である。方形の屋根を支えている柱列は，室内の間取りをそのまま地面に投影させながら斜面からの距離を保つ。それらは細かい柱でありながら，基礎，間仕切り，壁，パイプシャフトといった，建築の様々な水準の構成要素を凝縮させた「厚い」境界なのである。その境界の厚みと重なりは，隣り合う領域同士の新しい関係をつくっている。

（武井誠＋鍋島千恵／TNA）

Aires Mateus

2010

House in Leiria, Leiria, Portugal

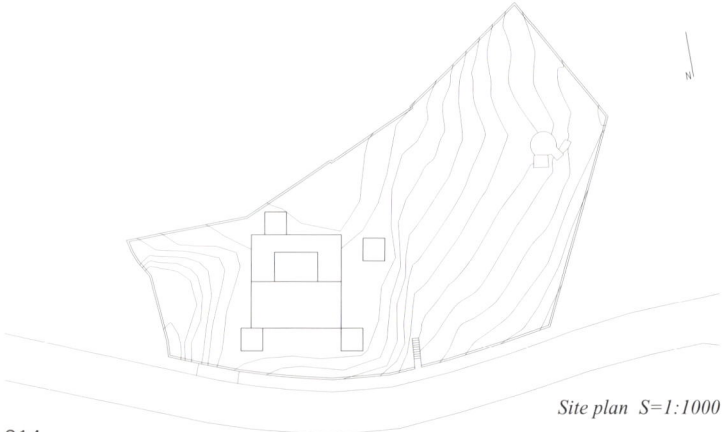

Overall view from southwest

Site plan S=1:1000

Ground floor: looking west. Terrace around void over court on basement

East-west section 1 S=1:400

North-south section 1

East-west section 2

North-south section 2

East-west section 3/south elevation

North-south section 3

East-west section 4/north elevation

North-south section 4/west elevation

Terrace on ground floor: looking east

216

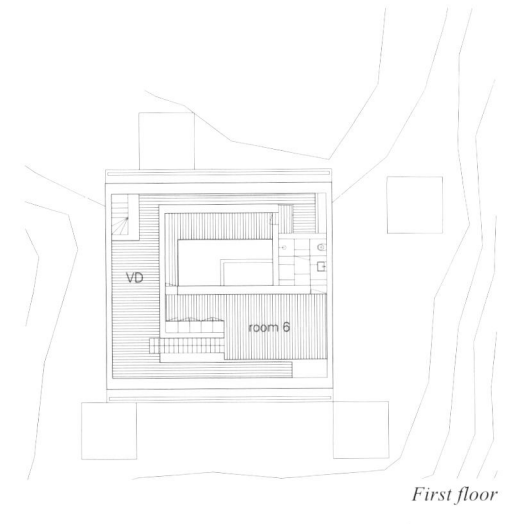

First floor

Ground floor S=1:400

Basement

Ground floor: dining room facing terrace

Living room on ground floor: looking toward dining room

217

Room 6 on first floor △▷

Staircase to room 6 on first floor

Basement: view of court from room 4

The site is o the outskirts of Leiria, in a high position overlooking the city.

The functions are banal: a house divided in private area with bedrooms, and social area with living-rooms. The private areas are at street level under the plot, around a central courtyard with rooms opening to private patios in a intimate environment. The living rooms are around a void, that collects light from above and gazes the castle at the city centre.

The house is a recognizable archetype emptied of its centre by the light designed by a three heighted courtyard that opens horizontally at the garden level. The bedroom courtyards, revealed in the garden, relate with this archetypal object providing different readings on its scale. Scale and volume are controlled in a chaotic context, with a clear identity that from its core relates with the historical legacy far away: the Leiria Castle.

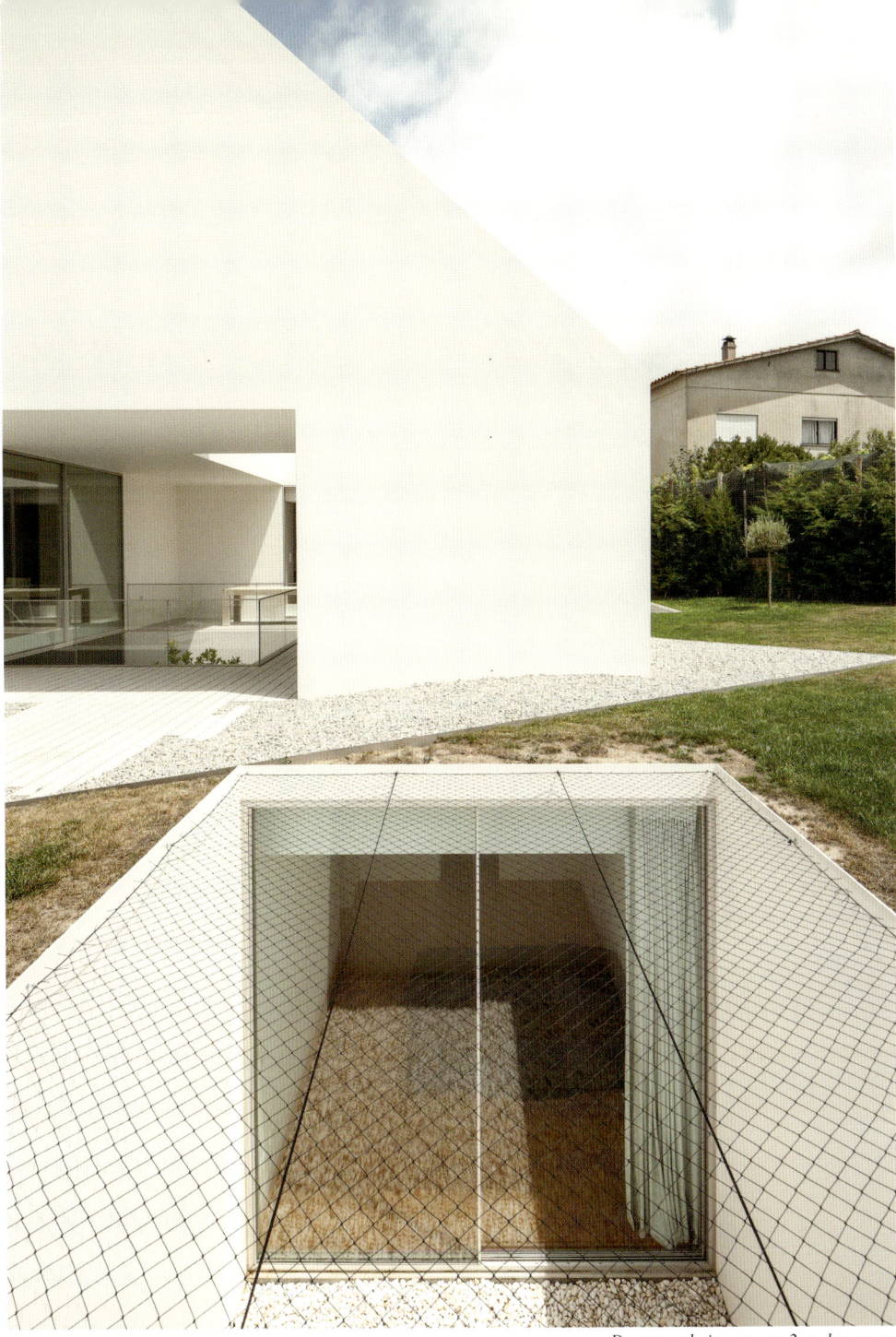

敷地はレイリアの街の郊外で，街を見下ろせる高い場所にある。

この住宅の機能は平凡なもので，寝室のあるプライベートな領域と居間のあるパブリックな領域に分かれている。プライベートな領域は，敷地下の道路レベルにあって，諸室は中庭の周りに配され，個別のパティオに面していて親密感のある場所となっている。居間は中庭上部のヴォイドを囲んでおり，ヴォイドには上部から光が取り込まれ，街の中心にある城を眺望できる。

庭のレベルで外につながる3層吹抜けの中庭からの光によって，この住宅は中心が空のアーキタイプとして認識できる。寝室に面する中庭は庭にさらされ，中心が空というアーキタイプのオブジェとしてスケールに異なる解釈を与えている。スケールとヴォリュームは，混沌としたコンテクストの中で明確なアイデンティティーを持ってコントロールされ，その根底では，遠く離れた歴史遺産であるレイリア城を想起させる。

Downward view: room 2 on basement

Room 4 on basement

Room 2 on basement

219

Andra Matin

2010

AM Residence, Jakarta, Indonesia

Overall view from east

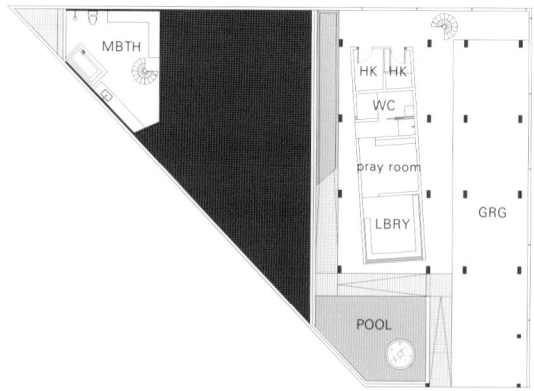

Ground floor S=1:400

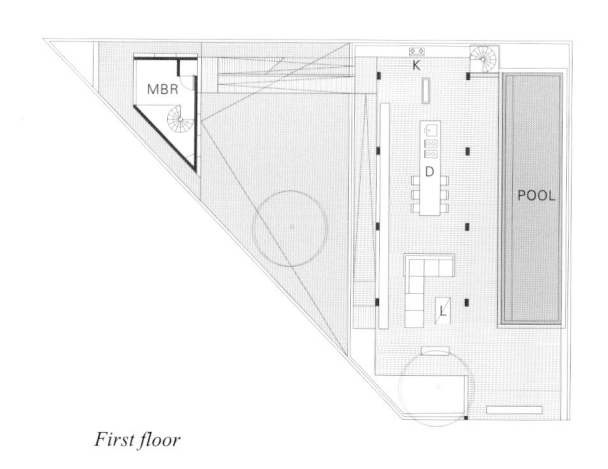

First floor

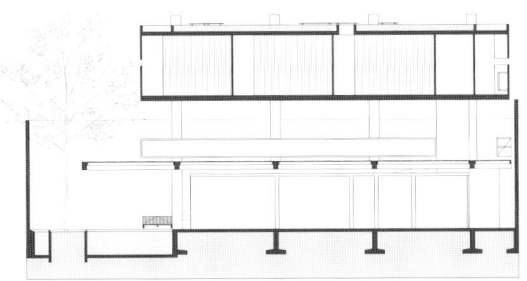

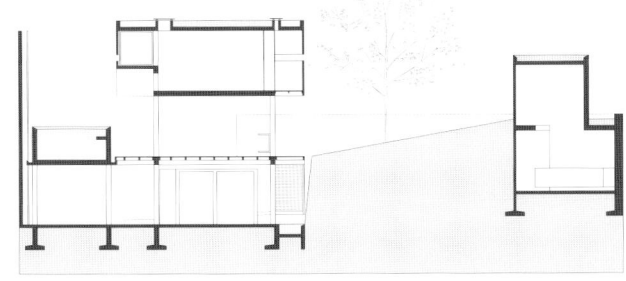

Longitudinal section S=1:300

Cross section

Dining/living room below, children's room above

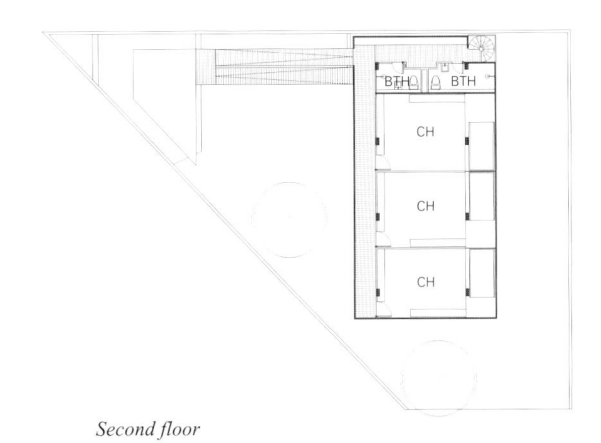

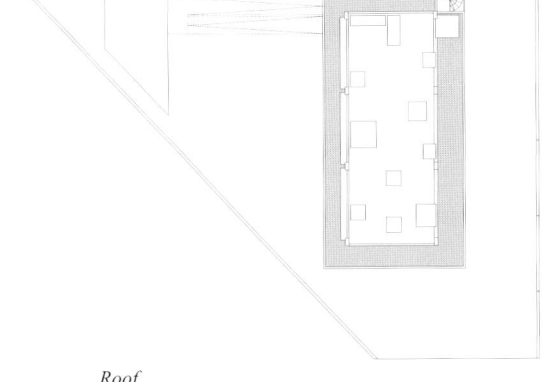

Second floor

Roof

Swimming pool: view from north. Living room on left

Semi-outdoor living/dining room on first floor

Semi-outdoor living/dining room on first floor

Alcove for bed at children's room

Children's room on second floor

Ramp connecting main building (right) and master bedroom (detached room, left)

View toward water court from library

Library on ground floor

The house is sited in a modest neighborhood where vegetations are lavish. It is comprised of exposed concrete and reclaimed ironwood for low maintenance reason. Strong connection between inside-outside is envisaged to bring nature closer with its residents.

The zoning is divided vertically: service and semi-public on ground level, communal in middle, and private spaces on top. The house is best described in cinematique journey: upon entering the wooden gate, visitors are greeted by a tranquil koi pond while a slated wooden ramp lures them to explore the level above. The ramp leads to an open common space where lies a massive timber table, swimming pool and lush greeneries. Two final ramps ascend to the sleeping quarters: master bedroom in the corner of the garden and children's above the main volume. The bedrooms sizes are shrunken to provide just enough space to sleep, and thus minimizing stimuli to allow optimum rest and giving maximum use of communal space for other activities.

この住宅は，緑豊かな閑静な地域に位置している。維持するのにあまり手がかからないことから，打ち放しコンクリートと硬質木材の再生材でできている。内部と外部の密接な関係によって，自然が住人にとって身近なものとなる。

ゾーニングは垂直になされている。サービスルームとセミパブリック空間は1階にあり，共有空間が中階に，プライベートな空間が最上階にある。この住宅は映画的体験として最もよく言い表すことができる。すなわち，木製の門を入ると，訪問者は穏やかな鯉の池に迎えられ，木製のスロープが上へと誘う。スロープは開放的な共有空間へと繋がり，大きな木製テーブル，スイミング・プール，青々とした緑がある。最後の二つのスロープを上ると寝室へと至る。主寝室は庭の角に位置し，子どもたちの寝室はメイン・ヴォリュームの上にある。寝室は小さく，寝るのに十分なだけの大きさであるため，刺激が最小となって最適な休息をもたらし，他の活動のための共有空間の利用を最大化している。

Master bathroom (below) and bedroom (above)

Spiral staircase between master bedroom (upper level) and bathroom (lower level)

Master bedroom

Kengo Kuma

2010

Glass/Wood House, U.S.A.

The site is located in Connecticut, U.S.A. The project is a renovation of the existing architecture and an addition of a new building accompanied with change in family composition. In New Canaan where the site is situated there are many residences that were designed by architects such as Philip Johnson and Marcel Breuer. Built in 1956, the existing house on the site is a house of the architect, John Black Lee, who was a friend of Johnson. It destined a succession of the beautiful glass covered architecture's spirit—New Canaan spirit. This was the second renovation following by Toshiko Mori in 1992.

Though the existing building was symmetric Palladian villa that stands alone in a forest, we tried to create 'intimacy' in the forest by adding perpendicularly placed new building and enclosing the territory in L-shape. (Johnson's *Glass House* is also built isolated.) L-shape is considered a model of the style in Japanese architecture which is similar to flight formation of geese. It enables two intersecting axes, framing of various spaces, lifting feeling of corners and a jump of consciousness by a rotating action.

In the new building, as a part of 'intimacy' we adopted a kind of mix structure that is made of wooden joist roof structure that sits on 3-inch by 6-inch steel flat-bar columns. Furthermore, by slightly placing columns away from corners, we tried to accelerate corners' transparency and a shift of notion by changing a direction.

In the existing building we substantially changed the inner plan, excluded symmetry and covered the exterior walls with louvers, so as to attain 'intimacy'. As substitute of isolated transparency achieved in 1950's we aimed at 'intimate transparency' and 'warm transparency'.
Kengo Kuma

Addition: view from west

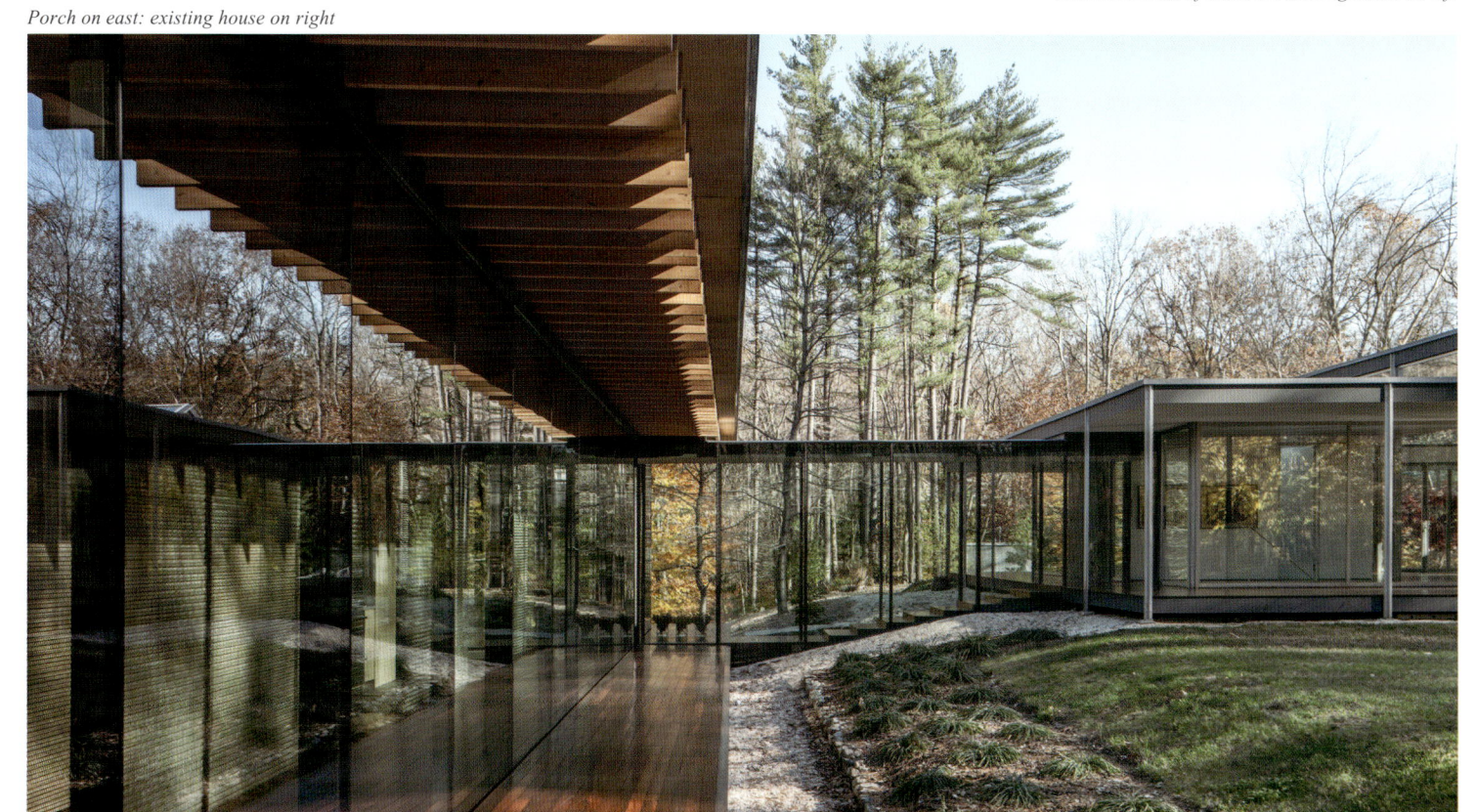

North elevation of addition: existing house on left

Porch on east: existing house on right

Existing house: living room and fireplace

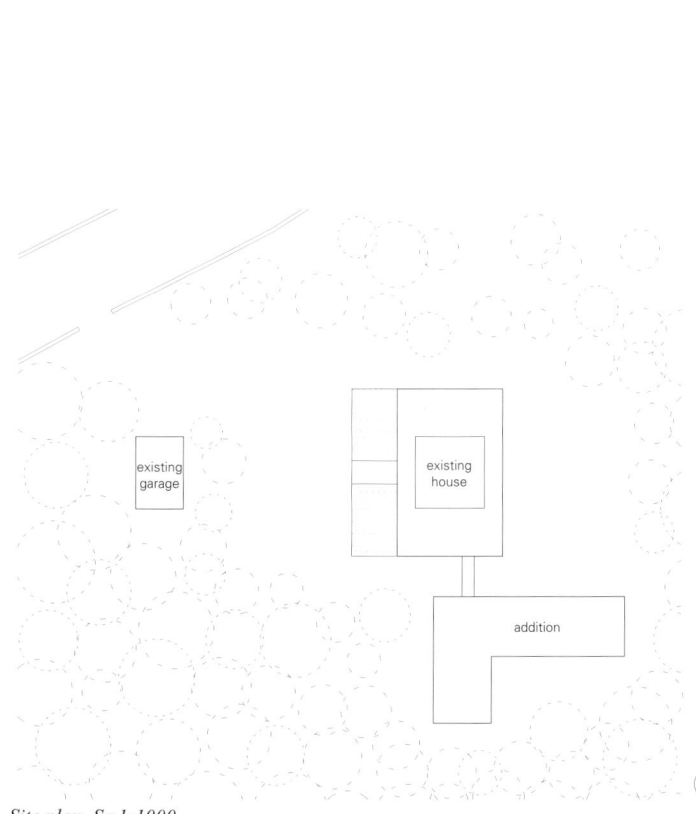

Site plan S=1:1000

Plan S=1:400

Connecting corridor: view toward existing house

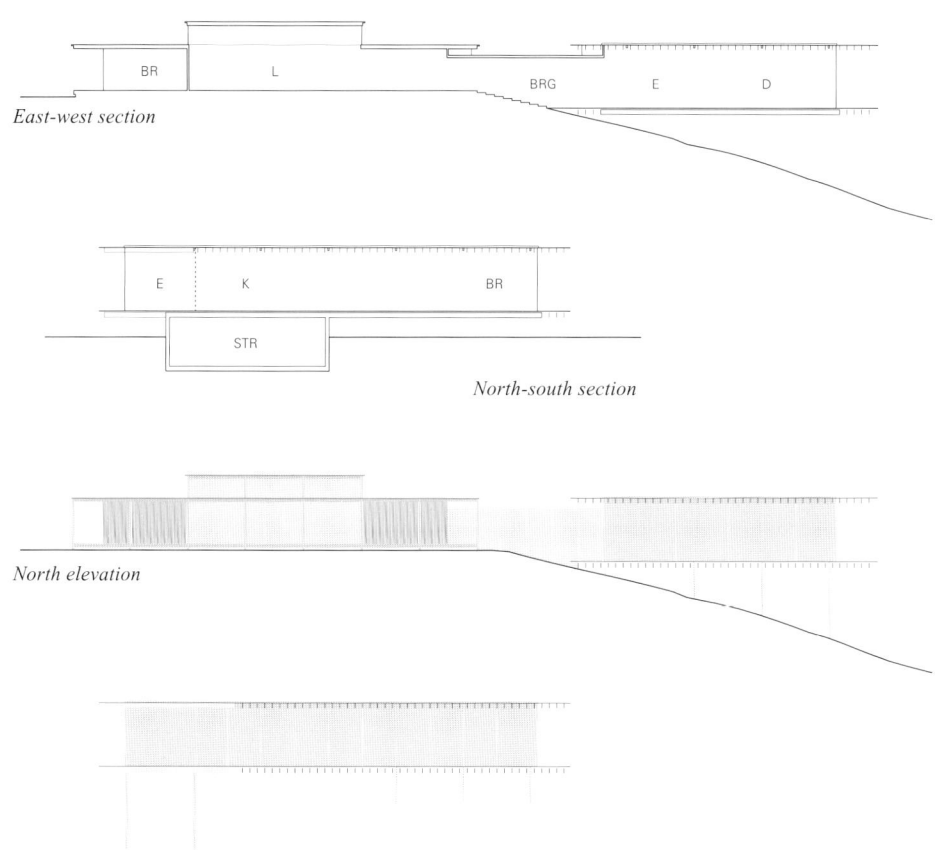

East-west section

North-south section

North elevation

West elevation S=1:400

　敷地は，アメリカ，コネチカット州。家族構成の変化に伴う既存建築の改修と，新棟の増築である。敷地のあるニューキャナンという町は，1950年代にフィリップ・ジョンソンやマルセル・ブロイヤーをはじめとする建築家が設計した住宅が数多く残る町であり，敷地に建つ既存建築もジョンソンと交友のあった建築家ジョン・ブラック・リーの自邸（1956年）で，その美しいガラス張りの建築の精神──ニューキャナンの精神──の継承をめざした。今回の改修は2度目で，1992年にトシコ・モリの設計で一度改修されている。

　既存建築は，森の中に孤立するシンメトリーなパラディオ形式のヴィラ建築であったが，直交する新棟の増築によってL字型に領域を囲い取り，森の中に一種の「親密さ」を創造しようと試みた（ジョンソンの「ガラスの家」も同様に孤立型である）。L字型は日本建築の雁行型配置の原型とも考えられ，二つの交差する軸線，様々な空間のフレーミング，コーナーの浮遊感，回転による意識のジャンプなどが可能となる。

　その「親密化」の一部として，新棟では3×6インチの鉄のフラットバーの柱の上に木のジョイスト構造の屋根が載るという，一種の混構造を採用した。さらに，コーナー部分では柱を隅部から微妙にずらすことでコーナーの透明性，方向転換による意識の転回をさらに加速しようと試みた。

　既存棟も内部プランを大幅に変えてシンメトリーを排し，外壁を木のルーバーで覆うことによって「親密化」を行った。1950年代の孤立した透明性に代わって，「親密な透明性」，「あたたかい透明性」の実現をめざした。

（隈研吾）

Porch: view toward dining room

Dining room of addition

Bedroom on south end

Kitchen: looking through steel mesh

View toward entry of addition from kitchen

Tadao Ando

2010

House in Utsubo Park, Osaka, Japan

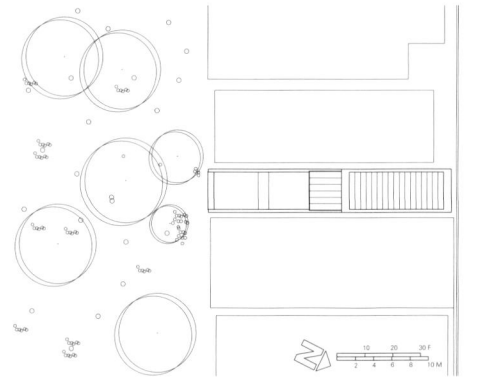

Site plan S=1:800

Specifically designed for a couple and their two dogs, this house is located in a corner of central Osaka that is bordered by a lush park on its southern side.

The main brief was to maximize the depth to which this lush greenery fronting the house could be experienced within, while making full use of its townhouse proportions of a 5-m plus width and 27-m depth.

A consequence of the site's narrow width was the layout's simplified spatial arrangement.

First, the scheme is arranged such that walls enclose the four sides of the site, a courtyard directly communicates with the park to the south, and another courtyard faces the entrance to the north. Interspaced between the two courtyards is the interior living zone—in the northern half of which is arranged various functions such as the stairs, kitchen, and bathroom; and in the southern half of which is arranged the living and dining area within a two-storey atrium space. A private zone is placed above this space and setback, with a roof terrace on the bedroom's southern side, and a study cantilevered over the northern courtyard.

The wall separating the park and courtyard has been further shrouded with green, while the floor on both the interior and exterior is lined with the same stone finish. This living space has been designed with the concept of a building acting systemically as a mechanism that draws 'Nature' in.
Tadao Ando

North elevation

Downward view of terrace facing on park

Fourth floor

Third floor

Second floor

First floor S=1:300

North elevation *West elevation*

South elevation *East elevation*

Section S=1:300

大阪都心部の緑豊かな公園の南に面する街区の一角を敷地とする，夫妻と2匹の犬のための専用住宅である。

間口5メートル余りに対し，奥行き27メートルという町屋的な敷地割りを活かしつつ，いかに前面の豊かな緑を住居深くまで取り込むかを主題に計画を進めた。

間口の狭い敷地ゆえ，空間構成の図式は単純である。まず敷地の四周を壁で囲い，南側に公園に連続するコートを，北側に玄関に面するコートを確保する。その二つのコートで挟まれたゾーンを住居として，北側半分に階段，水廻り等の機能諸室を集約，南側半分を2層吹き抜けのリビング・ダイニングとした。プライバシーを要する寝室はその上部にセットバックし，屋上テラスに南面するよう配置され，書斎は北側のエントランス・コートの上部に張り出すよう計画された。

公園とコートを隔てる壁は緑で覆われ，内外の床仕上げは全て同一の石貼りとなる。建物全体が〈自然〉を引き込む装置となるように意図した住まいである。
　　　　　　　　　　　　　　　　　（安藤忠雄）

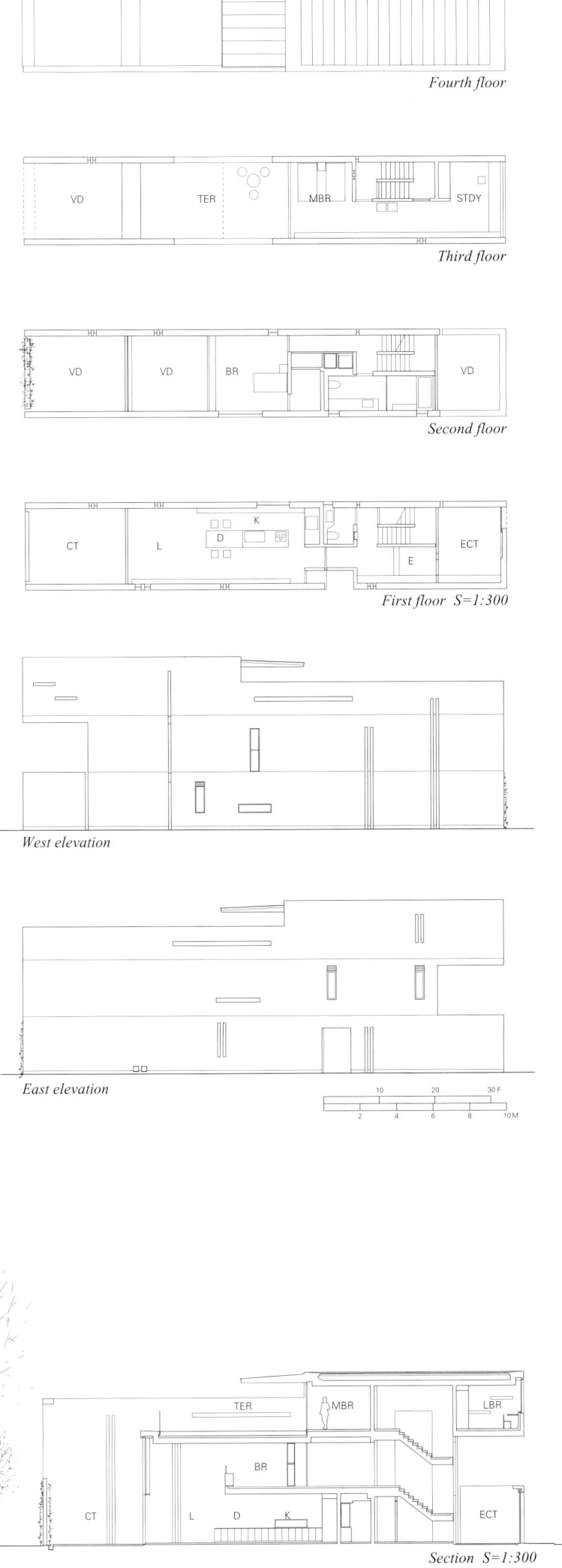

Living and dining room

View from living room to dining room

Court ▷

234

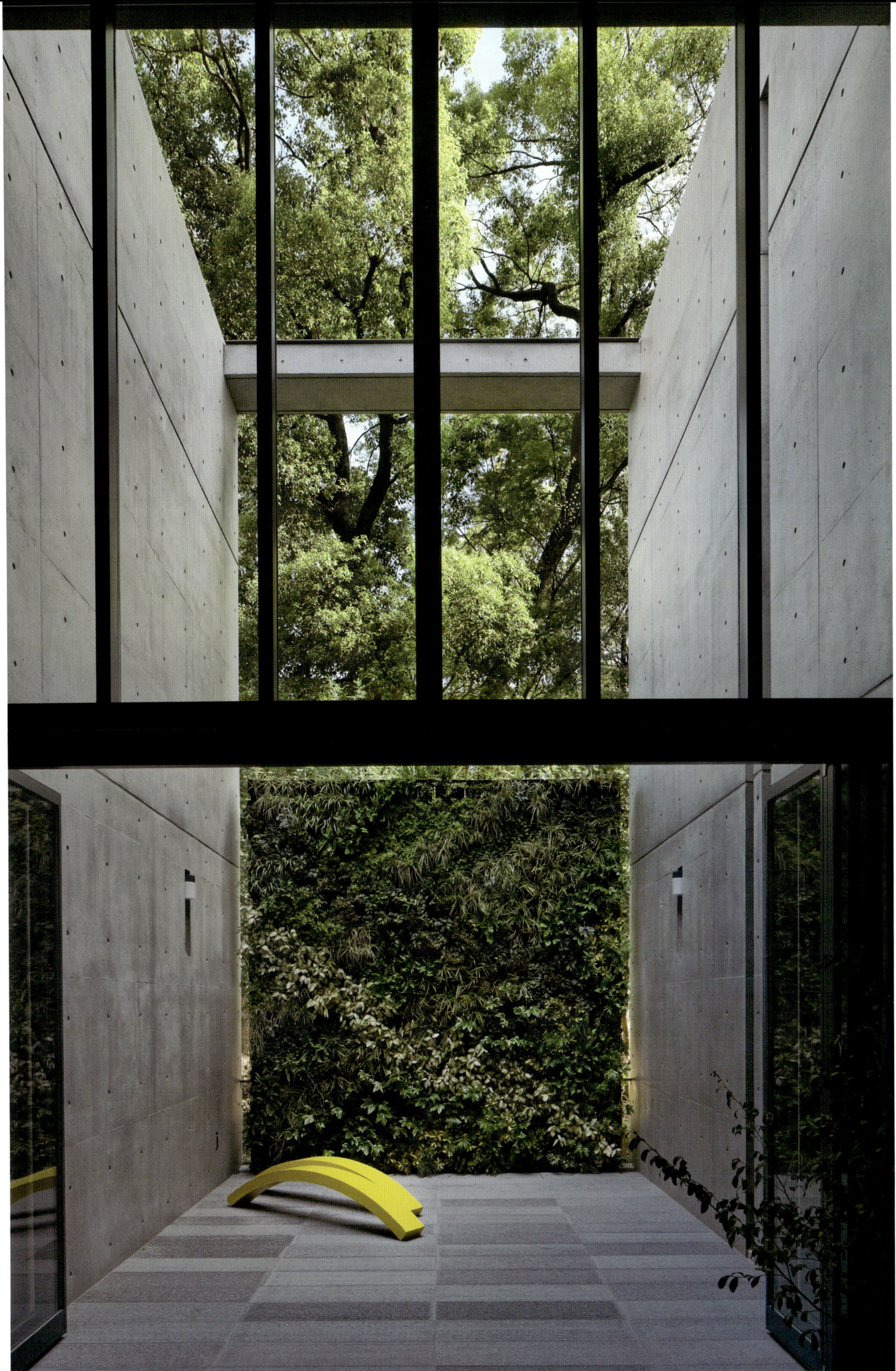

Court: view toward living room

View toward terrace from master bedroom

View toward court from entrance

Master bedroom on third floor

View toward study from master bedroom on third floor

Kengo Kuma

2010

Bamboo/Fiber, Japan

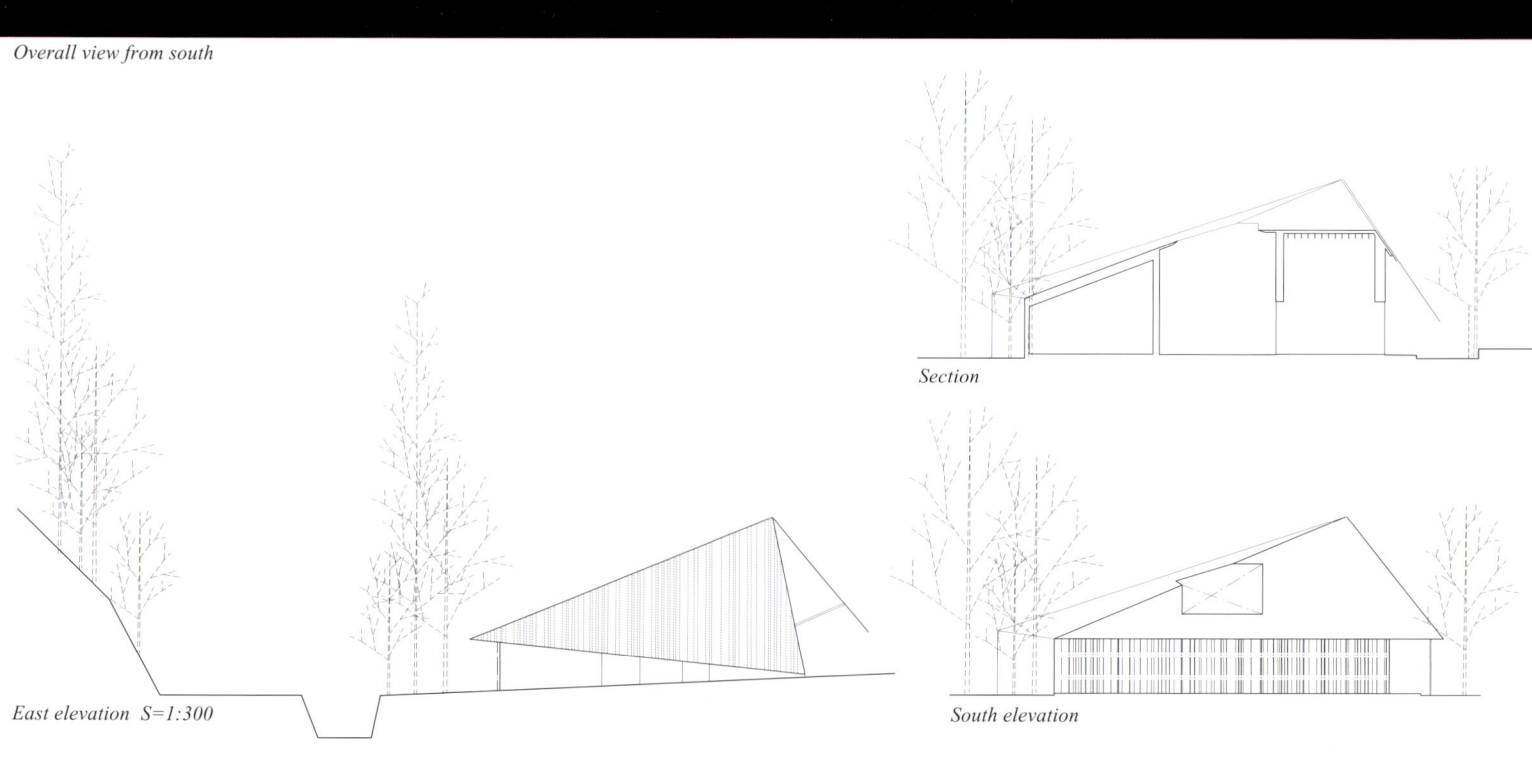

Overall view from south

East elevation S=1:300

Section

South elevation

Eaves of fiber reinforced plastics

Graveled approach with eaves on east

Site plan S=1:600

Hall

239

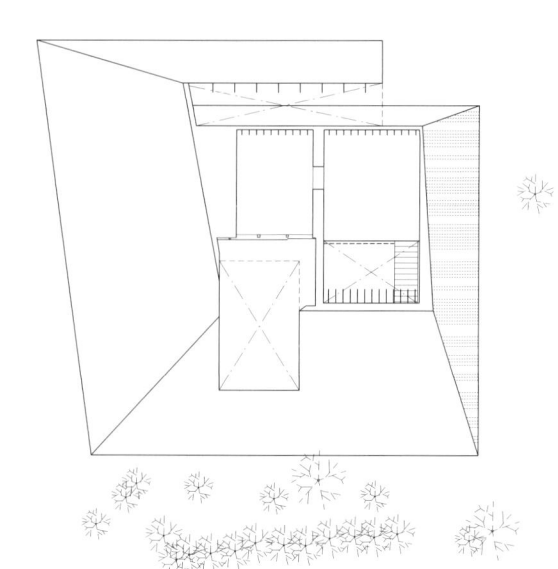

Second floor

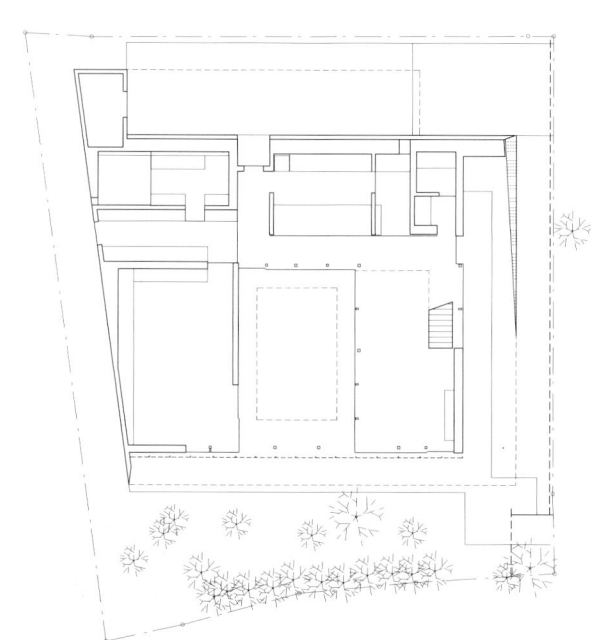

First floor S=1:300

Courtyard

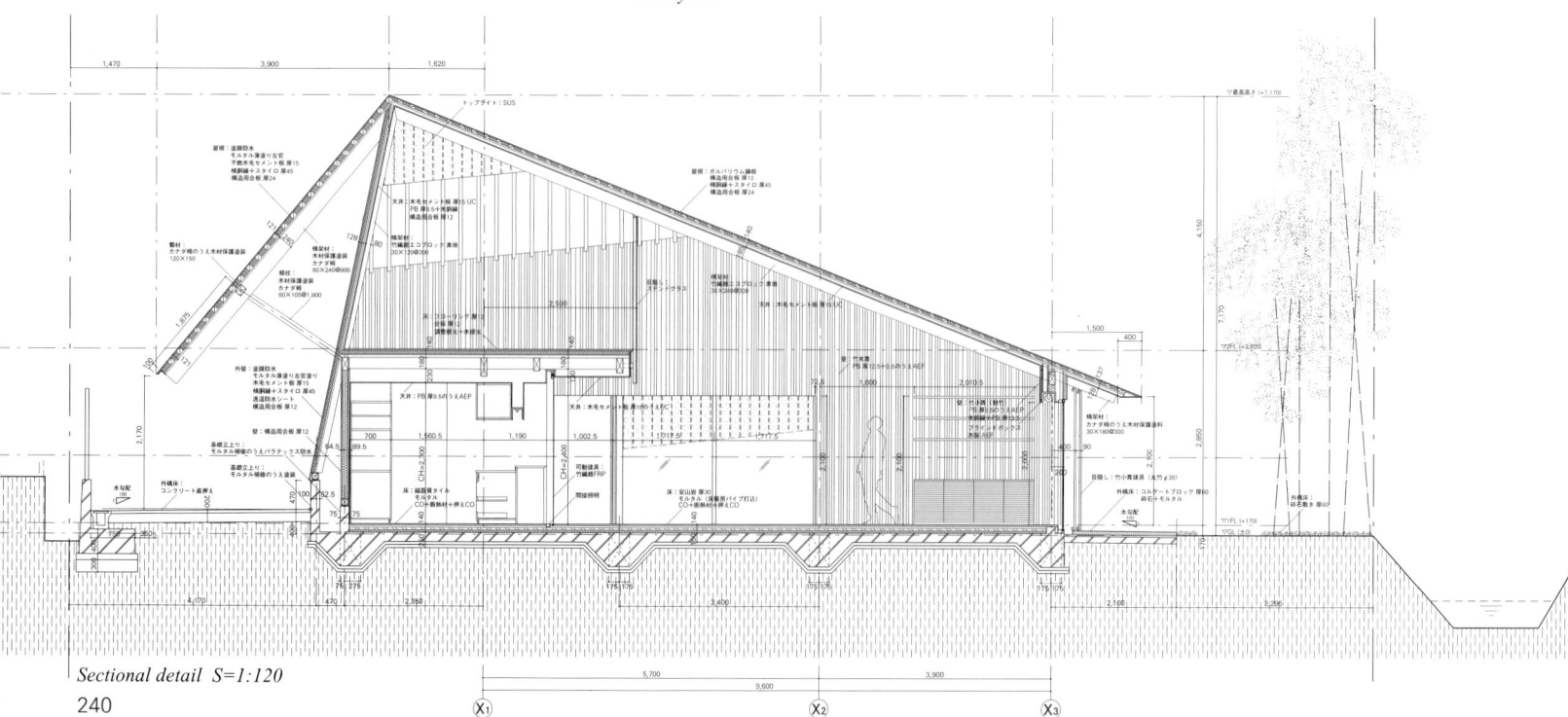

Sectional detail S=1:120

240

Hall: kitchen is behind partition of bamboo-fiber

View of hall through bamboo screen

Bedroom

Tatami room on second floor

敷地は，竹で覆われていた。この敷地で，竹に包まれた空間をつくってみたいと考えた。竹は建築で用いるには，大きな欠点のある材料である。乾燥すると簡単に割れてしまい，構造材としては使えないのである。竹をそのままではなく繊維にまで分解すると，様々な性質を与えることができた。竹の繊維を3,000トンのプレスで固形化した材料をみつけ，木とも竹とも違う独特な表情を持つその材料を，高強度・低伸縮である性質を利用し，大スパンの垂木として用いている。この竹の繊維は，FRPの芯材としても用いることができた。竹の繊維の上にプラスチック樹脂を塗り固めることで，半透明で琥珀色のFRPができる。この竹繊維FRPを，屋根の一部と間仕切りに用いた。さらに，竹の繊維を混入した和紙をみつけ，ロールブラインドとしている。

構造材でなければ，竹は古来より用いられてきた

The site was covered by bamboo. Here, I was inspired to make a space surrounded by bamboo. Bamboo has many deficits when used for architecture. As it easily cracks when dried, it could not be used for structural material. When we decomposed bamboo into fiber, we could give many characteristics to the substance. We found a bamboo material that its fiber was solidified with 3,000 ton press power. Using the strong and low elastic quality, we employed the material that has unique expression dissimilar from tree or bamboo for rafter of largely spanned space. The bamboo fiber could also be utilized as FRP's core material. Translucent amber-colored FRP is made by painting the bamboo fiber with plastic resin. We used the bamboo fiber FRP to a part of the roof and partition walls. Furthermore, we found washi (Japanese paper) that contains bamboo fiber and used it as a rolling blind.

Bamboo was used from old times as non-structural material, such as lining up bamboo for wickerwork pattern or foundation of earth walls. The earth walls of course would hide the bamboo when covered by dirt, so we decided to use the lined up bamboo as finish. When we aligned the bamboo, we realized that nodes' locations are strangely conspicuous. Where nodes are differs by each bamboo. When the same height bamboos are aligned, only nodes stand out. Of course, there is a design option to line up the bamboo, considering the position of nodes. However, here we varied the width of bamboo to 20 mm, 30 mm and 40 mm and adopted the method of giving differences to interval spaces. We thought it is more fitting layout to uneven natural materials.

When passing through the approach and entrance made of amber-colored bamboo fiber FRP, the space surrounded by bamboo rafters and bamboo walls appear. It is connected to bamboo forest that extends into outside of the site.

Skylight on second floor

材料である。竹を網代に並べたり，土壁の下地（竹小舞）にして用いてきた。この竹小舞は，土を塗ると当然見えなくなるのだが，竹の並んだ様子をそのまま仕上げとして用いることにした。竹小舞をつくり始め，整然と並んだ竹をみると，節の位置が妙に目立つことに気付いた。竹の節の位置は，1本ずつそれぞれ違う。等間隔に同じ巾の竹を並べると，節ばかりが目に付くのである。もちろん，節の位置をデザインしながら並べるという方法もあるのだが，ここでは竹の巾を変え（20，30，40ミリ），間隔もバラツキを与える方法を採用した。不均質な自然素材に対して，自然なレイアウトであると考えたのだ。

竹繊維FRPのつくる琥珀色のアプローチからエントランスを抜けると，竹の垂木と竹小舞に包まれた空間が現れる。外に拡がる竹林がつながっている。

Tatami room

Ryue Nishizawa

2011

Garden & House, Japan

It is a residence/office that is planned in the high density area having high-rise residence and office buildings. Two women who works on an editorial job wanted to work and live in the historical city environment. Concrete demand condition was an office, shared living space, individual room, guest room, bathroom and so on. We felt that this is a program in the middle of the function such as an office, a residence or a dormitory. The site had 8 x 4 meters extremely small rectangular shape and three sides of the site were surrounded by over 30 meter-high gigantic buildings without set back, which was a space like a bottom of the valley in between the gigantic buildings.

We wonder if we could design a building without walls because the width of the structure was subtract out of narrow site width if we built it by making structure walls as usual, and we felt the building would be very narrow. The final composition we selected is the plan that there are no walls, only horizontal slabs are vertically accumulated and a set of garden and room is arranged on each floor. We thought it makes open life that every room on each floor such as living room, private room, and bathroom has an exclusive garden to feel wind, to read or to enjoy the evening time. We can arrange rooms and gardens freely and distinctive relationship between rooms and gardens could be possible since rooms on each floor are smaller than slabs. We thought to design a transparent building without walls as a whole that we could feel maximally a bright environment in the dark site condition and happily and comfortably the special condition that we live in the center of the city as possible.
Ryue Nishizawa

West elevation facing street

Downward view: stacked garden

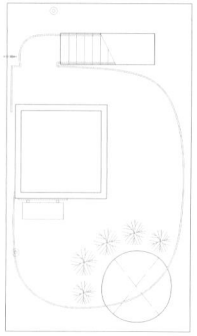

Roof

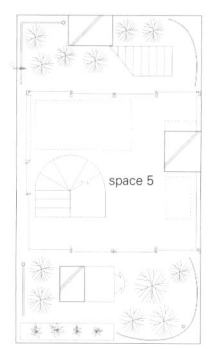

Fourth floor

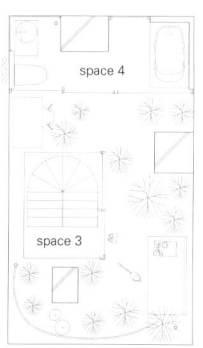

Third floor

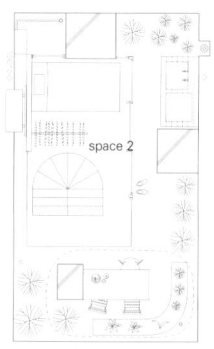

Second floor

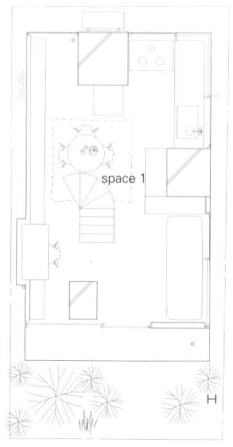

First floor S=1:150

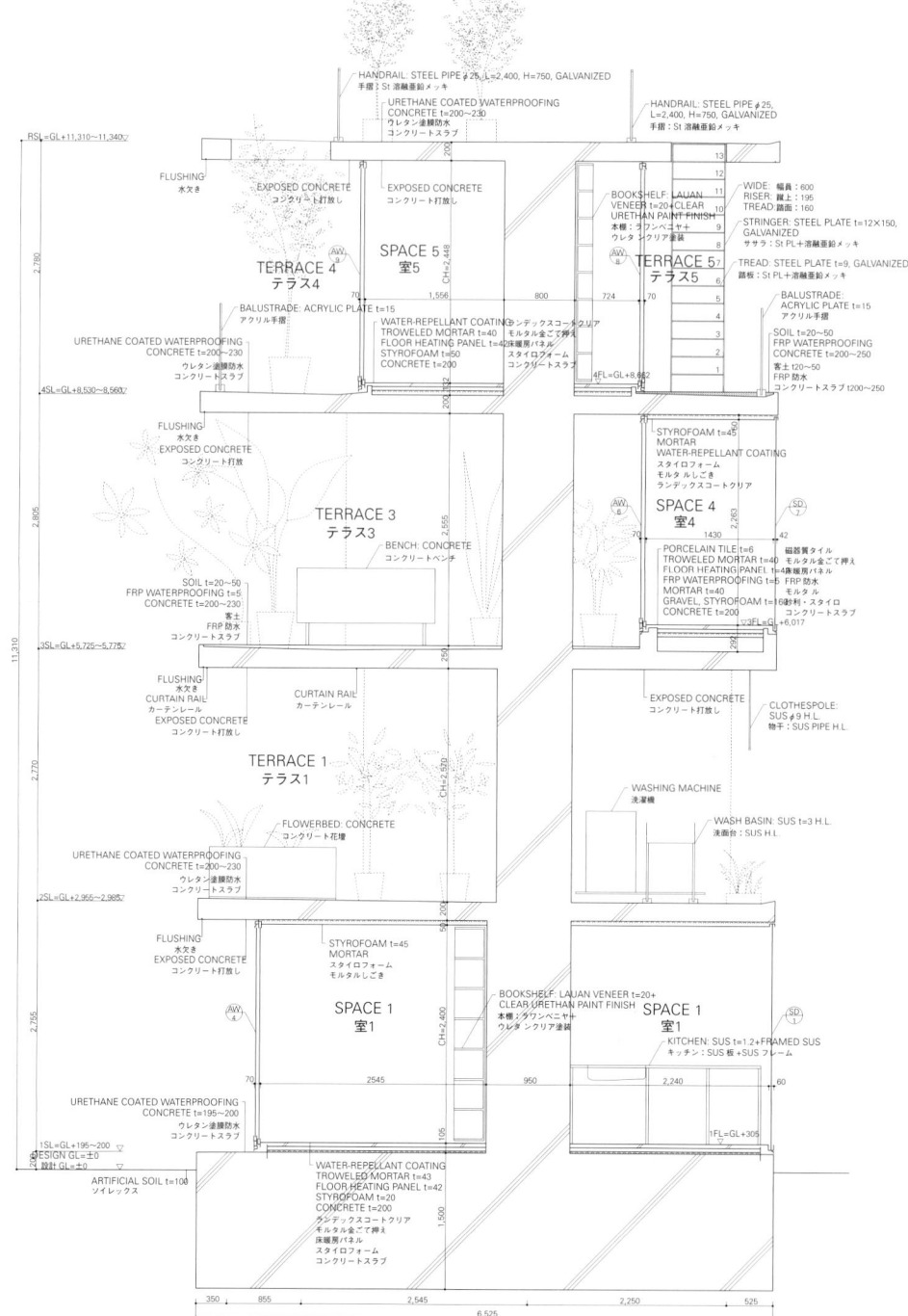

Sectional detail S=1:80

高層マンションやオフィスビルが多く建ち並ぶ高密度な街区に計画されている，住居兼オフィスである。住まい手は編集関係の仕事をしている女性二人で，歴史を持つ都市環境の中で仕事をしたり生活をしたりということを望まれた。具体的な要求条件としては，オフィス，共同リビングスペース，各個室，ゲストルーム，浴室，などであった。オフィスのような，住居のような，もしくは寮のような，いろいろな用途の中間のようなプログラムであると感じた。敷地は8×4メートルと極めて小さい長方形であり，左右と対面の敷地には高さ30メートルを越すたいへん巨大なビルがセットバックなしに建ち並んでいて，この敷地は巨大ビルに挟まれたまさに谷底のような空間であった。

普通に構造壁をつくって建物を考えると，狭い敷地幅員から構造の厚み分が更に差し引かれて，室内がたいへん狭くなると感じたので，壁がない建物を

つくれないかと考えた。最終的に選んだ構成は，各階壁なしのまま，水平スラブだけが垂直に積層されていき，各階に庭と個室がセットで配されるというものだ。各階の室はリビングだったり，各人のプライベートな室であったり，浴室であったりするが，そのどれもが専用の庭を持ち，屋外に出て風を感じたり，読書をしたり夕涼みをしたりといった開放的な生活ができるように考えた。各階の室はどれもスラブの大きさよりも小さいために，部屋と庭を自由な形で取ることができ，階によって異なる部屋と庭の関係をつくることが可能となった。全体として壁のない透明な建物であり，暗い敷地条件の中でも最大限に明るい環境を感じられるように，また町の中心に住むという特別な状況をなるべく楽しく快適に感じることができるようにと考えて設計している。

（西沢立衛）

Downward view of second floor

Second floor: view toward terrace from space 2

Terrace on fourth floor

Tadao Ando

2011

House in Monterrey, Monterrey, Mexico

Aerial view

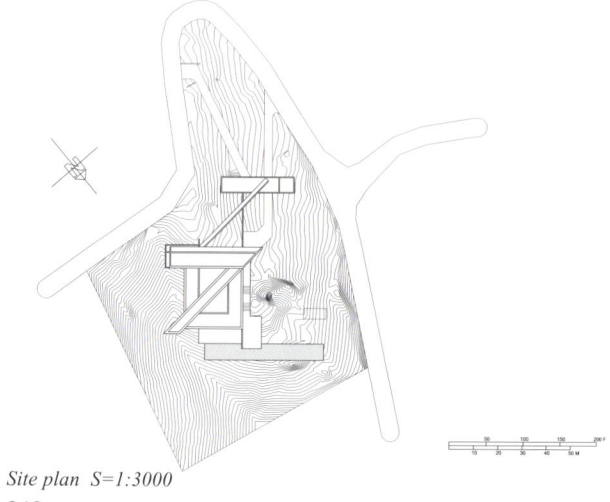

Site plan S=1:3000

Looking south from swimming pool

Swimming pool: looking northwest

Swimming pool. Master bedroom (left) and family dining room (right)

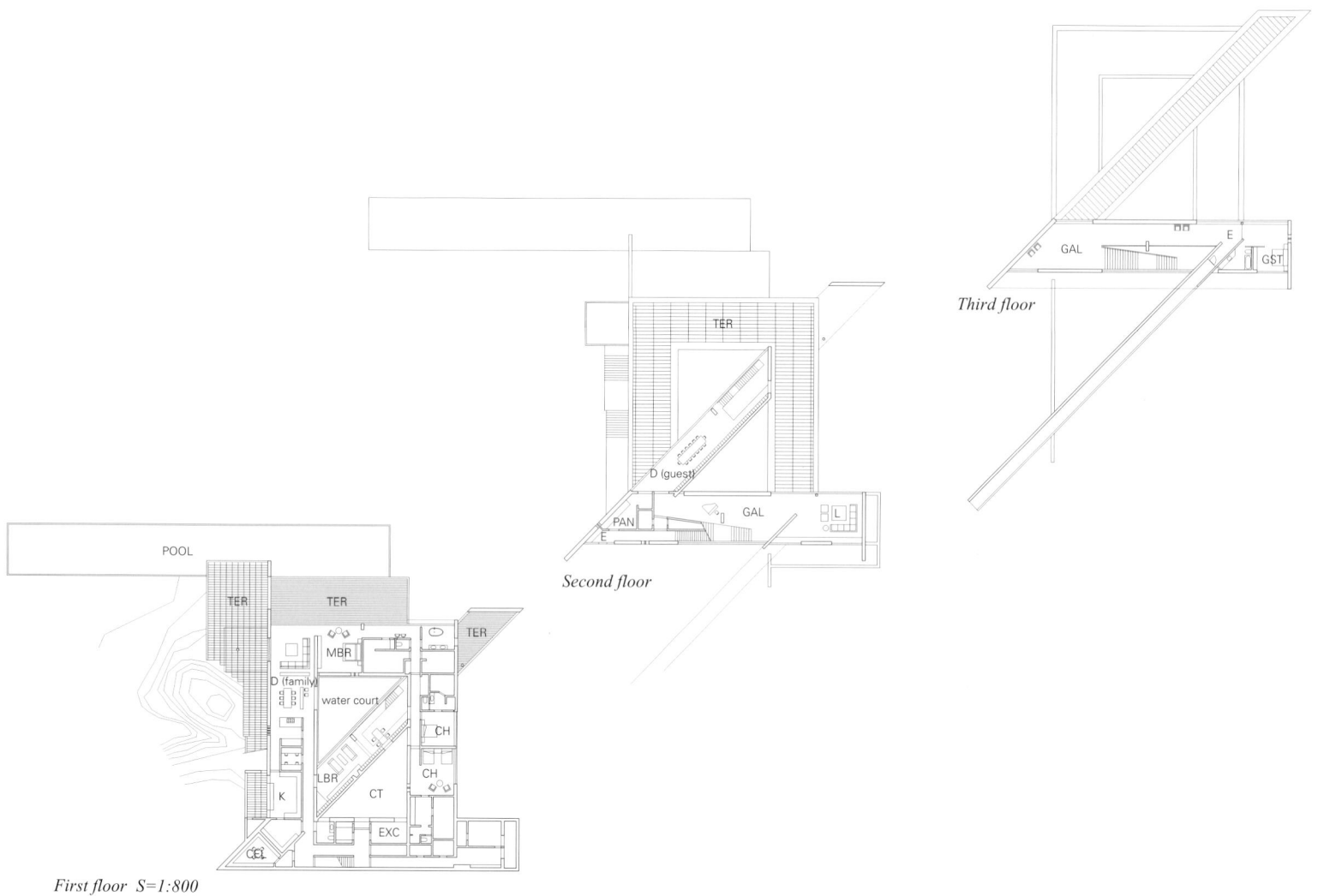

Third floor

Second floor

First floor S=1:800

Looking northeast from gallery on third floor

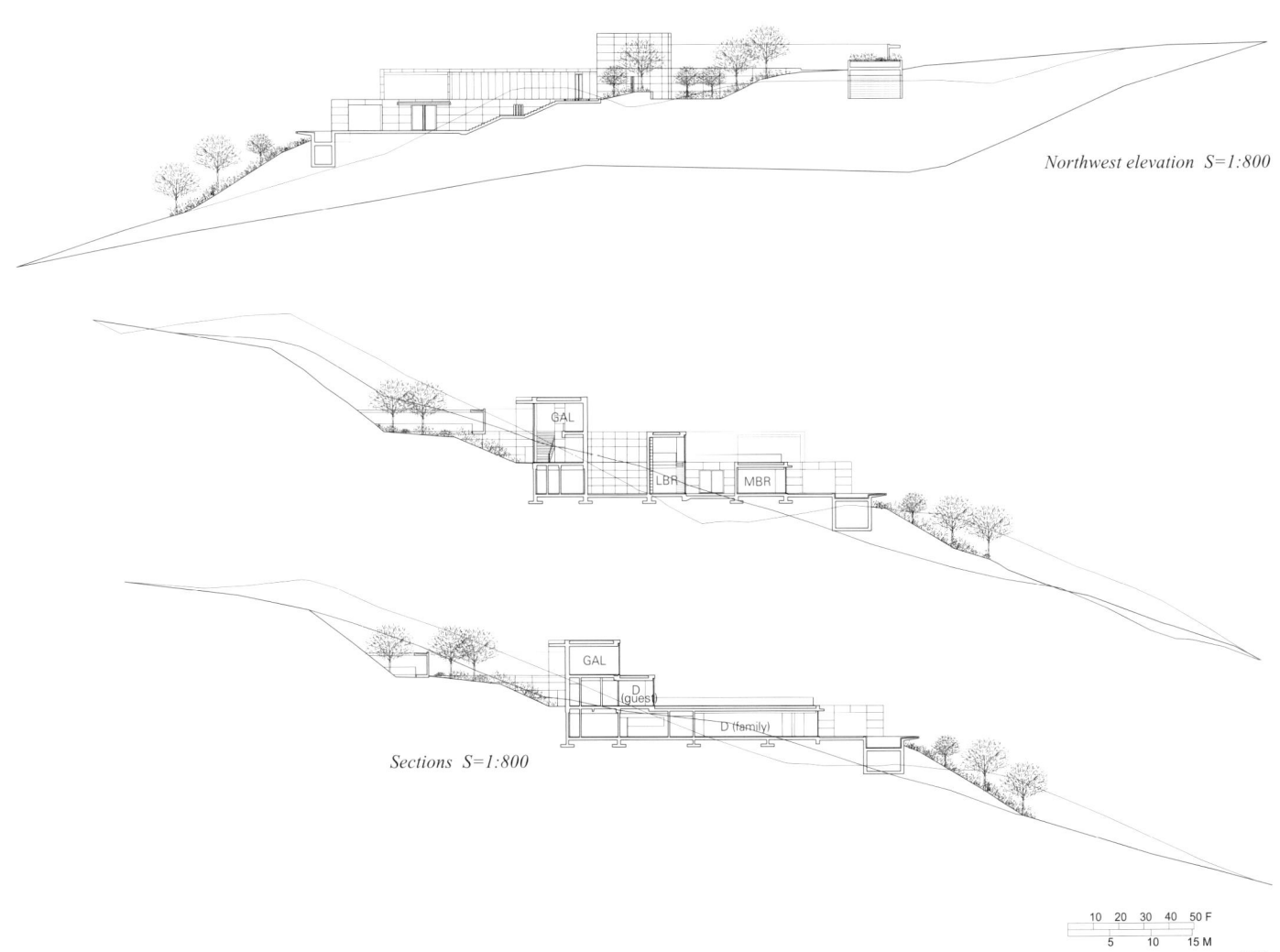

Northwest elevation S=1:800

Sections S=1:800

251

Family dining room on first floor

Master bedroom on first floor

Guest room on third floor

Looking down to the third largest industrial town in Mexico, Monterrey, the site is located at the foot of the mountains in a National Park. This is a residential project with a total floor area of 1,500 square meters.

At this site with a great view surrounded by abundant nature, the client requested a house which merges into the surrounding environment, bringing the beautiful views inside with perfect privacy. I conceived to realize the theme—open but closed to the outside—by using geometry corresponding to this theme.

The main square volume is set into the sloping site with the 'Z' element positioned above, running back toward the upper part of the slope. This three dimensional composition makes it possible to generate relationships between the different internal and external spaces, on the three different levels within this house. The private residential zone is at the lowest level and two triangular courtyards are surrounded by the square volume at the center.

The continuous volume of the public zone including a gallery space, forms a 'Z' as it climbs up the slope within the two story volume. There is a library at the axis of this residence which connects the private and public zones. At each level, various terraces which are generated as a result of this geometric composition dynamically draw the outside spaces in. The main approach from the upper part of the site is connected to the highest level of the public zone.

The great Mexican architect, Luis Barragán, achieved a marvelous architectural fusion of traditional and modern form. Barragán used simple vocabulary such as distinctive abstract forms and strong bright colors and achieved a modern Mexican architecture nobody can follow. I paid my best respect to him and conceived to develop his essences of modern architecture in my own way. The result is a dynamic 'Z' space where openness and closure, calmness and dynamism, and light and shadow cross over.
Tadao Ando

Main entrance

Gallery on second floor: looking northwest

Library on first floor: looking east

　敷地はメキシコ第三の産業都市であるモンテレイの市街地を見下ろす，山裾の国立公園内に位置する。延べ床面積約1,500平米の住宅の計画である。
　豊かな自然に囲まれた絶景の敷地に，クライアントは周辺環境に溶け込み，美しい眺望を存分に引き込みつつ，プライバシーの確保された住宅を望んだ。外部に対して開きつつ閉じること——これらの主題に呼応する幾何学により実現しようと考えた。
　建物は，斜面に埋め込むように配したロの字型のヴォリュームの一翼が，斜面上方に向かってZ字型にセットバックした形を持つ。この立体的構成により，住居内の三つの異なるレベルに，異なる内外空間の関係をつくることができる。プライベートの住居ゾーンは最下層部に，ヴォリュームによって囲まれた二つの三角形の中庭を中心に配置する。
　ギャラリーを含むパブリック・ゾーンは，そこから上の2層分のレベル内に，Z字型を描きつつ斜面に沿って上昇するヴォリュームの連続として展開する。プライベートとパブリックのゾーンをつなぐ基準軸から45度角度を振った棟には，この住居の核となるライブラリーが配されている。各レベルには幾何学的構成の結果生まれるテラスがさまざまな形で取り付き，建物内に外部空間をダイナミックに引き入れる。敷地上方からのメインアプローチは，パブリック・ゾーンの最上部に接続する。
　かつてメキシコに生きて，建築による伝統と現代の見事な融合を成し得た偉大なる建築家に，ルイス・バラガンがいる。バラガンの建築は独特の抽象形態，派手な色使いという，ある意味で単純なヴォキャブラリーを駆使しながら，誰にも真似できない，メキシコの近代建築をつくりあげた。その仕事に敬意を払い，そのエッセンスを私なりの方法で現代建築として展開させようと考えたのが，開放と閉鎖，静と動，光と影が交錯する，Z型によるダイナミックな住空間だった。

（安藤忠雄）

Evening view of library (first floor) and guest dining room (second floor)

Downward view of terrace on second floor

Sou Fujimoto

2011

House NA, Tokyo, Japan

South elevation

Looking east from living space 01: library on left above

House like Single Tree

House standing within a residential district in central Tokyo. To dwell in a house, amongst the dense urbanity of small houses and structures can be associated to living within a tree.

Tree has many branches, all being a setting for a place, and a source of activities of diverse scales. The intriguing point of a tree is that these places are not hermetically isolated but are connected to one another in its unique relativity. To hear one's voice from across and above, hopping over to another branch, a discussion taking place across branches by members from separate branches. These are some of the moments of richness encountered through such spatially dense living.

By stratifying floor plates almost furniture-like in scale, throughout the space, this house proposes living quarters orchestrated by its spatio-temporal relativity with one another, akin to a tree. The house can be considered a large single-room, and, if each plate is understood as rooms, it can equally be said that the house is a mansion of multifarious rooms. A unity of separation and coherence. Elements from furniture scales come together to collectively form scale of rooms, and further unto those of dwellings, of which renders the city. The steps between the plates at times will become seating and desks, at times as a device segmenting a territory, and at times each akin to leaves of the foliage filtering light down into the space. Providing intimacy for when two individuals chooses to be close to one another, or for a place afar still sharing each other's being. For when accommodating a group of guests, the distribution of people across the entire house will form a platform for a network type communication in space.

The white steel-frame structure itself shares no resemblance to a tree. Yet the life lived and the moments experienced in this space is a contemporary adaptation of the richness once experienced by the ancient predecessors from the time when they inhabited trees. Such is an existence between city, architecture, furniture and the body, and is equally between nature and artificiality.

Sou Fujimoto

South view from bedroom: bathroom on right above, sunroom on left

Entrance

〈1本の樹木のような住宅〉

東京都心の住宅地の中に建つ夫婦二人のための住宅。小さな家々が寄り集まった高密度な都市の中で1軒の家に住むことは，1本の樹木の中に住むことに似ているのではないだろうか。

樹木にはいくつかの枝がある。それぞれの枝の上には居場所があって，さまざまなスケールの活動の拠点となっている。樹木が面白い点は，それらのさまざまな居場所が，決して単体で独立しているのではなく，適度にお互いに関係を持ちあっているところだ。斜め上の場所から声が聞こえてきたり，となりの枝に飛び移ったり，またこの枝と向こうの枝とを両方使って何人かの人が談笑している。これはまさに，高密度で立体的に生活することの豊かさであろう。

この住宅は，家具のような小さな床プレートが立体的に空間の中に浮遊し積層することによって，そんな樹木のような立体的な関係性による生活の場所をつくり出す。家全体が大きなワンルームであるとも言えるし，床の数だけ部屋があるとするなら，十数個の部屋がある豪邸とも言える。分節性と一体性の同居。家具のスケールから，それらが集まって部屋のようなスケールとなり，さらに家のスケール，そして都市へと溶けていく。プレート同士の段差が椅子や机のように機能するときもあれば，領域を分節するときもあり，また光が差し込む木漏れ日の葉の1枚1枚ともなる。二人が同じ場所に寄りそうときもあれば，気配だけを感じつつそれぞれの居場所に逃げ込む時もある。友人が大勢来た時にはさまざまな床レベルにさまざまに人が分布して家全体がネットワーク状のコミュニケーションの場となる。

白い鉄骨でつくられたこのフレームは，それ自体，樹木に似ているわけではない。しかしここで行われる生活や体験は，太古の昔に人類が樹上で体験した豊かな立体的生活の現代的な再発見である。それは都市と建築と家具と身体のあいだであり，自然と人工のあいだである。

（藤本壮介）

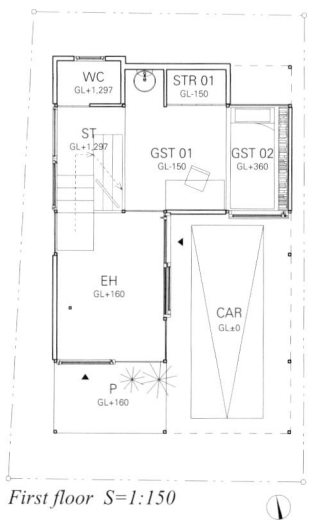

First floor S=1:150

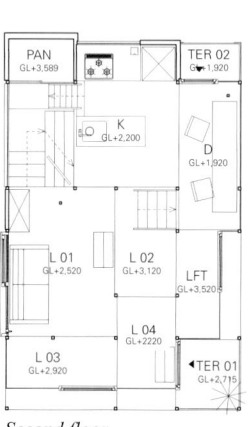

Second floor

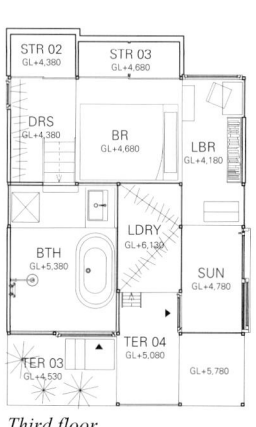

Third floor

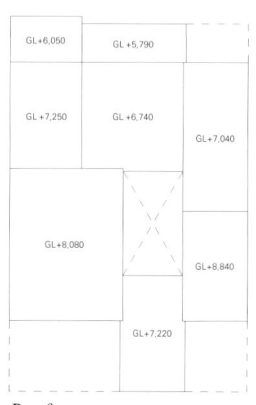

Roof

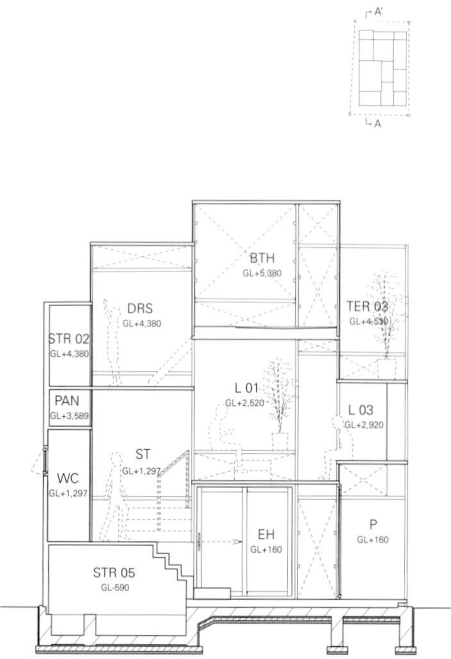

Section A-A'

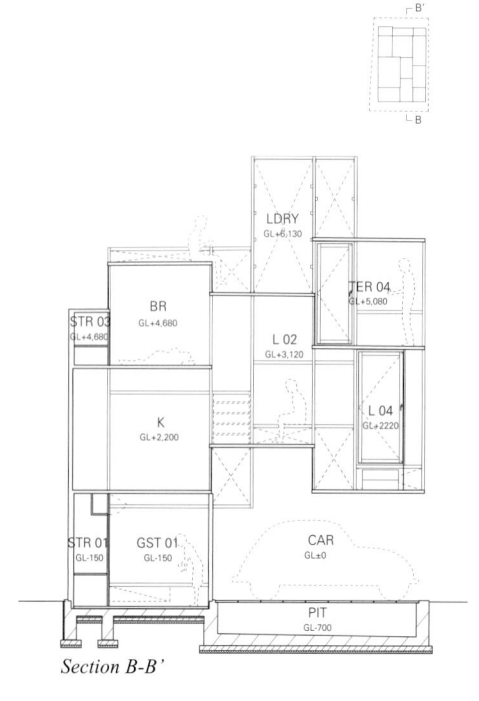

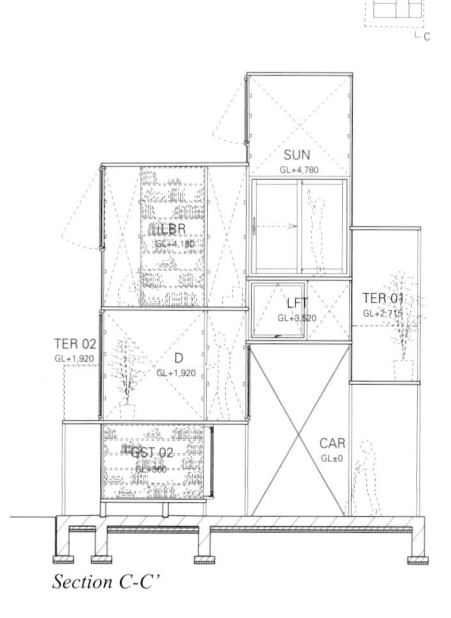

Section B-B'

Section C-C'

View from sunroom toward library below

Southeast corner: stratifying floor plates

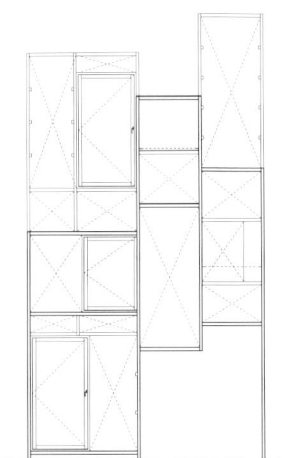

South elevation 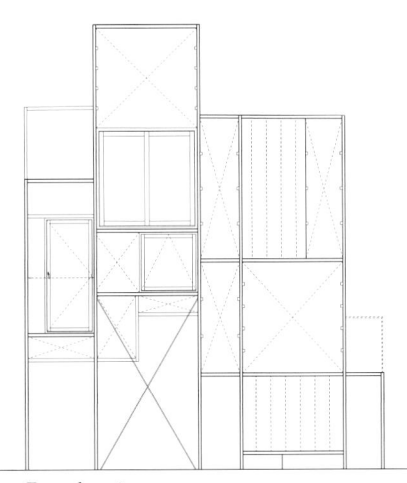 *East elevation* 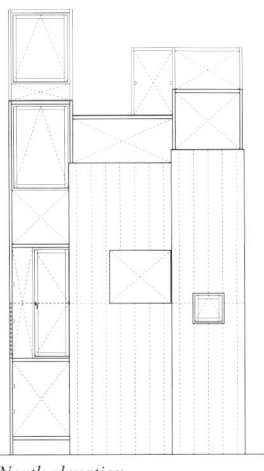 *North elevation* 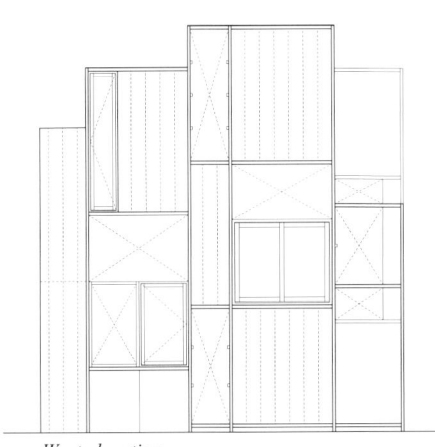 *West elevation*

Smiljan Radic

2012

Red Stone House, Santiago, Chile

Garden: view from east

South elevation S=1:400

Terrace/dining room (left) and garden (right)

Evening view: terrace (left), dining room (center) and living room (right)

Garden view from under bedroom wing

Upper floor

Upper floor

Lower floor S=1:600

This house is set in an existing garden with thirty-meter high trees that form shady interior space.

In a simple manner, the house incites its users to stroll through the garden. Its floor plan maintains a homogeneous horizontal level in the interior that corresponds to the upper elevation of the plot. The exposed reinforced concrete therefore emerges from the ground, allowing for the conventional limits of the closed yard it proposes to be altered.

This operation extends the perception of the space to the edges of the plot, bordered plants of smaller size and alters the conventional view of the trees that surround it.
Smiljan Radic

この住宅は以前からある庭の中に佇む。庭に並ぶ高さ30メートルの木々は室内に日陰の場を提供してくれる。

この建物はごく自然と，訪れた者に庭を通り抜けたくなるような気持ちにさせる。平面計画においては，室内の水平方向で，ある一定の高さを保持するようにした。それは建物上方の立面にも反映されている。一般的な囲われた庭にありがちな限られた領域にせぬよう注意を払いながら，打放しコンクリートを地面から立ち上げる。

こうした操作により，この住まいにおける空間認識は，敷地端部，さらにその境界上に生える小さな植物群にまで拡がっていく。また，この操作は敷地を取り囲む木々の眺望も一変させてくれる。
（スミルハン・ラディック）

Section B

Section A

Living room: stone can be revoluted to change relation of living and dining room (behind)

◁ △ *Staircase to study*

Study on upper floor

Study

Smiljan Radic　　　　　　　　　　　　　　　　2012

House for the Poem of the Right Angle, Vilches, Chile

View from southwest. Ramp to entrance on right

View from west. Sliding window of bedroom

The House for the Poem of the Right Angle shown in *Gallery MA*, Tokyo, November 2010, is the last refuge we have designed; it is a blind case facing a privileged landscape of mountains and oak woods.

The house assumes that the inhabitant knows where the river flows, but does not see it because he simply knows about it, it is permanently recognized at a distance.
Smiljan Radic

View from southeast

View from northeast

Kitchen (left) and courtyard (right)

Pair of skylight at living room

Courtyard: view toward kitchen on south

Living room

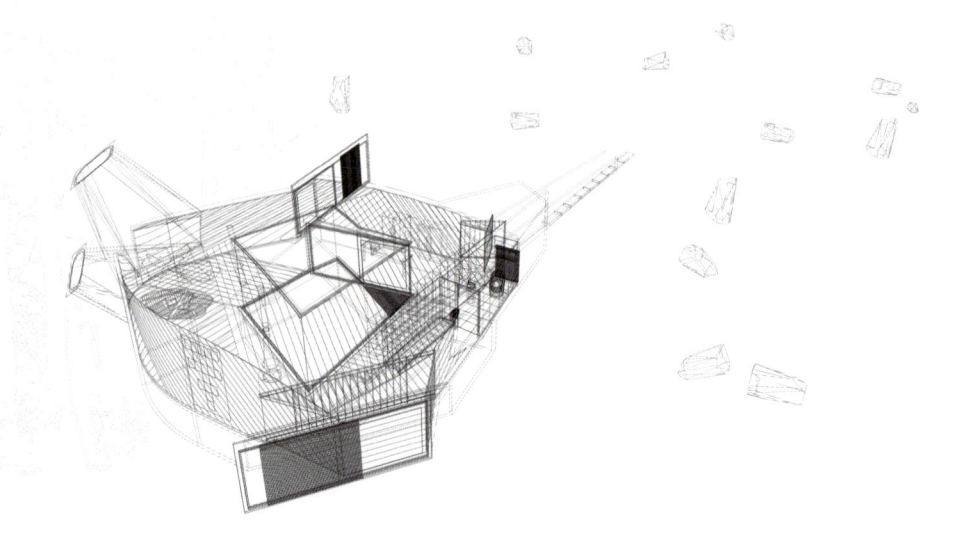

Isometric

Courtyard: view from kitchen

Plan

271

Looking east from bedroom

Bedroom on west

この「『直角の詩』のための住宅」は，東京・ギャラリー間で2010年11月に展示された，究極の隠れ家─山々の景観やナラの森といった恵まれた環境にありながら，それらに対して閉じた容器─である。

この住宅では，何処に川が流れているかを知るが故に，住まい手はあえてそれを視覚的には捉えようとしない，といった状況を仮定している。つまりここでは，川の存在は永久に縮まらない，ある一定の距離をおいて認識されるのだ。

（スミルハン・ラディック）

Children's bedroom

Bedrooms

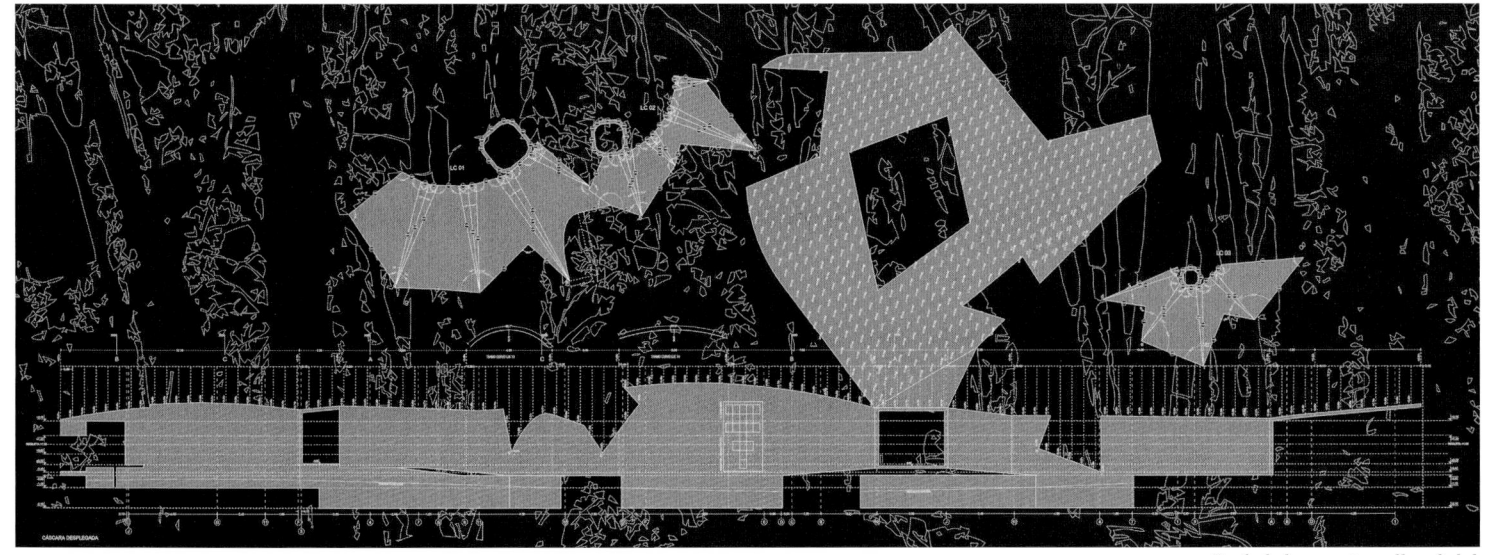

Exploded concrete wall and slab

Bercy Chen

2012

Edgeland Residence, Austin, Texas, U.S.A.

View from pool

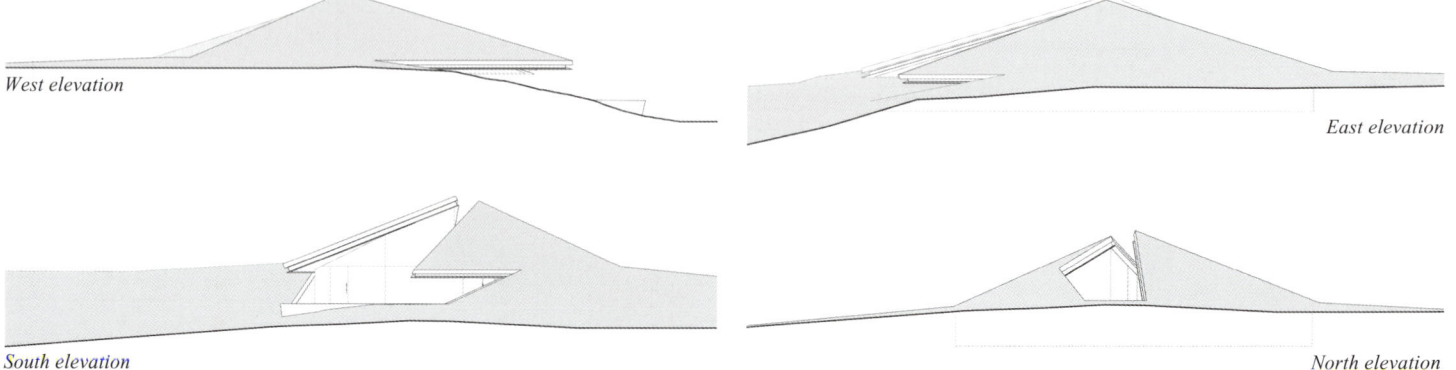

West elevation

East elevation

South elevation

North elevation

In an increasingly generic and de-natured world, we are interested in producing architecture tuned to the specificity of a place. *The Edgeland House* was commissioned by a science fiction writer fascinated by 21st century human habitation in the urban frontiers of abandoned industrial zones. Not unlike Col Charles Goodnight's first dug out at the JA ranch in 19th century Texas, the design is inspired by the vernacular of the "pit house", one of the oldest housing typology in North America used by Native Americans through the ages.

This brownfield reclaim project minimized disturbance to the site, as the previous excavations to remove a Chevron pipeline left a scar on the bluff, the two new green roofed wings sheltering each other from the sun is an attempt to heal the land by restoring the slope and bring wildlife back.

This approach addresses the climate of central Texas and utilize thermal capacity of earth to regulate temperature, while the linear courtyard down the center allows fresh air to flow between the bluff and the river below.

The courtyard is a theater for observing migrating humming birds, monarch butterflies, even ant colonies... etc, heightening one's awareness of nature in an urban setting. We collaborated with the Lady Bird Wildflower Center to reintroduce over 40 native species of wildflowers and grass to preserve the local ecosystem.

Living/dining room wing (right) and bedroom wing (left)

Living/dining room: view toward bedroom wing

Site plan

Roof

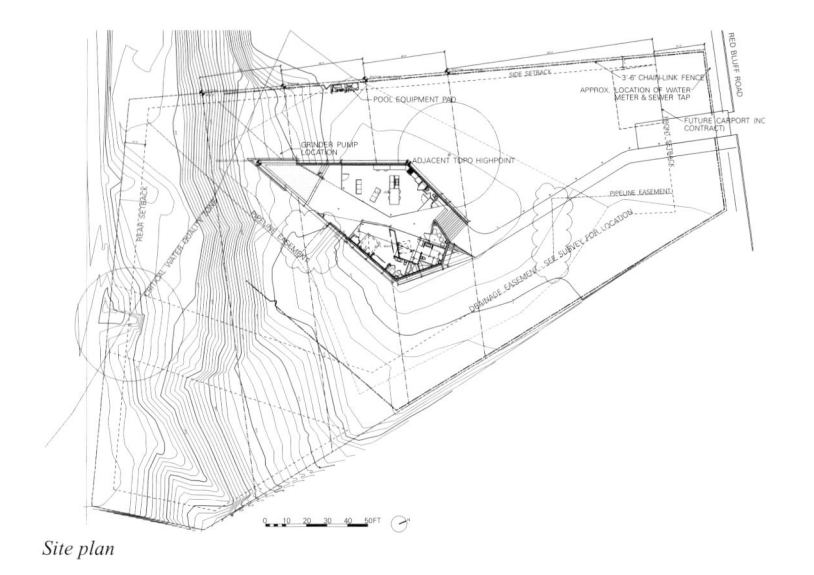

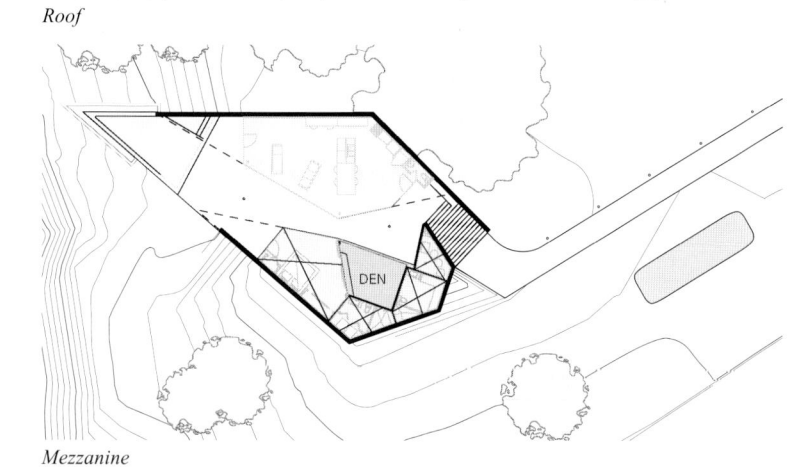

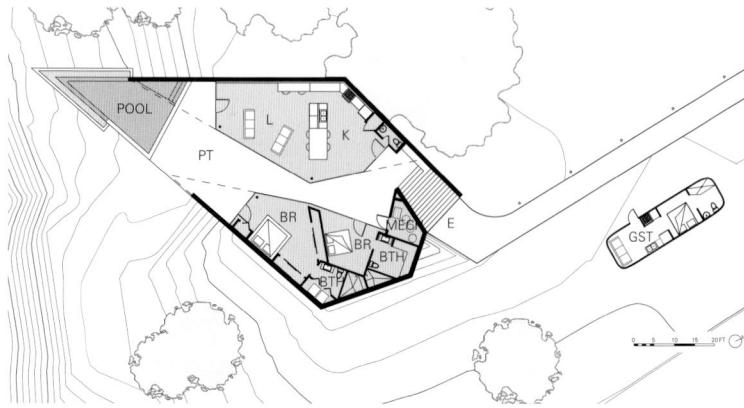

Mezzanine

First floor

Sections

　一層包括的に変化する世界に対し，場所の固有性と調和する建築をつくることがこの計画の出発点である。「エッジランド・ハウス」は21世紀の人類が住む都市のフロンティア，放棄された工業地域に魅了されたサイエンス・フィクション作家から依頼を受けたものである。これはテキサス州のJA牧場で19世紀に初めて建設された地下壕とよく似たもので，ヴァナキュラーな「竪穴式住居」から着想を得たものである。これは何世代にもわたり，アメリカ先住民が北アメリカで住み続けてきた最も古い居住形式の一つである。

　この計画ではブラウンフィールド（土壌汚染地域）を再生するため，敷地を乱さない方法が検討された。以前行われたシェブロン社のパイプライン撤去の際の掘削の傷跡が断崖にそのままの姿で残されているため，屋上を新しく緑化した2棟の住宅は，日射からお互いを保護すると共に，斜面を復元し野生動物を呼び戻すことによって大地を癒そうとしている。

　このようなアプローチは中央テキサスの気候を考慮したもので，温度を適温に保つため，土の持つ保温力が活用された。新鮮な空気が断崖とその下の川のあいだを流れるように，中央の中庭は直線状に計画された。

　中庭ではハチドリやオオカバマダラが移動する様子，あるいは蟻の巣などの自然を一望できる。都市空間において，ここは自然への意識を高めてくれる場所となる。この計画では地域の生態系を保全するために，レディ・バード・ワイルドフラワー・センターの協力によって，40種類に及ぶ野生植物や芝草が移植された。

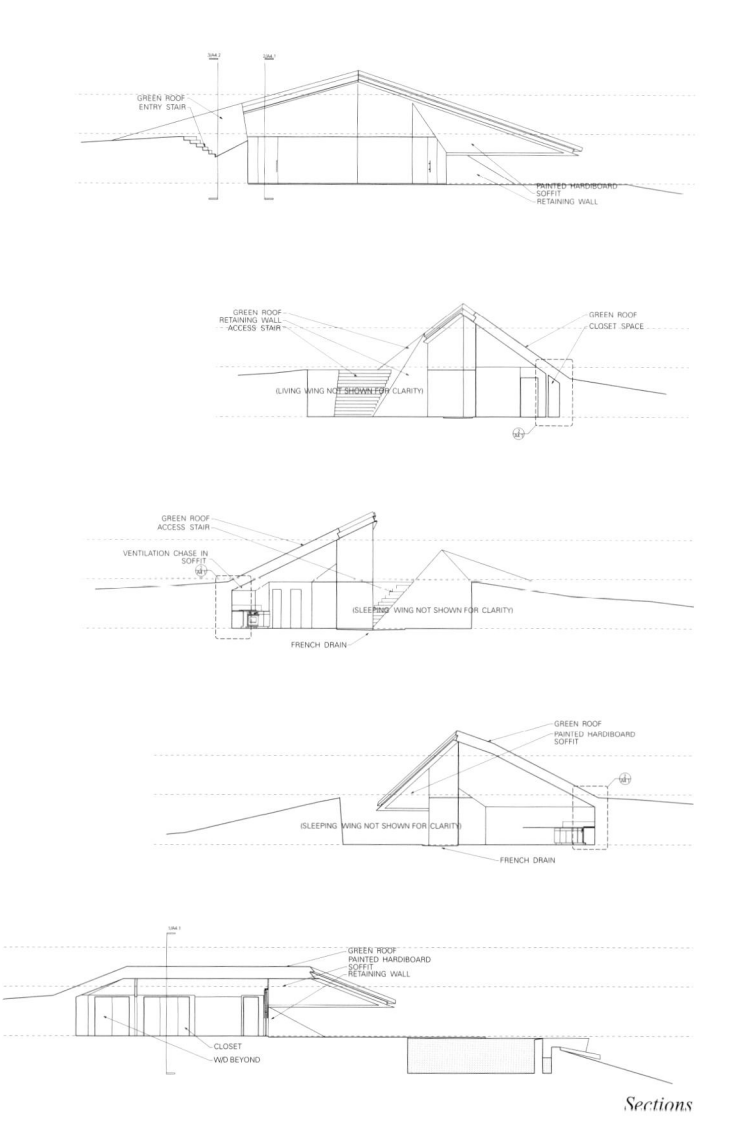

Living/dining room: looking west

◁ △ *Master bedroom*

SPBR Arquitetos　　　2013

Swimming Pool in São Paulo, São Paulo, Brazil

Street view from southeast

Patio: view toward street

Pool with cascade: view toward semi-outdoor dining room

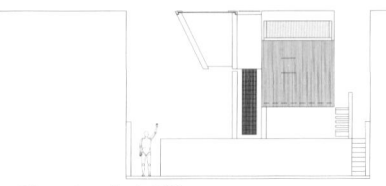

Elevation S=1:300

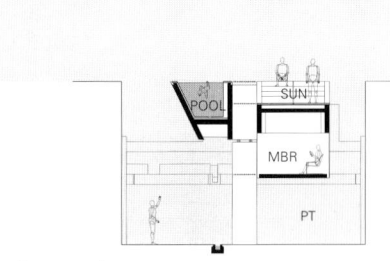

Cross section

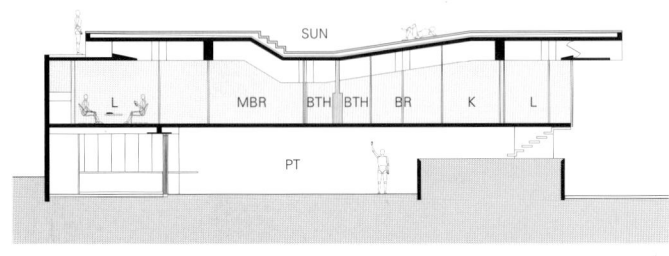

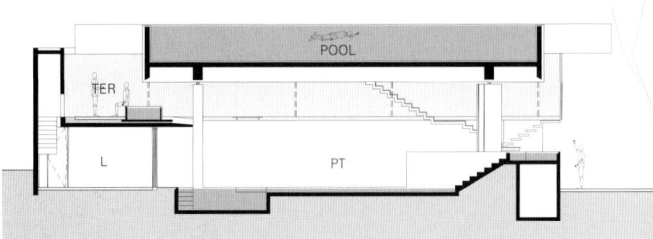

Longitudinal sections S=1:300

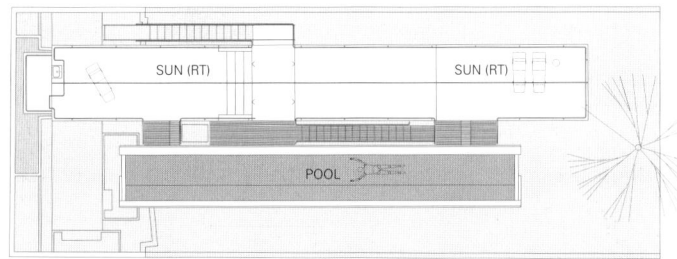

Level +5.60/+6.475

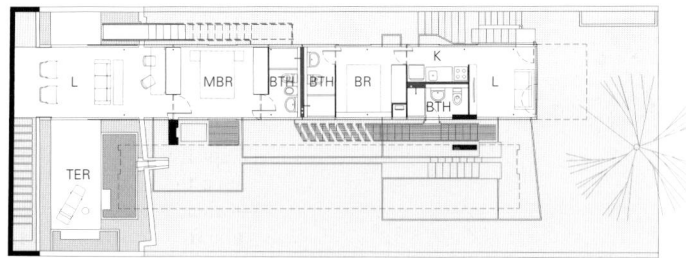

Level +2.80

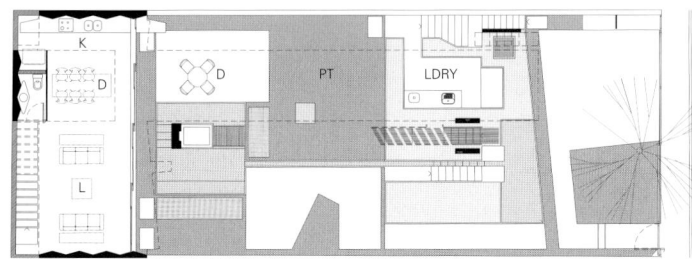

Level 0.00/+1.40 S=1:300

Patio. Steel staircase leading to roof terrace

Dug into Air—Swimming Pool in São Paulo
Clouds, drizzle, rain, snow or hail, in all its physical states water is related to sky.

However, if we are requested to think about a (swimming) pool, our imagination automatically starts to dig into the ground. Seas, lakes, and ponds explain the reason we react in that direction: essentially, a pool fells like a piece of a lake. It makes sense, the image corresponds to the word, water that rests smoothly on the ground. Water defines the surface.

But if I mention a specific type of pool, a water tank or a water tower, we first imagine an elevated volume of water, a pool detached from the ground level. In this case, hydrostatic pressure is a requirement to fulfill pipes, to supply water. Water level holds a potential possibility.

While walking on the ground, we could ask: where is the surface? In the specific sense of the word, surface has no layers or thickness. However, if one walks in a city like São Paulo (or New York), the ground level does not correspond to the surface anymore. There are some pieces

Living room

Kitchen

of the ground that haven't been touched by the sunlight for decades since buildings have permanently shaded them.

In this specific site, the neighborhood's average height is defined by the zoning code: 6 meters high. No side setbacks are required. The east neighbor building shades our site the entire morning until noon, when the west neighbor building starts to shade it for the whole afternoon. Therefore, if there is a pool to be built, exposed to the sunlight the whole day, it is crucial to define its surface: 6 meters above the ground level.

The assumption here is like to swim in a water tower and to enjoy that potential as a design possibility. One more water 'state' related to the sky of São Paulo.

Weekend House in City
São Paulo is a metropolis of 20 million people. It is approximately one hour from the coast. Because of severe traffic jams, its inhabitants spend hours commuting every day. On weekends, especially in the summer, hundreds of thousands drive to the beach causing jams on the roads as well.

In order to avoid being stuck in traffic during weekends, we received an unexpected but rather logical demand as a counterflow action: a weekend house in downtown São Paulo.

As an anti-FAR (floor area ratio) approach, a swimming pool, a solarium and a garden are the main elements of this project. In a properly inverted hierarchy, everything else on this program is complementary: a bedroom, a small apartment for a caretaker, and a space to cook and receive friends.

The site is very central, between an arterial avenue, Avenida Faria Lima, and a metropolitan infrastructural axis (road and railway) built on the Pinheiros river shore. Also, the site is exactly under the airport conical zone, meaning all flights coming from Rio de Janeiro fly over the site about each 7 minutes.

Pool and solarium were displayed as parallel volumes. Two columns were located in the 1 meter wide gap between them. The 12 meters span is faced on one side by beams supporting the pool and on the other by beams that support the solarium and also hang the floor underneath. Structurally, the mass of the pool counterweights the volume which holds inhabited spaces. In other words, water is balanced by the beach.

The ground level was kept free from any construction in order to achieve the maximum garden area ratio. As a result there are three different layers or three levels for three different moods: ground level (garden—introspective or encompassed by the site limits), apartment level (the only indoor space floating above the ground and underneath the pool), and rooftop (swimming pool and solarium, an extroverted or panoramic space).

This building and its program differs from the focus of traditional architectural projects in two ways: the metropolis becomes a possible place to stay and enjoy during the weekends and elements generally considered secondary in a big house become fundamental components.
Angelo Bucci

Patio, pool and living room (center)

Roof terrace (solarium) with swimming pool

〈空気に溶け込む—サンパウロのスイミング・プール〉
雲，霧雨，雨，雪，雹。これら全ての物理状態において，水は空と深く関わっている。

その一方で（スイミング）プールについて考える時，我々の想像力は大地へと反射的に向かう。海や湖沼の存在は，そのような関心の所在を解き明かす。プールとは小さな湖と同じく水を湛えるものである。自然の理。イメージと言語との符合。水は滑らかに地面へと溜まる。水はサーフェスを定義する。

また，貯水槽や貯水塔といった類のプールでは，空中における水の存在を想起する。プールは地面から切り離されるようにして存在している。ここでは配管に水を満たして供給するため，静水力学における水圧の力が要求される。水位には潜在的可能性が存在している。

地面を歩きながら自己へと問いかけてみる。サーフェスとは何を指すのか？　言葉の持つ意味に即して言えば，サーフェスにはレイヤーや厚みといった概念は存在しない。その一方，サンパウロ（や，ニューヨーク）のような都市を歩いてみると，地面とサーフェスとは符合しないことが分かる。いくつかの場所では建築物が地面に対し永遠にその影を落とすため，何十年ものあいだ日に当たることがなくなってしまっている。

この敷地では建築規制によって街区の平均高さは6メートルと定義されている。その一方で隣地斜線制限は不要と見なされた。東側の隣地の建築物は午前から昼間にかけて，西側の隣地の建築物は昼間から午後にかけて，敷地に影を落とす。そのためプールを建築しようとする場合には，日光を一日中浴びることができるようにサーフェスを地面から6メートル上空に浮かぶ平面，と定義しておく必要がある。

そこで想定されたのは，貯水塔で泳ぐことの楽しみを建築における潜在的可能性とすることである。これはサンパウロの空に現れる，もうひとつの水の「状態」と言える。

〈都市の週末住宅〉
サンパウロは2千万人の人口を抱える大都市である。海岸までの距離はおおよそ1時間。そのため，過酷な交通渋滞によって，居住者は毎日何時間もの通勤を強いられている。週末になると，特に夏の時期には，何十万もの人が海岸までドライブをするので渋滞は相変わらずである。

私たちに要求されたのは，このような週末の交通渋滞に巻き込まれるのを避けるために考えられた，意外にも合理的な対抗策である。それがサンパウロ市街地の週末住宅である。

FAR（容積率）を最大化するために，スイミング・プール，サンルーム及び庭が住宅の中心となるように計画された。ヒエラルキーを倒置させることにより，その他のプログラム，すなわち寝室，管理人室，友人を料理でもてなすゲスト・スペースは全て補完的なものとして計画された。

敷地は幹線道路であるファリア・リマ通りと，ピニェイロス川の河岸に面して建設された（道路と鉄道等の）都市交通軸線に挟まれた市街中心部にあたる。また，敷地は空港の円錐ゾーンの真下にあった。これはリオ・デ・ジャネイロからの全てのフライトが，7分おきに敷地上空を通過することを意味する。

プールとサンルームは平行したヴォリュームとして計画された。2本の柱がこれらヴォリュームの隙間1メートルに合わせて配置されている。12メートルのスパンは一方ではプールを支える梁と，他方ではサンルームを支える梁と交わり，その下のフロアを吊り上げる構造となっている。プールの質量が居住スペースを支持するヴォリュームと釣り合うように構造が計画された。すなわち，水とビーチ（ルーフ・テラス）はバランスがとれている。

地上レベルは構造物を設けないことにより，庭の面積が最も広く確保できるように計画された。その結果，各々異なる雰囲気を持つ3層の空間が異なるレベルに現れることになる。すなわち，地上レベル（庭—敷地境界線によって囲まれた内部的空間），住戸レベル（地表面の上空，プール下面に浮遊する唯一の内部空間）及び屋上（スイミング・プールとサンルーム，パノラマの広がる外部的空間）である。

この建築のプログラムは伝統建築が本来目的とするところとは次の2点で異なっている。すなわち，大都市で週末を楽しむことができうるという点において。そして，大きな住宅では副次的なものとして見なされがちな要素が，この建築では本質を構成しているという点においてである。

（アンジェロ・ブッチ）

Terrace on first floor: volume of swimming pool

doubleNegatives Architecture 2013

House in Nagohara, Minamisaku, Nagano, Japan

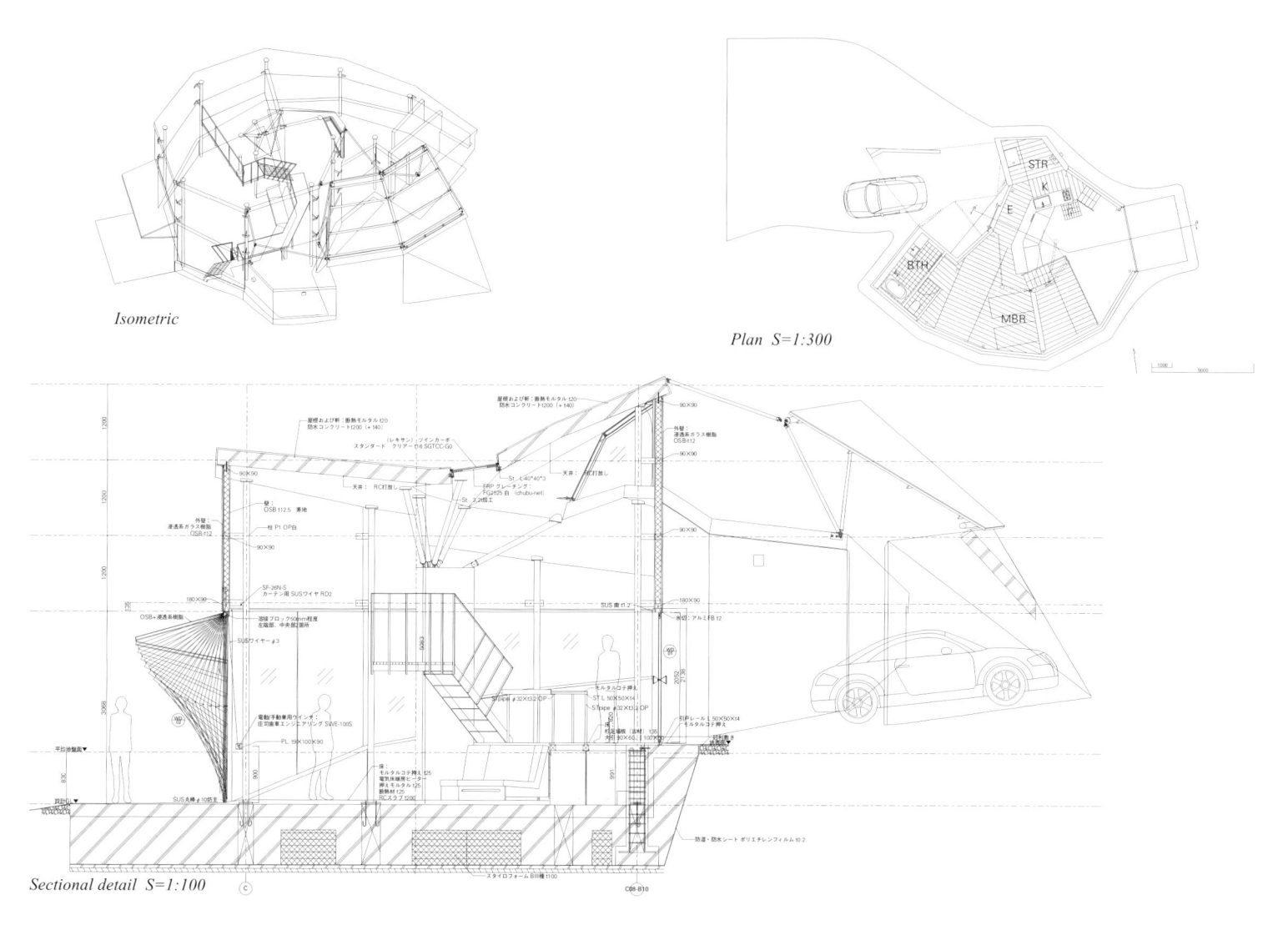

Isometric

Plan S=1:300

Sectional detail S=1:100

Architecture is an intellectual entity comprised of various components. It is even a network of agents, each progarmmed to satisfy one's unique purpose and the overall architectural plan. This house was created using a planning software "Corpora" (meaning aggregate/body), to put such architectural structure into practice.

The site is connected with grand nature, located on the eastern bases of Yatsugatake Mountains. The client uses the architecture as a married couple. There will be, at most, two groups of guests. They wished for a second house that is compact to maintain, has a relaxing openness, with multiple spaces and expansiveness achieved at the same time.

We assumed the "Super Eye," a conceptual omnidirectional vision, within the site's premises. "Super Eye" captures the space in polar coordinates, a point of the compass, site's undulations, tree and rock positions, and boundaries. We also consider this "Super Eye" as a structural node. Various local conditions are programmed as intentions of the architectural plan, working autonomously as agents of the planner: the visible distance which become the longest values of the structural material, joining within the sight of each other; generating support to work around structural instability; self selection; angle and joint tolerance for construction; the tendency for the western adjoining heights to be lower than the eastern side to deal with the strong western winds and flat roof regulations.

One "Super Eye" determines and generates the positioning of the new "Super Eye" by operating the angles and distance on the polar coordinates. The continuity of the changing angles and distances lead to an ordered structure framing. Because the exact characteristics and origins of this continuity is unknown, we experimented with different combinations of angles/lengths, shifting the initial position to simultaneously evaluate the part and the whole. The seemingly hard-to-encounter pricniples and conditions were forced to meet, serendipitously from the human eye, and inevitably by mathematics. Such was done to capture things that fall outside of a mere architect—values that are lost from our field of vision. The resulting structure framing becomes an artificial cavern that reflects the surrounding environment, with various conditions and points of view already incorporated within.

There is a glass opening along the local topography; a kitchen positioned at the intersection where the view openes up in all directions; and the spaces are gently sectioned by a continuing high table that can be used for multi-purposes. Two floor levels are connected to both the low and high sides of the site. The minimal living space, which is linked to the site's shape both physically and instinctively, achieves maximum space of activity for both the site's expansiveness and as an extention beyond the floors.

Sota Ichikawa / doubleNegatives Architecture

Overall view from south

View toward entrance on west

Living/dining room

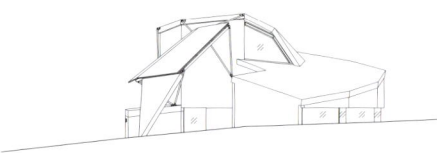

West elevation S=1:300　　　*South elevation*

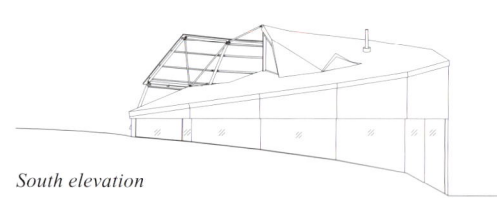

Master bedroom

建築は，様々な部位が集まった知的な総体である。各部位が如何にあるべきか，設計意図がプログラムされたエージェントたちのネットワークと言ってもいい。この住宅は，そのような建築の成り立ちを実践する設計ソフトウェア「Corpora」（総体・身体の意）によって創造されている。

敷地は八ヶ岳山麓東側に位置し，雄大な自然と繋がっている。クライアントは夫婦で建物を使用。最大2組のゲストを迎える。目の行き届くコンパクトさ，静養の為の開放感，複数の居場所と広さが同時に獲得できるようなセカンドハウスが望まれた。

全方向を視る概念的な視点「Super Eye」（超眼）を敷地内に想定する。「Super Eye」は空間を極座標で捉え，方位，敷地の起伏，樹木や岩の位置，建設範囲等を感知する。同時に，「Super Eye」は構造の結節点と考える。互いの視界内で結びつき，構造部材の最長値となる視界距離，構造不安定を回避する補完生成，自己淘汰，施工のための許容接続数や角度，強い西風や陸屋根禁止条例に対応するための隣接高さが西く東となる傾向，といった局所条件が設計意図としてプログラムされ，設計者のエージェントとして自律する。

Terrace: folding wall is opened

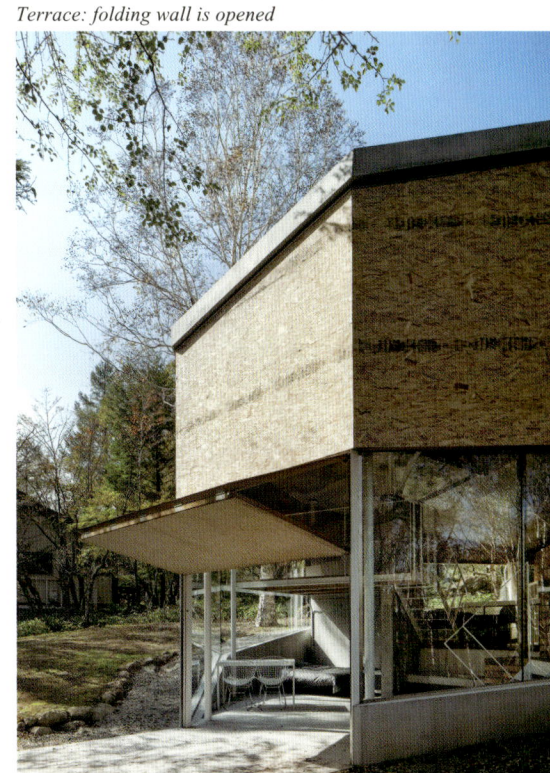

View from entrance

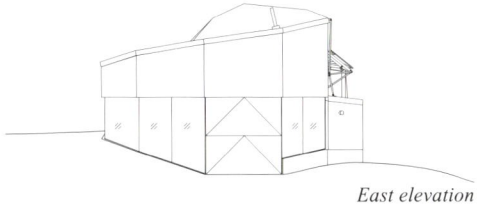

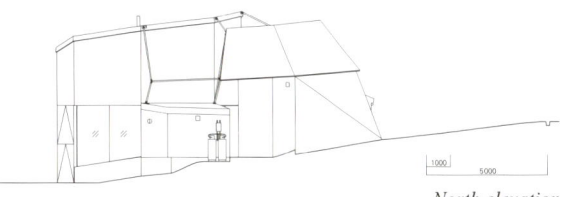

East elevation

North elevation

Site plan S=1:800

　一つの「Super Eye」は極座標的な角度と距離の操作によって，新たな「Super Eye」の位置を決め生成する。この角度と距離の変化の連続性は，秩序を持った構造フレームを導く。「どこから，どのような連続性であるべきか」ということは未知であるため，初期配置をずらしながら，生成角度・長さのあらゆる組合せを試行し，部分と全体を同時に評価していく。出会うことが難しそうな原理と条件を，人間から見れば奇跡的に，数理的には必然的に出会わせる。一建築家の外にあるもの，私たちの視点からは掴みきれない価値をすくい取るべく。こうして生成選択された構造フレームは，様々な条件や視点が織り込み済みの，敷地環境が反射されたいわば人工の洞窟となる。

　地形に沿ってガラス開口とし，ほぼ全方向に視界が抜ける交点にキッチンを配置，連続した多目的なハイテーブルで緩やかに空間を仕切る。二つの床レベルは，敷地の高低両側に繋げる。感覚的にも物理的にも，敷地形状と連続した最小限の居住空間は，敷地全体の広がりと，床の延長としての敷地を，最大限の活動空間として獲得している。

（市川創太／dNA）

View from living/dining room

Ryue Nishizawa

2013

Terasaki House, Kanagawa, Japan

Overall view from southeast

Site plan S=1:1000

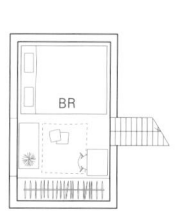

First floor S=1:200

Basement

Courtyard

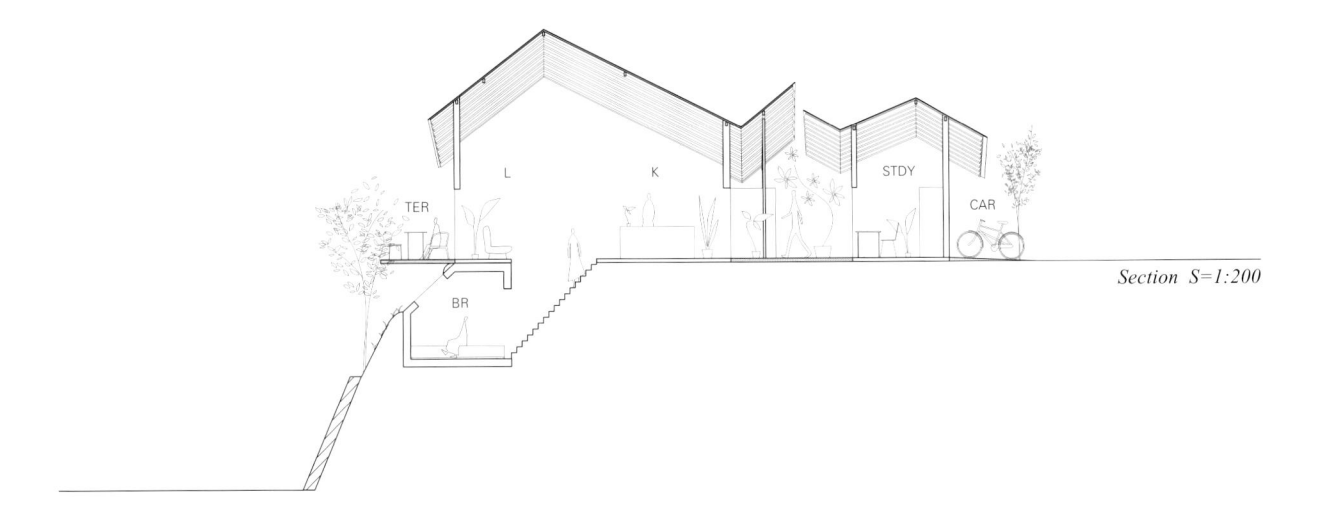

Section S=1:200

Kitchen: view toward living room

The house sits on top of a valley on the outskirts of Tokyo. Surrounded by numerous farms and a large public park, the area is teeming with ample greenery. Within such an environment, we found this site to be particularly appealing. Located on the edges of a valley, it is close to a large park, with unobstructed views and spatial openness. To take advantage of the site's unique and favorable conditions, including its light, great views, and richly green surroundings, we developed a plan for a single-story house with a courtyard. We placed a large roof over the rooms and the courtyard, and created an open space where the indoors extend to the courtyard and beyond. The roof is shaped in an elongated strip along the narrow site that stretches to the north and south. However, instead of placing a single large roof, we designed it so that it curves and bends into a shape that is different from a single gabled or sloping roof, and gently envelops the indoors with a warm atmosphere. Also, the design integrates both shadow and light in the indoor spaces, by capturing light through the openings of the roof.

Our goal is to create a comfortable living space protected by its framework, with a sense of transparency that continues into the structure's fertile surrounding context.
Ryue Nishizawa

Dining room

View from study toward living/dinihg/kitchen through courtyard

東京近郊の, 丘の上に建つ住宅である。周辺には大きな公園や農園などがあり, 豊かな緑に恵まれている。その中でもこの敷地は, 丘の端に位置していて, 大きな公園をすぐ近くに持ち, 開かれた眺望の良さと空間的な開放感を持つ, 特別な魅力があった。そのような恵まれた条件, 明るい光, 眺めの良さ, 緑豊かな周辺環境といった, 土地がもつ諸条件をよく取り込みたいと考えて, いろいろスタディした結果, 中庭形式の平屋建ての平面構成を考えた。部屋と中庭を一つにまとめるような大きな屋根を架けて, 室内と中庭, 外が連続してゆくような, 開放的な空間を考えた。敷地が南北に細長いので, 屋根は敷地形状に沿って長く伸びて行く形状となるが, 単に長い大屋根を1枚架けるというのではなく, それを割ったり曲げたりして, 切妻や方流れといった単一勾配屋根とは違う断面形状とし, 室内をつつみこむような雰囲気をつくり出した。また同時に, 屋根を割ったその裂け目から光を取り込んで, 影と光が同居する屋根下空間を考えた。

架構によって包まれた, 落ち着いた居住空間でありながら, 周辺環境の豊かさにつながってゆく透明感を併せ持つ空間を目指している。

(西沢立衛)

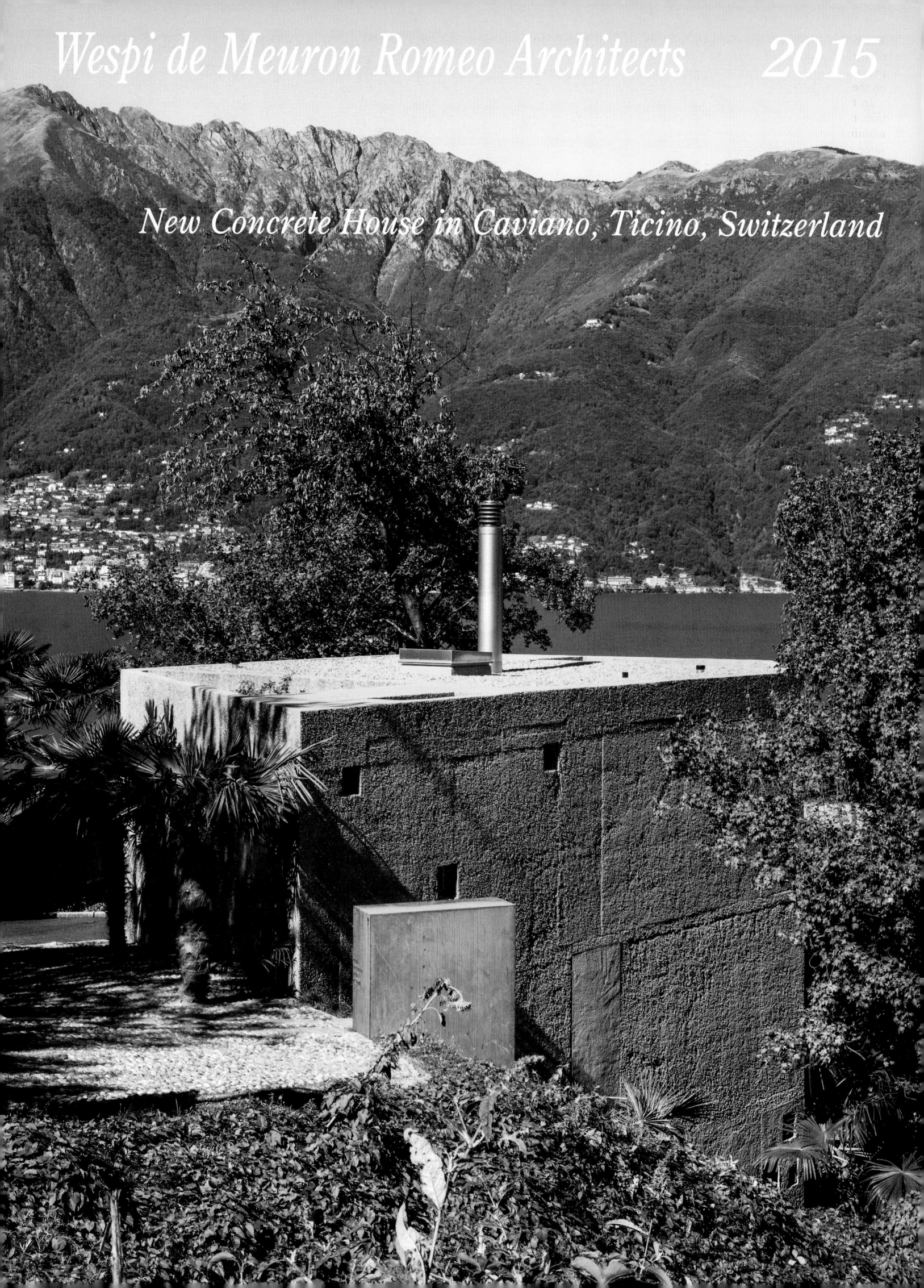

Wespi de Meuron Romeo Architects   2015

New Concrete House in Caviano, Ticino, Switzerland

The house, designed as a residence for a family of three persons, was built in the immediate proximity of the architecture office in Caviano on the Lake Maggiore.

In terms of adequate architectural densification, new living space should be created on a remaining area of just 128 square meters, on the same plot as the architecture office was built in 1981, without damaging the existing qualities. On the contrary, an enrichment of the outer spatial situation should be generated with reasonable densification in context with the existing building.

The building laws determined the outer form of the building, what often happens when leftover plots are developed. The minimal distance to the road, the minimal distance to the forest, the minimal building distance to the architecture office as well as the right to build on the limit to the southwest neighbour, create an irregular pentagonal form of totally 79 square meters surface.
A clear rectangle of 48 square meters surface, which is the isolated interior, was integrated in this irregular form.

The polygonal exterior shape and the steep topography of the site let the building appear as an archaic stone block in middle of the forest, this is reinforced by the rough washed concrete surfaces becoming darker by the weathering.

To the mountain-sided street, the construction presents itself as a closed, simple one-storey volume. The only opening towards, the street is the raw steel gate leading to the entrance court.

A 3-meter wide forecourt with a natural stone pavement and two palms connects the house to the street and upgrade it spatially.

To the valley-side, the house appears as a narrow 3-storey tower.

The house is organised on three floors: the top floor on the street level accommodates the entrance, the main living area and dining with the open kitchen, on two sides it's completely closed and on the other two sides it's completely vitrified towards the courtyards.

The entrance courtyard on the mountainside protects the house against insight from the street and in the meantime it lets the sunlight in.

The inner courtyard on the seaside releases the view to the lake and the mountains through a big roofed opening; while it's closed wall surfaces reflect the sunlight to the inside.

Both courtyards, each with a wisteria, let the living room becomes a "garden" room and let the inhabitants experience in an unusual intense way the varying atmospheres of the weather and the light.

A skylight above the staircase allows light to penetrate into the lower floor, which accommodates two bedrooms, each with its own outdoor loggia, the bathroom and the stairs to the cellar, where is the technique and a workspace.

Partial north elevation

◁ *View from east. House on top of steep hillside*

Downward view from south

View toward dining room: inner courtyard on left

Level -1

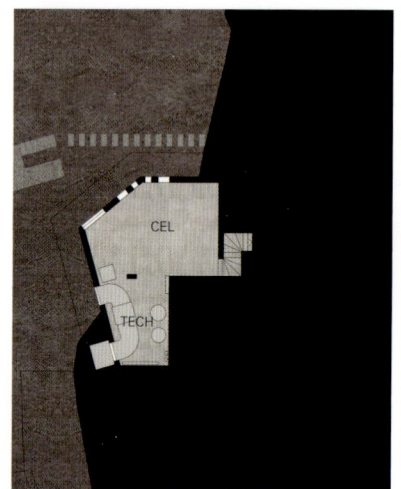

Roof

Level -2

Level 0 S=1:300

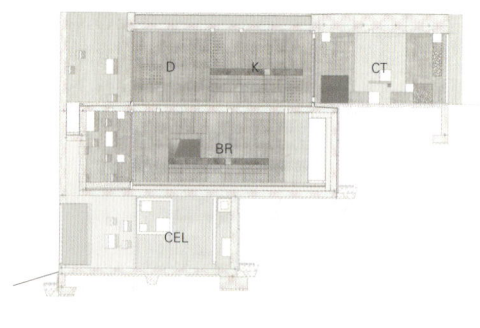

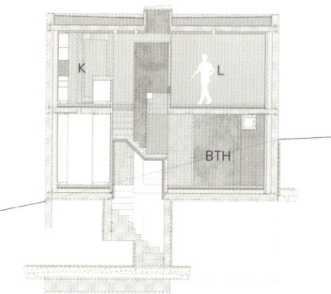

Sections S=1:250

294

Living room

Skylight above staircase

Bedroom on level -1

この住宅は三人家族の住まいとして設計され、マッジョーレ湖畔、カヴィアーノの設計事務所のごく近くに建てられた。

適切な建築の密度という点では、新しい住まいに残された敷地はたったの128平米であった。これは1981年に建てられた設計事務所の敷地を、既存の質を損なうことなく共有するという条件に基づくものである。これとは対照的に、既存の建物との関係において適度な密度を保ちながら屋外の空間的状況を充実させる必要もあった。

取り残された敷地が開発される際によく起こることだが、建物の形態は建築法規によって決定した。道路への最小距離、森林への最小距離、建物から建築事務所までの最小距離、そして南西方向の建築の築造制限に基づいて、総面積79平米の不等辺五角形がつくられた。独立した室内空間である48平米の整った長方形がこの不等辺の形態に統合された。

五角形の形態と急勾配の敷地の地形によって、この建物は森林のまっただ中に佇む、いにしえの石材としてあらわれる。洗い出し仕上げが施された肌理の粗いコンクリートの表面が風化によって色が濃くなることで印象は深まっていく。

山側の通りへは、この建物は閉鎖的で単純な平屋のヴォリュームとしてあらわれる。通りに面している唯一の開口部は、エントランスコートに続く粗鋼製の門扉である。

自然石の舗装が施された幅3メートルの前庭と2本の椰子の木が住宅と通りをつなぎ、住宅の空間の質を高めている。

谷側へは、この家は幅の狭い3階建ての塔のようにあらわれる。

この住宅は3階建てである。道路レベルの最上階には玄関、メインのリビングルームとオープンキッチンつきのダイニングルームが置かれる。二面は完全に遮蔽され、残りの二面は庭に面して総ガラス張りになっている。

山側の前庭は通りからの視線を遮る一方で、採光を確保する役割を果たす。

湖畔に面した中庭では、大きな屋根つきの開口部の向こう側に湖と山々を望むことができる。中庭を囲う壁面で反射した光は内部へと射しこむ。

前庭、中庭のどちらの庭にも藤が植えられ、リビングルームが「ガーデン」ルームとなる。住まい手は移ろいゆく空模様と光を他では味わえない強烈な方法で体験することとなる。

階段の天窓からは光が下階に向かって降り注ぐ。下階にはロッジア付きの寝室が二つと、各種設備と作業場のある地下室へつながる階段がある。

Photographic Credits
All photographs: GA photographers;
Yukio Futagawa: pp.9-13, 20-25, 82-87, 92-97, 102-107, 112-117, 140-149, 156 left, 157-161, 172-177, 182-201, 206, 207 right, 232-237, 248-255
Yoshio Futagawa: pp.54-59, 64-69, 88-91, 108-111, 120-121, 123 right top, left bottom, 128-139, 150-155, 162-171, 178-181, 202-205, 214-219, 226-231, 238-243, 260-287, 292-295
Katsumasa Tanaka: p.207 left, pp.208-213, 220-225, 244-247, 256-259